Eureka Math Study Guide

Other Books

WHEATLEY PORTFOLIO

English, Grades K–5, Second Edition

English, Grades 6–8, Second Edition

English, Grades 9–12, Second Edition

ALEXANDRIA PLAN

United States History, Grades K–2

World History, Grades K–2

United States History, Grades 3–5

World History, Grades 3–5

Eureka Math Study Guide
Grade 4

JB JOSSEY-BASS™
A Wiley Brand

Cover design by Chris Clary
Cover image: Vincent van Gogh (1853–1890), The Starry Night. Saint Rémy, June 1889. Oil on canvas, $29 \times 36\frac{1}{4}''$ (73.7 × 92.1 cm). Acquired through the Lillie P. Bliss Bequest.
Location: The Museum of Modern Art, New York, NY, U.S.A.
Digital Image © The Museum of Modern Art / Licensed by SCALA / Art Resource, NY

Published by Jossey-Bass
A Wiley Brand
One Montgomery Street, Suite 1000, San Francisco, CA 94104-4594–www.josseybass.com

Jossey-Bass books and products are available through most bookstores. To contact Jossey-Bass directly, call our Customer Care Department within the U.S. at 800-956-7739, outside the U.S. at 317-572-3986, or fax 317-572-4002.

For more information about *Eureka Math*, visit www.eureka-math.org.

Wiley publishes in a variety of print and electronic formats and by print-on-demand. Some material included with standard print versions of this book may not be included in e-books or in print-on-demand. If this book refers to media such as a CD or DVD that is not included in the version you purchased, you may download this material at http://booksupport.wiley.com. For more information about Wiley products, visit www.wiley.com.

Library of Congress Cataloging-in-Publication Data

Eureka math study guide. A story of units, grade 4 education edition / Great Minds—First edition.
    pages   cm
    Includes bibliographical references and index.
    ISBN 978-1-118-81186-3 (paperback)
    1. Mathematics—Study and teaching (Preschool)—Standards—United States.   I. Great Minds
QA135.6.E83 2015
372.7'2—dc23

                                                                2014029344

Printed in the United States of America

FIRST EDITION
PB *Printing* 10 9 8 7 6 5 4 3 2 1

Contents

Introduction

When do you know you really understand something? One test is to see if you can explain it to someone else—well enough that *they* understand it. *Eureka Math* routinely requires students to "turn and talk" and explain the math they learned to their peers.

That is because the goal of *Eureka Math* (which you may know as the EngageNY math modules) is to produce students who are not merely literate, but fluent, in mathematics. By fluent, we mean not just knowing what process to use when solving a problem but understanding why that process works.

Here's an example. A student who is fluent in mathematics can do far more than just name, recite, and apply the Pythagorean theorem to problems. She can explain why $a^2 + b^2 = c^2$ is true. She not only knows the theorem can be used to find the length of a right triangle's hypotenuse, but can apply it more broadly—such as to find the distance between any two points in the coordinate plane, for example. She also can see the theorem as the glue joining seemingly disparate ideas including equations of circles, trigonometry, and vectors.

By contrast, the student who has merely memorized the Pythagorean theorem does not know why it works and can do little more than just solve right triangle problems by rote. The theorem is an abstraction—not a piece of knowledge, but just a process to use in the limited ways that she has been directed. For her, studying mathematics is a chore, a mere memorizing of disconnected processes.

Eureka Math provides much more. It offers students math knowledge that will serve them well beyond any test. This fundamental knowledge not only makes wise citizens and competent consumers, but it gives birth to budding physicists and engineers. Knowing math deeply opens vistas of opportunity.

A student becomes fluent in math—as they do in any other subject—by following a course of study that builds their knowledge of the subject, logically and thoroughly. In *Eureka Math*, concepts flow logically from PreKindergarten through high school. The "chapters" in the story of mathematics are "A Story of Units" for the elementary grades, followed by "A Story of Ratios" in middle school and "A Story of Functions" in high school.

This sequencing is joined with a mix of new and old methods of instruction that are proven to work. For example, we utilize an exercise called a "sprint" to develop students' fluency with standard algorithms (routines for adding, subtracting, multiplying, and dividing whole numbers and fractions). We employ many familiar models and tools such as the number line and tape diagrams (aka bar models). A newer model highlighted in the curriculum is the number bond (illustrated below), which clearly shows how numbers are comprised of other numbers.

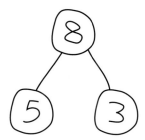

Eureka Math is designed to help accommodate different types of classrooms and serve as a resource for educators, who make decisions based on the needs of students. The "vignettes" of teacher-student interactions included in the curriculum are not scripts, but exemplars illustrating methods of instruction recommended by the teachers who have crafted our curricula.

Eureka Math has been adopted by districts from East Meadows, New York, to Lafayette, Los Angeles, to Chula Vista, California. At Eureka Math we are excited to have created the most transparent math curriculum in history—every lesson, all classwork, and every problem is available online.

Many of us have less than joyful memories of learning mathematics: lots of memorization, lots of rules to follow without understanding, and problems that didn't make any sense. What if a curriculum came along that gave children a chance to avoid that math anxiety and replaced it with authentic understanding, excitement, and curiosity? Like a New York educator attending one of our trainings said: "Why didn't I learn mathematics this way when I was a kid? It is so much easier than the way I learned it!"

Eureka!

Lynne Munson
Washington, DC

From the Writers

To Our Fellow Teachers:

Storytelling is as old as time and brings excitement to many, including my two-year-old son, who giggles at silly monkey characters in his books, and my fourth-graders, who beg me to read the next chapter of a mystery book. Unfortunately, mathematics is rarely taught as a coherent story but instead as a jumble of topics taught from year to year. Because students enjoy stories so much, why not tell mathematics as a story? That's just what we did.

Classroom teachers and mathematicians from across the country gathered to tell a coherent story of mathematics in the form of a three-part narrative, *Eureka Math*. I've been honored to lead the Grade 4 installment of that trilogy. The mathematics comes to life with each successive lesson just as a main character develops with each successive chapter. Students are encouraged to reason about mathematics using precise language and develop stronger mental math skills.

The models used aren't quick and easy exit strategies but a strong foundation for building conceptual understanding. For example, the area model has its roots in PreKindergarten as students begin to talk about the space inside a figure. As understanding about the concept of area grows, students are able to use the area model to multiply and divide multi-digit whole and decimal numbers. This way standard algorithms aren't just a rote series of steps but rather a logical sequence with connections to number sense.

We—the writers, editors, teachers, and mathematicians—share this chapter in the story of mathematics with you. May it deepen your understanding of mathematics, provide foundation for your teaching, and help countless children to become better at mathematics.

Kelly Alsup
Chicago, IL
Grade 4 lead writer/editor
Eureka Math/Great Minds

Foreword

TELLING THE STORY OF MATH

Each module in *Eureka Math* builds carefully and precisely on the content learned in the previous modules and years, weaving the knowledge learned into a coherent whole. This produces an effect similar to reading a good novel: The storyline, even after weeks of not reading, is easy to pick up again because the novel pulls the reader back into the plot immediately–the need to review is minimal because the plot brings out and adds to what has already happened. This cumulative aspect of the plot, along with its themes, character development, and composition, are all part of the carefully thought-out design of the *Eureka Math* curriculum.

So what is the storyline? One can get a sense of how the story evolves by studying the major themes of A *Story of Units*, A *Story of Ratios*, and A *Story of Functions*.

A *Story of Units* investigates how concepts including place value, algorithms, fractions, measurements, area, and so on can all be understood by relating and manipulating types of units (e.g., inches, square meters, tens, fifths). For example, quantities expressed in the same units can be added: 3 apples plus 4 apples equals 7 apples. Likewise, 3 fifths plus 4 fifths is 7 fifths. Whole number multiplication, as in "3 fives = 15 ones," is merely another form of converting between different units, as when we state that "1 foot = 12 inches." These similarities between concepts drive the day-to-day theme throughout the PreK–5 curriculum: each type of unit (or building block) is handled the same way through the common features that all units share. Understanding the commonalities and like traits of these building blocks makes it much easier to sharply contrast the differences. In other words, the consistency of manipulation of different units helps students see the connection in topics. No longer is every new topic separate from the previous topics studied.

A *Story of Ratios* moves students beyond problems that involve one-time calculations using one or two specific measurements to thinking about proportional relationships that hold for a whole range of measurements. The proportional relationships theme shows up every day during middle school as students work with ratios, rates, percentages, probability, similarity, and linear functions. A *Story of Ratios* provides the transition years between students thinking of a specific triangle with side lengths 3 cm, 4 cm, and 5 cm in elementary school to a broader view in high school for studying the set of all triangles with side lengths in a 3:4:5 ratio (e.g., 6:8:10, 9:12:15).

A *Story of Functions* generalizes linear relationships learned in middle school to polynomial, rational, trigonometric, exponential, and logarithmic functions in high school. Students study the properties of these functions and their graphs, and model with them to move explicitly from real-world scenarios to mathematical representations. The algebra learned in middle school is applied in rewriting functions in different forms and solving equations derived from one or more functions. The theme drives students to finish high school knowing not only how to manipulate the major functions used in college but also to be fully capable of modeling real-life data with an appropriate function in order to make predictions and answer questions.

The many "little eurekas" infused in the storyline of *Eureka Math* help students learn how to wield the true power of mathematics in their daily lives. Experiencing these "aha moments" also convinces students that the mathematics that drives innovation and advancement in our society is within their reach.

Scott Baldridge
Lead writer and lead mathematician, *Eureka Math*
Loretta Cox Stuckey and Dr. James G. Traynham Distinguished Professor of Mathematics,
Louisiana State University
Co-director, Gordon A. Cain Center for Science, Technology,
Engineering, and Mathematical Literacy

How to Use This Book

As a self-study resource, these *Eureka Math* Study Guides are beneficial for teachers in a variety of situations. They introduce teachers who are brand new to either the classroom or the *Eureka Math* curriculum not only to *Eureka Math* but also to the content of the grade level in a way they will find manageable and useful. Teachers already familiar with the curriculum will also find this resource valuable as it allows a meaningful study of the grade-level content in a way that highlights the connections between modules and topics. The guidebooks help teachers obtain a firm grasp on what it is that students should master during the year. The structure of the book provides a focus on the connections between the standards and the descriptions of mathematical progressions through the grade, topic by topic. Teachers therefore develop a multifaceted view of the standards from a thorough analysis of the guide.

The *Eureka Math* Study Guides can also serve as a means to familiarize teachers with adjacent grade levels. It is helpful for teachers to know what students learned in the grade level below the one they are currently teaching as well as the one that follows. Having an understanding of the mathematical progression across grades enhances the teacher's ability to reach students at their level and ensure they are prepared for the next grade.

For teachers, schools, and districts that have not adopted *Eureka Math*, but are instead creating or adjusting their own curricular frameworks, these grade-level study guides offer support in making critical decisions about how to group and sequence the standards for maximal coherence within and across grades. *Eureka Math* serves as a blueprint for these educators; in turn, the study guides present not only this blueprint but a rationale for the selected organization.

The *Eureka Math* model provides a starting point from which educators can build their own curricular plan if they so choose. Unpacking the new standards to determine what skills students should master at each grade level is a necessary exercise to ensure appropriate choices are made during curriculum development. The *Eureka Math* Study Guides include lists of student outcomes mapped to the standards and are key to the unpacking process. The overviews of the modules and topics offer narratives rich with detailed descriptions of how to teach specific skills needed at each grade level. Users can have confidence in the interpretations of the standards presented, as well as the sequencing selected, due to the rigorous review process that occurred during the development of the content included in *Eureka Math*.

This *Eureka Math* Study Guide contains the following:

Introduction to Eureka Math (chapter 1): This introduction consists of two sections: "Vision and Storyline" and "Advantages to a Coherent Curriculum."

Major Mathematical Themes in Each Grade Band (chapter 2): The first section presents year-long curriculum maps for each grade band (with subsections addressing A *Story of Units*, A *Story of Ratios*, and A *Story of Functions*). It is followed by a detailed examination of math concept development for PreK to Grade 5. The chapter closes with an in-depth description of how alignment to the instructional shifts and the standards of mathematical practice is achieved.

Grade-Level Content Review (chapter 3): The key areas of focus and required fluencies for a given grade level are presented in this chapter, along with a rationale for why topics are grouped and sequenced in the modules as they are. The Alignment Chart lists the standards that are addressed in each module of the grade.

Curriculum Design (chapter 4): The approach to modules, lessons, and assessment in A *Story of Units* is detailed in this chapter. It also provides a wealth of information about how to achieve the components of instructional rigor demanded by the new standards: fluency, concept development, and application.

Approach to Differentiated Instruction (chapter 5): This chapter describes the approach to differentiated instruction used in A *Story of Units*. Special populations such as English language learners, students with disabilities, students performing above grade level, and students performing below grade level are addressed.

Grade-Level Module Summary and Unpacking of Standards (chapter 6): This chapter presents information from the modules to provide an overview of the content of each and explain the mathematical progression. The standards are translated for teachers, and a fuller picture is drawn of the teaching and learning that should take place through the school year.

Mathematical Models (chapter 7): This chapter presents information on the mathematical models used in A *Story of Units*.

Terminology (chapter 8): The terms included in this list were compiled from the New or Recently Introduced Terms portion of the Terminology section of the Module Overviews. Terms are listed by grade level and module number where they are introduced in A *Story of Units*. The chapter also offers descriptions, examples, and illustrations associated with the terms.

Eureka Math Study Guide

CHAPTER 1

Introduction to Eureka Math

VISION AND STORYLINE

Eureka Math is a comprehensive, content-rich PreK–12 curriculum and professional development platform. It follows the focus and coherence of the new college- and career-ready standards and carefully sequences the mathematical progressions into expertly crafted instructional modules.

The new standards and progressions set the frame for the curriculum. We then shaped every aspect of it by addressing the new instructional shifts that teachers must make. Nowhere are the instructional shifts more evident than in the fluency, application, concept development, and debriefing sections that characterize lessons in the PreK–5 grades of *Eureka Math*. Similarly, Eureka's focus in the middle and high school grades on problem sets, exploration, Socratic discussion, and modeling helps students internalize the true meaning of coherence and fosters deep conceptual understanding.

Eureka Math is distinguished not only by its adherence to the new standards, but also by its foundation in a theory of teaching math that has been proven to work. This theory posits that mathematical knowledge is conveyed most effectively when it is taught in a sequence that follows the story of mathematics itself. This is why we call the elementary portion A *Story of Units*, followed by A *Story of Ratios* in middle school, and A *Story of Functions* in high school. Mathematical concepts flow logically from one to the next in this curriculum.

The sequencing has been joined with proven methods of instruction. These methods drive student understanding beyond process to deep mastery of mathematical concepts. The goal of *Eureka Math* is to produce students who are fluent, not merely literate, in mathematics.

In spite of the extensiveness of these resources, *Eureka Math* is not meant to be prescriptive. Rather, we offer it as a basis for teachers to hone their own craft. Great Minds believes deeply in the ability of teachers and in their central, irreplaceable role in shaping the classroom experience. To support and facilitate that important work, *Eureka Math* includes both scaffolding hints to help teachers support Response to Intervention (RTI) and maintains a consistent lesson structure that allows teachers to focus their energy on engaging students in the mathematical story.

In addition, the online version of *Eureka Math* (www.eureka-math.org) features embedded video that demonstrates classroom practices. The readily navigable online version includes progressions-based search functionality to permit navigation between standards and related lessons, linking all lessons in a particular standards strand or mathematical progression and learning trajectory. This functionality also helps teachers identify and remediate gaps in prerequisite knowledge, implement RTI tiers, and provide support for students at a variety of levels.

The research and development on which *Eureka Math* is based was made possible through a partnership with the New York State Education Department, for which this work was originally created. The department's expert review team, including renowned mathematicians who helped write the new standards, progressions, and the much-touted "Publishers' Criteria" (http://achievethecore.org/page/686/publishers-criteria) strengthened an already rigorous development process. We are proud to offer *Eureka Math*, an extended version of that work, to teachers all across the country.

ADVANTAGES TO A COHERENT CURRICULUM

Great Minds believes in the theory of teaching content as a coherent story from PreK to Grade 12—one that is sequential, scaffolded, and logically cohesive within and between grades. Great Minds' *Eureka Math* is a program with a three-part narrative, from A *Story of Units* (PreK–5) to A *Story of Ratios* (6–8) to A *Story of Functions* (9–12). This curriculum shows Great Minds' commitment to provide educators with the tools necessary to move students between grade levels so that their learning grows from what comes before and after.

A coherent curriculum creates a common knowledge base for all students that supports effective instruction across the classroom. Students' sharing of a base of knowledge engenders a classroom environment of common understanding and learning. This means that the effectiveness of instruction can be far more significant than when topics are taught as discrete unrelated items, as teachers can work with students to achieve a deep level of comprehension and shared learning.

This cohesiveness must be based on the foundation of a content-rich curriculum that is well organized and thoughtfully designed in order to facilitate learning at the deepest level. A coherent curriculum should be free of gaps and needless repetition, aligned to standards but also vertically and horizontally linked across lessons and grade levels. What students learn in one lesson prepares them for the next in a logical sequence. In addition, what happens in one second-grade classroom in one school closely matches what happens in another second-grade classroom, creating a shared base of understanding across students, grades, and schools.

Lack of coherence can lead to misalignment and random, disordered instruction that can prove costly to student learning and greatly increase the time that teachers spend on preparation, revisions, and repetition of material. The model of a sequential, comprehensive curriculum, such as *Eureka Math*, brings benefits within the uniformity in time spent on content, approach to instruction, and lesson structure, facilitating a common base of knowledge and an environment of shared understanding.

The commitment to uniformity influenced Great Minds' approach to creating *Eureka Math*. This curriculum was created from a single vision spanning PreK–12, with the same leadership team of mathematicians, writers, and project managers overseeing and coordinating the development of all grades at one time. By using the same project team throughout the course of *Eureka Math's* development, Great Minds was able to ensure that *Eureka Math* tells a comprehensive story with no gaps from grade to grade or band to band.

CHAPTER 2

Major Mathematical Themes in Each Grade Band

This chapter presents the year-long curriculum maps for each grade band in the *Eureka Math* curriculum: A *Story of Units*, A *Story of Ratios*, and A *Story of Functions*. These maps illustrate the major mathematical themes across the entire mathematics curriculum. The chapter also includes a detailed examination of the math concept development for A *Story of Units*, highlighting the significance of the unit. The chapter closes with an in-depth description of how the curriculum is aligned to the Instructional Shifts and the Standards for Mathematical Practice.

YEAR-LONG CURRICULUM MAPS FOR EACH GRADE BAND

The curriculum map is a chart that shows, at a glance, the sequence of modules comprising each grade of the entire curriculum for a given grade band. The map also indicates the approximate number of instructional days designated for each module of each grade. It is important for educators to have knowledge of how key topics are sequenced from PreK through Grade 12. The maps for the three grade bands in figures 2.1 to 2.3 reveal the trajectories through the grades for topics such as geometry, fractions, functions and statistics, and probability.

MATH CONTENT DEVELOPMENT FOR PREK–5: A STORY OF UNITS

The curricular design for A *Story of Units* is based on the principle that mathematics is most effectively taught as a logical, engaging story. At the elementary level, this story's main character is the basic building block of arithmetic, the unit. Themes like measurement, place value, and fractions run throughout the storyline, and each is given the amount of time proportionate to its role in the overall story. The story climaxes when students learn to add, subtract, multiply, and divide fractions; and to solve multi-step word problems with multiplicative and additive comparisons.

	PreKindergarten	Kindergarten	Grade 1	Grade 2
20 days	M1: Counting to 5 (45 days)	M1: Numbers to 10 (43 days)	M1: Sums and Differences to 10 (45 days)	M1: Sums and Differences to 20 (10 days)
				M2: Addition and Subtraction of Length Units (12 days)
20 days				M3: Place Value, Counting, and Comparison of Numbers to 1,000 (25 days)
20 days	M2: Shapes (15 days)	*M2: 2D and 3D Shapes (12 days)	M2: Introduction to Place Value Through Addition and Subtraction Within 20 (35 days)	M4: Addition and Subtraction Within 200 with Word Problems to 100 (35 days)
20 days	M3: Counting to 10 (50 days)	M3: Comparison of Length, Weight, Capacity, and Numbers to 10 (38 days)		
20 days			M3: Ordering and Comparing Length Measurements as Numbers (15 days)	M5: Addition and Subtraction Within 1,000 with Word Problems to 100 (24 days)
20 days		M4: Number Pairs, Addition and Subtraction to 10 (47 days)	M4: Place Value, Comparison, Addition and Subtraction to 40 (35 days)	M6: Foundations of Multiplication and Division (24 days)
20 days	M4: Comparison of Length, Weight, Capacity, and Numbers to 5 (35 days)			
			M5: Identifying, Composing, and Partitioning Shapes (15 days)	M7: Problem Solving with Length, Money, and Data (30 days)
20 days	M5: Addition and Subtraction Stories and Counting to 20 (35 days)	M5: Numbers 10–20 and Counting to 100 (30 days)	M6: Place Value, Comparison, Addition and Subtraction to 100 (35 days)	
				M8: Time, Shapes, and Fractions as Equal Parts of Shapes (20 days)
20 days		M6: Analyzing, Comparing, and Composing Shapes (10 days)		

*Please refer to grade-level descriptions to identify partially labeled modules and

Key:	Geometry	Number

Figure 2.1 Grades PreK–5 Year-Long Curriculum Map: A Story of Units

Grade 3	Grade 4	Grade 5	
M1: Properties of Multiplication and Division and Solving Problems with Units of 2–5 and 10 (25 days)	M1: Place Value, Rounding, and Algorithms for Addition and Subtraction (25 days)	M1: Place Value and Decimal Fractions (20 days)	20 days
M2: Place Value and Problem Solving with Units of Measure (25 days)	*M2: Unit Conversions (7 days)	M2: Multi-Digit Whole Number and Decimal Fraction Operations (35 days)	20 days
	M3: Multi-Digit Multiplication and Division (43 days)		20 days
M3: Multiplication and Division with Units of 0, 1, 6–9, and Multiples of 10 (25 days)		M3: Addition and Subtraction of Fractions (22 days)	20 days
M4: Multiplication and Area (20 days)	M4: Angle Measure and Plane Figures (20 days)	M4: Multiplication and Division of Fractions and Decimal Fractions (38 days)	20 days
M5: Fractions as Numbers on the Number Line (35 days)	M5: Fraction Equivalence, Ordering, and Operations (45 days)		20 days
		M5: Addition and Multiplication with Volume and Area (25 days)	20 days
M6: Collecting and Displaying Data (10 days)			
M7: Geometry and Measurement Word Problems (40 days)	M6: Decimal Fractions (20 days)	M6: Problem Solving with the Coordinate Plane (40 days)	20 days
	M7: Exploring Measurement with Multiplication (20 days)		20 days

the standards corresponding to all modules.

Number and Geometry, Measurement	Fractions

	Grade 6	Grade 7	Grade 8	
20 days	M1: Ratios and Unit Rates (35 days)	M1: Ratios and Proportional Relationships (30 days)	M1: Integer Exponents and the Scientific Notation (20 days)	**20 days**
20 days			M2: The Concept of Congruence (25 days)	**20 days**
20 days	M2: Arithmetic Operations Including Division of Fractions (25 days)	M2: Rational Numbers (30 days)	M3: Similarity (25 days)	**20 days**
20 days	M3 Rational Numbers (25 days)	M3: Expressions and Equations (35 days)		**20 days**
20 days	M4: Expressions and Equations (45 days)		M4: Linear Equations (40 days)	**20 days**
20 days		M4: Percent and Proportional Relationships (25 days)		**20 days**
20 days			M5: Examples of Functions from Geometry (15 days)	
20 days	M5: Area, Surface Area, and Volume Problems (25 days)	M5: Statistics and Probability (25 days)	M6: Linear Functions (20 days)	**20 days**
20 days		M6: Geometry (35 days)	M7: Introduction to Irrational Numbers Using Geometry (35 days)	**20 days**
20 days	M6: Statistics (25 days)			**20 days**

Key:	Number	Geometry	Ratios and Proportions	Expressions and Equations	Statistics and Probability	Functions

Figure 2.2   Grades 6–8 Year-Long Curriculum Map: A Story of Ratios

Few U.S. textbooks paint mathematics as a dynamic, unfolding tale. They instead prioritize teaching procedures and employ a spiraling approach, in which topics are partially taught and then returned to—sometimes years later—with the unrealistic expectation that students will somehow connect the dots. But teaching procedures as skills without a rich context is ineffective. Students can too easily forget procedures and will fail if they do not have deeper, more concrete knowledge from which they can draw.

THE SIGNIFICANCE OF THE UNIT

Even as new concepts are introduced to students, the overarching theme remains: defining the basic building block, the unit. Studying, relating, manipulating, and converting the unit allows students to add, subtract, complete word problems, multiply, divide, and understand concepts like place value, fractions, measurements, area, and volume. Students learn that unit-based procedures are transferable and can thus build on their knowledge in new ways. The following progressions demonstrate how the curriculum moves from the introductory structures of addition, through place value and multiplication, to operations with fractions and beyond.

	Grade 9 – Algebra I	Grade 10 – Geometry	Grade 11 – Algebra II	Grade 12 – Precalculus and Advanced Topics	
20 days	M1: Relationships Between Quantities and Reasoning with Equations and Their Graphs (40 days)	M1: Congruence, Proof, and Constructions (45 days)	M1: Polynomial, Rational, and Radical Relationships (45 days)	M1: Complex Numbers and Transformations (40 days)	20 days
20 days					20 days
20 days	M2: Descriptive Statistics (25 days)	M2: Similarity, Proof, and Trigonometry (45 days)	M2: Trigonometric Functions (20 days)	M2: Vectors and Matrices (40 days)	20 days
20 days	M3: Linear and Exponential Functions (35 days)		M3: Functions (45 days)		20 days
20 days		M3: Extending to Three Dimensions (15 days)		M3: Rational and Exponential Functions (25 days)	20 days
20 days	M4: Polynomial and Quadratic Expressions, Equations and Functions (30 days)	M4: Connecting Algebra and Geometry through Coordinates (20 days)		M4: Trigonometry (20 days)	20 days
20 days		M5: Circles with and Without Coordinates (25 days)	M4: Inferences and Conclusions from Data (40 days)	M5: Probability and Statistics (25 days)	20 days
10 days	M5: A Synthesis of Modeling with Equations and Functions (20 days)				10 days

Figure 2.3   Grades 9-12 Year-Long Curriculum Map: A Story of Functions

Numbers through 10

Initially, in PreKindergarten and Kindergarten, one object is one unit: "Let's count the frogs! The frog is one unit: 1 frog, 2 frogs, 3 frogs …" Students then relate numbers to each other and to 5 and 10. For example, in building a growth pattern (a stair-shaped structure) of unit cubes representing each number to 10 and having a color change at 5, students see that 7 is 1 unit more than 6, 1 less than 8, 2 more than 5, and 3 less than 10. That is, it can be broken into 1 and 6, or 2 and 5. Then 7 can be a unit to manipulate ("I can break it apart into 3 and 4") to be formed ("I can add 1 more to 6"), and related ("It needs 3 more to be 10").

Addition and Subtraction

In order to add 8 and 6, for example, students form a unit of 10 and add the remainder: $8 + 6 = 8 + (2 + 4) = (8 + 2) + 4 = 10 + 4 = 14$. They extend that skill by adding $18 + 6$, $80 + 60$, $800 \text{ kg} + 600 \text{ kg}$, and 8 ninths + 6 ninths. This idea is easily transferable to more complex units. Adding mixed units (e.g., 2 dogs 4 puppies + 3 dogs 5 puppies) means adding like units just as in 2 tens 4 ones + 3 tens 5 ones, 2 feet 4 inches + 3 feet 5 inches, 2 hours 4 minutes + 3 hours 50 minutes, and so on.

Place Value and the Standard Algorithms

With regard to this overarching theme, the place value system is an organized, compact way to write numbers using *place value units* that are powers of 10: ones, tens, hundreds, and so on. Explanations of all standard algorithms hinge on the manipulation of these place value units and the relationships between them (e.g., 10 tens = 1 hundred).

Multiplication

One of the earliest, easiest methods of forming a new unit is by creating groups of another unit. Kindergarten students take a stick of 10 linking cubes and break it into twos. "How many cubes are in your stick?" "Ten!" "Break it and make twos." "Count your twos with me: '1 two, 2 twos, 3 twos' ... We made 5 twos!" Groups of 4 apples, for example, can be counted: 1 four, 2 fours, 3 fours, 4 fours. Relating the new unit to the original unit develops the idea of multiplication: 3 groups of 4 apples equal 12 apples (or 3 fours are 12). Manipulating the new unit brings out other relationships: 3 fours + 7 fours = 10 fours or $(3 \times 4) + (7 \times 4) = (3 + 7) \times 4$.

Fractions

Forming fractional units is exactly the same as the procedure for multiplication, but the "group" can now be the amount when a whole unit is subdivided equally: A segment of length 1 can be subdivided into 4 segments of equal length, each representing the unit 1 fourth. The new unit can then be counted and manipulated just like whole numbers: 3 fourths + 7 fourths = 10 fourths.

Word Problems

Forming units to solve word problems is one of the most powerful examples of this overarching theme. Consider the following situation:

Each bottle holds 900 ml of water.
A bucket holds 6 times as much water as a bottle.
A glass holds 1/5 as much water as a bottle.

We can use the bottle capacity to form a unit pictorially and illustrate the other quantities with relationship to that unit:

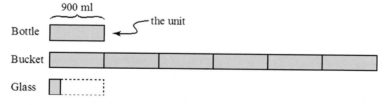

The unit can then be used to answer word problems about this situation, such as, "How much more does the bucket hold than 4 bottles?" (2 units or 1800 ml).

Once the units are established and defined, the task is simply manipulating them with arithmetic. With this repetition of prior experiences, the student realizes that he or she has seen this before.

HOW A STORY OF UNITS ALIGNS WITH THE INSTRUCTIONAL SHIFTS

A *Story of Units* is structured around the essential Instructional Shifts needed to implement the new college- and career-ready standards. These principles, articulated as three shifts (focus, coherence, and rigor), help educators understand what is required to implement the necessary changes. Rigor refers to the additional shifts of fluency, conceptual understanding, and application—and all three are done with a dual-intensity emphasis on practicing and understanding. All three Instructional Shifts are required to teach the new standards.

Shift 1: Focus—"Focus deeply on only the concepts that are prioritized in the standards."

A *Story of Units* follows the focus of the standards by relating every arithmetic idea back to understanding the idea of a unit:

- What the definition of the unit is in particular cases (e.g., whole numbers, fractions, decimals, measurements)
- Commonalities between all units (they can be added, subtracted, multiplied, and so on)
- The unique features of some units (e.g., a rectangle's area units, as opposed to its length units, can be calculated quickly by multiplying length measurements of the rectangle)

It is the study of the commonalities between units that drives the focus of A *Story of Units* so that the concepts that students learn are the ones prioritized by the standards. The commonalities form the interconnectedness of the math concepts and enable students to more easily transfer their mathematical skills and understanding across grades. Perhaps surprising, it is also the focused study of the commonalities between types of units that makes the contrast between these different types more pronounced. That is, by understanding the commonalities between types of units, students develop their ability to compare and contrast the types of units. The focus drives an understanding of the commonalities and the differences in the ways that arithmetic can be used to manipulate numbers.

Evidence of focus is seen as well in the integral use of the Partnership for Assessment of Readiness for College and Careers (PARCC) Content Emphases to focus on the major work of the grade level. Each module begins with the Focus Grade Level Standards clearly stating the clusters of standards that are emphasized in the material. As noted in the Publishers' Criteria, approximately three-quarters of the work is on the major clusters where students should be most fluent. Supporting clusters are interwoven as connecting components in core understanding while additional clusters introduce other key ideas.

Shift 2: Coherence—"Principals and teachers carefully connect the learning within and across grades so that … students can build new understanding onto foundations built in previous years."

A *Story of Units* is not a collection of topics. Rather, the modules and topics in the curriculum are woven through the progressions of the standards. A *Story of Units* carefully prioritizes and sequences those standards with a deliberate emphasis on mastery of the outlined major cluster standards. As students complete each module, this meticulous sequencing enables them to transfer their mathematical knowledge and understanding to new, increasingly challenging concepts.

Module Overview charts show how topics are aligned with standards to create an instructional sequence that is organized precisely to build on previous learning and to support future learning.

The teaching sequence chart for each topic outlines the instructional path by stating the learning objectives for each lesson. The sequence of problems in the material is structured to help teachers analyze the mathematics for themselves and help them with differentiated instruction. As students advance from simple to more complex concepts, the different problems provide opportunities for teachers to (1) break problems down for students struggling with a next step or (2) stretch problems out for those hungry for greater challenges.

Coherence is supported as well through the use of a finite set of concrete and pictorial models. As a result, students develop increasing familiarity with this limited set of consistently used models over the years. In second grade, for example, they use number disks (aka place value disks) to represent place value; that model remains constant through the third, fourth, and fifth grades. As new ideas are introduced, the consistent use of the same model leads students to more rapid and deeper understanding of new concepts.

Shift 3: Rigor—"Pursue, with equal intensity, three aspects of rigor in the major work of each grade: conceptual understanding, procedural skill and fluency, and applications."

The three-pronged nature of rigor undergirds a main theme of the Publishers' Criteria. Fluency, deep understanding, and application with equal intensity must drive instruction for students to meet the standards' rigorous expectations.

FLUENCY

"Students are expected to have speed and accuracy with simple calculations; teachers structure class time and/or homework time for students to memorize, through repetition, core functions."

Fluency represents a major part of the instructional vision that shapes A Story of Units; it is a daily, substantial, and sustained activity. One or two fluencies are required by the standards for each grade level, and fluency suggestions are included in most lessons. Implementation of effective fluency practice is supported by the lesson structure.

Fluency tasks are strategically designed for the teacher to easily administer and assess. A variety of suggestions for fluency activities are offered, such as mental math activities and interactive drills. Throughout the school year, such activities can be used with new material to strengthen skills and enable students to see their accuracy and speed increase measurably each day.

CONCEPTUAL UNDERSTANDING

"Students deeply understand and can operate easily within a math concept before moving on. They learn more than the trick to get the answer right. They learn the math."

Conceptual understanding requires far more than performing discrete and often disjointed procedures to determine an answer. Students must not only learn mathematical content; they must also be able to access that knowledge from numerous vantage points and communicate about the process. In A Story of Units, students use writing and speaking to solve mathematical problems, reflect on their learning, and analyze their thinking. Several times a week, the lessons and homework require students to write their solutions to word problems. Thus, students learn to express their understanding of concepts and articulate their thought processes through writing. Similarly, they participate in daily debriefings and learn to verbalize the patterns and connections between the current lesson and their previous learning, in addition to listening to and debating their peers' perspectives. The goal is to interweave the learning of new concepts with reflection time into students' everyday math experience.

At the module level, *sequence is everything*. Standards within a single module and modules across the year carefully build on each other to ensure that students have the requisite understanding to fully access new learning goals and integrate them into their developing schemas of understanding. The deliberate progression of the material follows the critical instructional areas outlined in the introduction of the standards for each grade.

APPLICATION

"Students are expected to use math and choose the appropriate concept for application even when they are not prompted to do so."

A *Story of Units* is designed to help students understand how to choose and apply mathematics concepts to solve problems. To achieve this, the modules include mathematical tools and diagrams that aid problem solving, interesting problems that encourage students to think quantitatively and creatively, and opportunities to model situations using mathematics. The goal is for students to see mathematics as connected to their environment, other disciplines, and the mathematics itself. Ranges of problems are presented within modules, topics, and lessons that serve multiple purposes:

- Single-step word problems that help students understand the meaning of a particular concept.
- Multistep word problems that support and develop instructional concepts and allow for cross-pollination of multiple concepts into a single problem.
- Exploratory tasks designed to break potential habits of rigid thinking. For example, asking students to draw at least three different triangles with a 15-inch perimeter encourages them to think of triangles other than equilaterals. Geometry problems with multiple solution paths and mental math problems that can be solved in many ways are further examples.

The Problem Sets are designed so that there is a healthy mix of PARCC type I, II, and III tasks:

Type I: Such tasks include computational problems, fluency exercises, conceptual problems, and applications, including one-step and multistep word problems.

Type II: These tasks require students to demonstrate reasoning skills, justify their arguments, and critique the reasoning of their peers.

Type III: For these problems, students must model real-world situations using mathematics and demonstrate more advanced problem-solving skills.

Dual intensity—"Students are practicing and understanding. There is more than a balance between these two things in the classroom—both are occurring with intensity."

A *Story of Units* achieves this goal through a balanced approach to lesson structure. Each lesson is structured to incorporate ten to twenty minutes of fluency activities, while the remaining time is devoted to developing conceptual understanding or applications—or both.

New conceptual understanding paves the way for new types of fluency. A *Story of Units* starts each grade with a variety of relevant fluency choices from the previous grade. As the year progresses and new concepts are taught, the range of choices grows. Teachers can—and are expected to—adapt their lessons to provide the intense practice with the fluencies that their students most need. Thus, A *Story of Units* doesn't wait months to spiral back to a concept. Rather, once a concept is learned, it is immediately spiraled back into the daily lesson structure through fluency and applications.

HOW A STORY OF UNITS ALIGNS WITH THE STANDARDS FOR MATHEMATICAL PRACTICE

Like the Instructional Shifts, each standard for mathematical practice is integrated into the design of A *Story of Units*.

1. **Make sense of problems and persevere in solving them.**

   An explicit way in which the curriculum integrates this standard is through its commitment to consistently engaging students in solving multistep problems. Purposeful integration of a variety of problem types that range in complexity naturally invites children to analyze givens, constraints, relationships, and goals. Problems require students to organize their thinking through drawing and modeling, which necessitates critical self-reflection on the actions they take to problem-solve. On a more foundational level, concept sequence, activities, and lesson structure present information from a variety of novel perspectives. The question, "How can I look at this differently?" undergirds the organization of the curriculum, each of its components, and the design of every problem.

2. **Reason abstractly and quantitatively.**

   The use of tape diagrams is one way in which A Story of Units provides students with opportunities to reason abstractly and quantitatively. For example, consider the following problem:

   > *A cook has a bag of rice that weighs 50 pounds. The cook buys another bag of rice that weighs 25 pounds more than the first bag. How many pounds of rice does the cook have?*

   To solve this problem, the student uses a tape diagram to abstractly represent the first bag of rice. To make a tape diagram for the second bag, the student reasons to decide whether the next bar is bigger, smaller, or the same size—and then must decide by how much. Once the student has drawn the models on paper, the fact that these quantities are presented as bags in the problem becomes irrelevant as the student shifts focus to manipulating the units to get the total. The unit has appropriately taken over the thought process necessary for solving the problem.

   Quantitative reasoning also permeates the curriculum as students focus in on units. Consider the problem "6 sevens plus 2 sevens is equal to 8 sevens." The unit being manipulated in this sequence is sevens.

3. **Construct viable arguments and critique the reasoning of others.**

   Time for debriefing is included in every daily lesson plan and represents one way in which the curriculum integrates this standard. During debriefings, teachers lead students in discussions or writing exercises that prompt children to analyze and explain their work, reflect on their own learning, and make connections between concepts. In addition to debriefings, partner sharing is woven throughout lessons to create frequent opportunities for students to develop this mathematical practice. Students use drawings, models, numeric representations, and precise language to make their learning and thinking understood by others.

4. **Model with mathematics.**

A first-grade student represents "3 students were playing. Some more came. Then there were 10. How many students came?" with the number sentence $3 + \square = 10$. A fourth-grade student represents a drawing of 5 halves of apples with an expression and writes $5 \times \frac{1}{2}$. Both students are modeling with mathematics. This is happening daily in word problems. Students write both "situation equations" and "solution equations" when solving word problems. In doing so, they are modeling MP.2, reason abstractly and quantitatively.

5. **Use appropriate tools strategically.**

Building students' independence with the use of models is a key feature of A Story of Units, and our approach to empowering students to use strategic learning tools is systematic. Models are introduced and used continuously so that eventually students use them automatically. The depth of familiarity that students have with the models not only ensures that they naturally become a part of students' schema but also facilitates a more rapid and deeper understanding of new concepts as they are introduced.

Aside from models, tools are introduced in Kindergarten and reappear throughout the curriculum in every concept. For example, rulers are tools that kindergartners use to create straight edges that organize their work and evenly divide their papers. They will continue to use them through Grade 5.

6. **Attend to precision.**

In every lesson of every module across the curriculum, students are manipulating, relating, and converting units and are challenged not only to use units in these ways but also to specify which unit they are using. Literally anything that can be counted can be a unit: There might be 3 frogs, 6 apples, 2 fours, 5 tens, 4 fifths, 9 cups, or 7 inches. Students use precise language to describe their work: "We used a paper clip as a unit of length." Understanding the unit is fundamental to their precise, conceptual manipulation. For example, 27 times 3 is not simply 2 times 3 and 7 times 3; rather, it should be thought of as 2 tens times 3 and 7 ones times 3. Specificity and precision with the unit is paramount to conceptual coherence and unity.

7. **Look for and make use of structure.**

There are several ways in which A Story of Units weaves this standard into the content of the curriculum. One way is through daily fluency practice. Sprints, for example, are intentionally patterned fluency activities. Students analyze the pattern of the sprint and use its discovery to assist them with automaticity—for example, "Is the pattern adding one or adding ten? How does knowing the pattern help me work faster?"

An example from a PreK lesson explicitly shows how concepts and activities are organized to guide students in identification and use of structure. In this lesson, the student is charged with the problem of using connecting cubes to make stairs for a bear to get up to his house. Students start with one cube to make the first stair. To make the second stair, students place a second cube next to the first but quickly realize that the two "stairs" are equal in height. In order to carry the bear upward, they must add another cube to the second stair so that it becomes higher than the first.

8. **Look for and express regularity in repeated reasoning.**

   Mental math is one way in which A Story of Units *brings this standard to life. It begins as early as first grade, when students start to make tens. Making ten becomes both a general method and a pathway for quickly manipulating units through addition and subtraction. For example, to mentally solve 12 + 3, students identify the 1 ten and add 10 + (2 + 3). Isolating or using ten as a reference point becomes a form of repeated reasoning that allows students to quickly and efficiently manipulate units.*

   In summary, the Instructional Shifts and the Standards for Mathematical Practice help establish the mechanism for thoughtful sequencing and emphasis on key topics in A Story of Units. It is evident that these pillars of the new standards combine to support the curriculum with a structural foundation for the content. Consequently, A Story of Units is artfully crafted to engage teachers and students alike while providing a powerful avenue for teaching and learning mathematics.

CHAPTER 3

Grade-Level Content Review

The Grade-Level Content Review begins with a list of modules developed to deliver instruction aligned to the standards at a given grade level. This introductory component is followed by three sections: the Summary of Year, the Rationale for Module Sequence, and the Alignment Chart with the grade-level standards. The Summary of Year portion of each grade level contains four pieces of information:

- The critical instructional areas for the grade
- The Key Areas of Focus for the grade band
- The Required Fluencies for the grade
- The Major Standard Emphasis Clusters for the grade

The Rationale for Module Sequence portion of each grade level provides a brief description of the instructional focus of each module for that grade and explains the developmental sequence of the mathematics.

The Alignment Chart for each grade lists the standards that are addressed in each module of the grade. Throughout the alignment charts, when a cluster is included without a footnote, it is taught in its entirety; there are also times when footnotes are relevant to particular standards within a cluster. All standards for each grade have been carefully included in the module sequence. Some standards are deliberately included in more than one module so that a strong foundation can be built over time.

The Grade-Level Content Review offers key information about grade-level content and provides a recommended framework for grouping and sequencing topics and standards.

Sequence of Grade 4 Modules Aligned with the Standards

Module 1: Place Value, Rounding, and Algorithms for Addition and Subtraction

Module 2: Unit Conversions and Problem Solving with Metric Measurement

Module 3: Multi-Digit Multiplication and Division

Module 4: Angle Measure and Plane Figures

Module 5: Fraction Equivalence, Ordering, and Operations

Module 6: Decimal Fractions

Module 7: Exploring Measurement with Multiplication

Summary of Year

Fourth-grade mathematics is about (1) developing understanding and fluency with multi-digit multiplication and developing understanding of dividing to find quotients involving multi-digit dividends; (2) developing an understanding of fraction equivalence, addition and subtraction of fractions with like denominators, and multiplication of fractions by whole numbers; and (3) understanding that geometric figures can be analyzed and classified based on their properties, such as having parallel sides, perpendicular sides, particular angle measures, and symmetry.

Key Areas of Focus for Grades 3–5: Multiplication and division of whole numbers and fractions–concepts, skills, and problem solving.

Required Fluency: 4.NBT.4 Add and subtract within 1,000,000.

Major Standard Emphasis Clusters

Operations and Algebraic Thinking

- Use the four operations with whole numbers to solve problems.

Number and Operations in Base Ten

- Generalize place value understanding for multi-digit whole numbers.
- Use place value understanding and properties of operations to perform multi-digit arithmetic.

Number and Operations–Fractions

- Extend understanding of fraction equivalence and ordering.
- Build fractions from unit fractions by applying and extending previous understandings of operations on whole numbers.
- Understand decimal notation for fractions, and compare decimal fractions.

RATIONALE FOR MODULE SEQUENCE IN GRADE 4

In Grade 4, students extend their work with whole numbers. They begin with large numbers using familiar units (tens and hundreds) and develop their understanding of thousands by building knowledge of the pattern of *times ten* in the base-ten system on the place value chart (4.NBT.1). In Grades 2 and 3, students focused on developing the concept of composing and decomposing place value units within the addition and subtraction algorithms. Now, in Grade 4, they see those (de)compositions through the lens of multiplicative comparison (e.g., 1 thousand is 10 times as much as 1 hundred). They next apply their broadened understanding of patterns on the place value chart to compare, round, add, and subtract. The module culminates with solving multistep word problems involving addition and subtraction modeled with tape diagrams that focus on numerical relationships.

The algorithms continue to play a part in Module 2 as students relate place value to metric units. This module helps students draw similarities:

1 ten	= 10 ones
1 hundred	= 10 tens
1 hundred	= 100 ones
1 meter	= 100 centimeters
1 thousand	= 1,000 ones
1 kilometer	= 1,000 meters
1 kilogram	= 1,000 grams
1 liter	= 1,000 milliliters

Students work with metric measurement in the context of the addition and subtraction algorithms, mental math, place value, and word problems. Customary units are used as a context for fractions in Module 5.

In Module 3, measurements provide the concrete foundation behind the distributive property in the multiplication algorithm: 4 × (1 m 2 cm) can be made physical using ribbon, where it is easy to see the 4 copies of 1 m and the 4 copies of 2 cm. Likewise, 4 × (1 ten 2 ones) = 4 tens 8 ones. Students then turn to the place value table with number disks to develop efficient procedures for multiplying and dividing one-digit whole numbers and use the table with number disks to understand and explain why the procedures work. Students also solve word problems throughout the module as they select and accurately apply appropriate methods to estimate, mentally calculate, or use the procedures they are learning to compute products and quotients.

Module 4 focuses as much on solving unknown angle problems using letters and equations as it does on building, drawing, and analyzing two-dimensional shapes in geometry. Students have used letters and equations to solve word problems in earlier grades. They continue to do so in Grade 4, and now they also learn to solve unknown-angle problems: work that challenges students to build and solve equations to find unknown angle measures. First, students learn the definition of *degree* and learn how to measure angles in degrees using a circular protractor. From the definition of *degree* and the fact that angle measures are additive, the following rudimentary facts about angles naturally follow:

1. **The sum of angle measurements around a point is 360 degrees.**

2. **The sum of angle measurements on a line is 180 degrees.**

Hence, from these two facts, students see that vertical angles are equal. Armed only with these facts, they are able to generate and solve equations as in figure 3.1:

Find the unknown angle x.

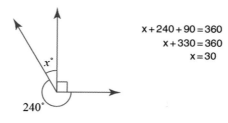

$$x + 240 + 90 = 360$$
$$x + 330 = 360$$
$$x = 30$$

Figure 3.1

Unknown-angle problems help to unlock algebraic concepts for students because such problems are visual. The x clearly stands for a specific number. If a student wished, he or she could place a protractor down on that angle and measure it to find x. But that destroys the joy of deducing the answer and solving the puzzle independently.

Module 5 centers on equivalent fractions and operations with fractions. We use fractions when there is a given unit, the *whole unit*, but we want to measure using a smaller unit, the *fractional unit*. To prepare students to explore the relationship between a fractional unit and its whole unit, examples of such relationships in different contexts were already carefully established earlier in the year:

360 degrees in	1 complete turn
100 centimeters in	1 meter
1,000 grams in	1 kilogram
1,000 milliliters in	1 liter

The beauty of fractional units, once defined and understood, is that they behave just as all other units do:

- 3 fourths + 5 fourths = 8 fourths just as 3 meters + 5 meters = 8 meters
- 4 × 3 fourths = 12 fourths just as 4 × 3 meters = 12 meters.

Students add and subtract fractions with like units using the area model and the number line. They multiply a fraction by a whole number where the interpretation is as repeated addition; for example, 3 fourths + 3 fourths = 2 × 3 fourths. Through this introduction to fraction arithmetic, they gradually come to understand fractions as units they can manipulate, just as they do whole numbers. Throughout the module, customary units of measurement provide a relevant context for the arithmetic.

Module 6, on decimal fractions, starts with the realization that decimal place value units are simply special fractional units; for example, 1 tenth = $\frac{1}{10}$, 1 hundredth = $\frac{1}{100}$. Fluency plays an important role in this topic as students learn to relate $\frac{3}{10}$ = 0.3 = 3 tenths. They also recognize that 3 tenths is equal to 30 hundredths and subsequently have their first experience adding and subtracting fractions with unlike units, for example, 3 tenths + 4 hundredths = 30 hundredths + 4 hundredths.

The year ends with a module focused on multiplication and measurement as students solve multistep word problems. Exploratory lessons support conceptual understanding of the relative sizes of measurement units. Students explore conversion in hands-on settings and subsequently apply those conversions to solve multistep word problems involving all operations and multiplicative comparison.

ALIGNMENT TO THE STANDARDS AND PLACEMENT OF STANDARDS IN THE MODULES

Module and Approximate Number of Instructional Days	Standards Addressed in Grade 4 Modules[1]
Module 1: Place Value, Rounding, and Algorithms for Addition and Subtraction (25 days)	**Use the four operations with whole numbers to solve problems.[2]** 4.OA.3 Solve multistep word problems posed with whole numbers and having whole-number answers using the four operations, including problems in which remainders must be interpreted. Represent these problems using equations with a letter standing for the unknown quantity. Assess the reasonableness of answers using mental computation and estimation strategies including rounding. **Generalize place value understanding for multi-digit whole numbers. (Grade 4 expectations in this domain are limited to whole numbers less than or equal to 1,000,000.)** 4.NBT.1 Recognize that in a multi-digit whole number, a digit in one place represents ten times what it represents in the place to its right. *For example, recognize that 700 ÷ 70 = 10 by applying concepts of place value and division.* 4.NBT.2 Read and write multi-digit whole numbers using base-ten numerals, number names, and expanded form. Compare two multi-digit numbers based on meanings of the digits in each place, using >, =, and < symbols to record the results of comparisons. 4.NBT.3 Use place value understanding to round multi-digit whole numbers to any place. **Use place value understanding and properties of operations to perform multi-digit arithmetic.[3]** 4.NBT.4 Fluently add and subtract multi-digit whole numbers using the standard algorithm.
Module 2: Unit Conversions and Problem Solving with Metric Measurement (7 days)	**Solve problems involving measurement and conversion of measurements from a larger unit to a smaller unit.[4]** 4.MD.1 Know relative sizes of measurement units within one system of units including km, m, cm; kg, g; lb, oz.; l, ml; hr, min, sec. Within a single system of measurement, express measurements in a larger unit in terms of a smaller unit. Record measurement equivalents in a two-column table. *For example, know that 1 ft is 12 times as long as 1 in. Express the length of a 4 ft snake as 48 in. Generate a conversion table for feet and inches listing the number pairs (1, 12), (2, 24), (3, 36), ...* 4.MD.2 Use the four operations to solve word problems involving distances, intervals of time, liquid volumes, masses of objects, and money, including problems involving simple fractions or decimals, and problems that require expressing measurements given in a larger unit in terms of a smaller unit. Represent measurement quantities using diagrams such as number line diagrams that feature a measurement scale.
Module 3: Multi-Digit Multiplication and Division (43 days)	**Use the four operations with whole numbers to solve problems.** 4.OA.1 Interpret a multiplication equation as a comparison, e.g., interpret 35 = 5 × 7 as a statement that 35 is 5 times as many as 7 and 7 times as many as 5. Represent verbal statements of multiplicative comparisons as multiplication equations. 4.OA.2 Multiply or divide to solve word problems involving multiplicative comparison, e.g., by using drawings and equations with a symbol for the unknown number to represent the problem, distinguishing multiplicative comparison from additive comparison. (See Standards Glossary, Table 2.) 4.OA.3 Solve multistep word problems posed with whole numbers and having whole-number answers using the four operations, including problems in which remainders must be interpreted. Represent these problems using equations with a letter standing for the unknown quantity. Assess the reasonableness of answers using mental computation and estimation strategies including rounding.

(Continued)

Module and Approximate Number of Instructional Days	Standards Addressed in Grade 4 Modules[1]
	Gain familiarity with factors and multiples. 4.OA.4 Find all factor pairs for a whole number in the range 1–100. Recognize that a whole number is a multiple of each of its factors. Determine whether a given whole number in the range 1–100 is a multiple of a given one-digit number. Determine whether a given whole number in the range 1–100 is prime or composite. **Use place value understanding and properties of operations to perform multi-digit arithmetic. (Grade 4 expectations in this domain are limited to whole numbers less than or equal to 1,000,000.)[5]** 4.NBT.5 Multiply a whole number of up to four digits by a one-digit whole number, and multiply two two-digit numbers, using strategies based on place value and the properties of operations. Illustrate and explain the calculation by using equations, rectangular arrays, and/or area models.[6] 4.NBT.6 Find whole-number quotients and remainders with up to four-digit dividends and one-digit divisors, using strategies based on place value, the properties of operations, and/or the relationship between multiplication and division. Illustrate and explain the calculation by using equations, rectangular arrays, and/or area models. **Solve problems involving measurement and conversion of measurements from a larger unit to a smaller unit.[7]** 4.MD.3 Apply the area and perimeter formulas for rectangles in real world and mathematical problems. For example, find the width of a rectangular room given the area of the flooring and the length, by viewing the area formula as a multiplication equation with an unknown factor.
Module 4: Angle Measure and Plane Figures (20 days)	**Geometric measurement: understand the concept of an angle and measure angles.** 4.MD.5 Recognize angles as geometric shapes that are formed wherever two rays share a common endpoint, and understand concepts of angle measurement: a. An angle is measured with reference to a circle with its center at the common endpoint of the rays, by considering the fraction of the circular arc between the points where the two rays intersect the circle. An angle that turns through 1/360 of a circle is called a "one-degree angle," and can be used to measure angles. b. An angle that turns through n one-degree angles is said to have an angle measure of n degrees. 4.MD.6 Measure angles in whole-number degrees using a protractor. Sketch angles of specified measure. 4.MD.7 Recognize angle measure as additive. When an angle is decomposed into non-overlapping parts, the angle measure of the whole is the sum of the angle measures of the parts. Solve addition and subtraction problems to find unknown angles on a diagram in real world and mathematical problems, e.g., by using an equation with a symbol for the unknown angle measure. **Draw and identify lines and angles, and classify shapes by properties of their lines and angles.** 4.G.1 Draw points, lines, line segments, rays, angles (right, acute, obtuse), and perpendicular and parallel lines. Identify these in two-dimensional figures. 4.G.2 Classify two-dimensional figures based on the presence or absence of parallel or perpendicular lines, or the presence or absence of angles of a specified size. Recognize right triangles as a category, and identify right triangles. 4.G.3 Recognize a line of symmetry for a two-dimensional figure as a line across the figure such that the figure can be folded along the line into matching parts. Identify line-symmetric figures and draw lines of symmetry.

Module and Approximate Number of Instructional Days	Standards Addressed in Grade 4 Modules[1]

Module 5: Fraction Equivalence, Ordering, and Operations[8] (45 days)	**Generate and analyze patterns.**
	4.OA.5 Generate a number or shape pattern that follows a given rule. Identify apparent features of the pattern that were not explicit in the rule itself. *For example, given the rule "Add 3" and the starting number 1, generate terms in the resulting sequence and observe that the terms appear to alternate between odd and even numbers. Explain informally why the numbers will continue to alternate in this way.*
	Extend understanding of fraction equivalence and ordering. (Grade 4 expectations in this domain are limited to fractions with denominators 2, 3, 4, 5, 6, 8, 10, 12, and 100.)
	4.NF.1 Explain why a fraction a/b is equivalent to a fraction $(n \times a)/(n \times b)$ by using visual fraction models, with attention to how the number and size of the parts differ even though the two fractions themselves are the same size. Use this principle to recognize and generate equivalent fractions.
	4.NF.2 Compare two fractions with different numerators and different denominators, e.g., by creating common denominators or numerators, or by comparing to a benchmark fraction such as 1/2. Recognize that comparisons are valid only when the two fractions refer to the same whole. Record the results of comparisons with symbols >, =, or <, and justify the conclusions, e.g., by using a visual fraction model.
	Build fractions from unit fractions by applying and extending previous understanding of operations on whole numbers.
	4.NF.3 Understand a fraction a/b with $a > 1$ as a sum of fractions $1/b$.
	  a. Understand addition and subtraction of fractions as joining and separating parts referring to the same whole.
	  b. Decompose a fraction into a sum of fractions with the same denominator in more than one way, recording each decomposition by an equation. Justify decompositions, e.g., by using a visual fraction model. *Examples: 3/8 = 1/8 + 1/8 + 1/8; 3/8 = 1/8 + 2/8; 2 1/8 = 1 + 1 + 1/8 = 8/8 + 8/8 + 1/8.*
	  c. Add and subtract mixed numbers with like denominators, e.g., by replacing each mixed number with an equivalent fraction, and/or by using properties of operations and the relationship between addition and subtraction.
	  d. Solve word problems involving addition and subtraction of fractions referring to the same whole and having like denominators, e.g., by using visual fraction models and equations to represent the problem.
	4.NF.4 Apply and extend previous understandings of multiplication to multiply a fraction by a whole number.
	  a. Understand a fraction a/b as a multiple of 1/b. For example, use a visual fraction model to represent 5/4 as the product 5 × (1/4), recording the conclusion by the equation 5/4 = 5 × (1/4).
	  b. Understand a multiple of a/b as a multiple of 1/b, and use this understanding to multiply a fraction by a whole number. For example, use a visual fraction model to express 3 × (2/5) as 6 × (1/5), recognizing this product as 6/5. (In general, n × (a/b) = (n × a)/b.)
	  c. Solve word problems involving multiplication of a fraction by a whole number, e.g., by using visual fraction models and equations to represent the problem. *For example, if each person at a party will eat 3/8 of a pound of roast beef, and there will be 5 people at the party, how many pounds of roast beef will be needed? Between what two whole numbers does your answer lie?*
	Represent and interpret data.
	4.MD.4 Make a line plot to display a data set of measurements in fractions of a unit (1/2, 1/4, 1/8). Solve problems involving addition and subtraction of fractions by using information presented in line plots. *For example, from a line plot find and interpret the difference in length between the longest and shortest specimens in an insect collection.*

Module and Approximate Number of Instructional Days	Standards Addressed in Grade 4 Modules[1]
Module 6: Decimal Fractions (20 days)	**Understand decimal notations for fractions, and compare decimal fractions. (Grade 4 expectations in this domain are limited to fractions with denominators 2, 3, 4, 5, 6, 8, 10, 12, and 100.)[9]** 4.NF.5 Express a fraction with denominator 10 as an equivalent fraction with denominator 100, and use this technique to add two fractions with respective denominators 10 and 100. *For example, express 3/10 as 30/100, and add 3/10 + 4/100 = 34/100.* (Students who can generate equivalent fractions can develop strategies for adding fractions with unlike denominators in general. But addition and subtraction with unlike denominators in general is not a requirement at this grade.) 4.NF.6 Use decimal notation for fractions with denominators 10 or 100. *For example, rewrite 0.62 as 62/100; describe a length as 0.62 meters; locate 0.62 on a number line diagram.* 4.NF.7 Compare two decimals to hundredths by reasoning about their size. Recognize that comparisons are valid only when the two decimals refer to the same whole. Record the results of comparisons with the symbols >, =, or <, and justify the conclusions, e.g., by using a visual model. **Solve problems involving measurement and conversion of measurements from a larger unit to a smaller unit.[10]** 4.MD.2 Use the four operations to solve word problems involving distances, intervals of time, liquid volumes, masses of objects, and money, including problems involving simple fractions or decimals, and problems that require expressing measurements given in a larger unit in terms of a smaller unit. Represent measurement quantities using diagrams such as number line diagrams that feature a measurement scale.
Module 7: Exploring Measurement with Multiplication (20 days)	**Use the four operations with whole numbers to solve problems.** 4.OA.1 Interpret a multiplication equation as a comparison, e.g., interpret 35 = 5 × 7 as a statement that 35 is 5 times as many as 7 and 7 times as many as 5. Represent verbal statements of multiplicative comparisons as multiplication equations. 4.OA.2 Multiply or divide to solve word problems involving multiplicative comparison, e.g., by using drawings and equations with a symbol for the unknown number to represent the problem, distinguishing multiplicative comparison from additive comparison. (See Standards Glossary, Table 2.) 4.OA.3 Solve multistep word problems posed with whole numbers and having whole-number answers using the four operations, including problems in which remainders must be interpreted. Represent these problems using equations with a letter standing for the unknown quantity. Assess the reasonableness of answers using mental computation and estimation strategies including rounding. **Solve problems involving measurement and conversion of measurements from a larger unit to a smaller unit.[11]** 4.MD.1 Know relative sizes of measurement units within one system of units including km, m, cm; kg, g; lb, oz.; l, ml; hr, min, sec. Within a single system of measurement, express measurements in a larger unit in terms of a smaller unit. Record measurement equivalents in a two-column table. *For example, know that 1 ft is 12 times as long as 1 in. Express the length of a 4 ft snake as 48 in. Generate a conversion table for feet and inches listing the number pairs (1, 12), (2, 24), (3, 36), …* 4.MD.2 Use the four operations to solve word problems involving distances, intervals of time, liquid volumes, masses of objects, and money, including problems involving simple fractions or decimals, and problems that require expressing measurements given in a larger unit in terms of a smaller unit. Represent measurement quantities using diagrams such as number line diagrams that feature a measurement scale.

CHAPTER 4

Curriculum Design

Curriculum design details the approach to modules, lessons, and assessment in *A Story of Units*. This chapter describes the key elements in the modules, as well as the role each plays in successful implementation of the new standards. We provide a wealth of information about how to achieve the components of instructional rigor (fluency, concept development, and application) that the standards demand.

APPROACH TO MODULE STRUCTURE

One of the first steps in designing a curriculum to implement the standards is to determine the grouping and sequencing of the standards at each grade level. This process should be well thought out, and decisions should be based on sound rationale. It is imperative that standards for a particular grade level be structured appropriately and addressed adequately.

Making key information available to classroom teachers in each module or unit of study helps to ensure successful implementation of the standards. The authors of the curriculum included numerous features to assist teachers not only in their day-to-day classroom activities but also in developing their understanding of the mathematics content and the standards.

Each module has four primary parts: Module Overview, Topic Overviews, Lessons, and Assessments:

- The Module Overview, rich with valuable information, introduces the key components of each module. It outlines the progression of the lessons from the beginning of the module to the end. The components of the overview are as follows:
  - The opening narrative explains the progression of the mathematics through the module topic by topic.
  - Distribution of Instructional Minutes is a diagram that suggests a possible distribution of class time based on the emphasis of particular lesson components in different lessons throughout the module.
  - Focus Grade-Level Standards are the major standards that the module targets.

- Foundational Standards are prerequisite knowledge that support the Focus Grade-Level Standards. These include standards addressed prior to the module that are essential for student learning and understanding. This section can be helpful in preparing for teaching lessons and for addressing any gaps that might crop up, especially during the first couple of years of implementation.
  - Focus Standards for Mathematical Practice act as a guide to create a well-rounded, standards-aligned classroom environment. This module element highlights which of the eight Standards for Mathematical Practice are a focus of the module and explains how each is addressed in the module.
  - Overview of Module Topics and Lesson Objectives lists each topic in the module, along with the associated standards and lesson objectives. The chart provides the number of days allotted for coverage of each topic. The chart also notes when the Mid-Module and End-of-Module Assessments should be administered during the module and how much time is allotted for each.
  - Terminology consists of both new and recently introduced terms and familiar terms and symbols. Descriptions, examples, and illustrations of the terms are included in this section.
  - Suggested Tools and Representations provides teachers with a list of the models, manipulatives, diagrams, and so forth that are recommended to teach the content of the module.
  - The Assessment Summary gives key information about the assessments of the module, including where within the module they are given and what standards are addressed.

- The Topic Overview lists the Focus Standards associated with the topic. It also provides a narrative similar to that found in the Module Overview but with information regarding specific lessons within the topic. The overview also offers Coherence Links, which reference other modules in the curriculum giving teachers access to foundational and more advanced material related to the topic. A chart detailing the objectives for each lesson is the final feature of the overview.

- Lessons and Assessments are the remaining primary parts of the module. The sections that follow detail these module components.

APPROACH TO LESSON STRUCTURE

Fluency, concept development, and application, all components of instructional rigor, are demanded by the new standards (see Instructional Shifts in chapter 2) and should be layered into daily lessons to help guide students through the mathematics. Lessons must be structured to incorporate fluency activities along with the development of conceptual understanding, procedural skills, and problem solving. Ideally, these components are taught through the deliberate progression of material from concrete to pictorial to abstract. All stages of instruction ought to be designed to help students reach higher and higher levels of understanding. The lesson design in A *Story of Units* reflects these ideals and is an exemplary model of how to achieve the demands the standards necessitates.

Through a balanced approach to lesson design, A *Story of Units* supports the development of an increasingly complex understanding of the mathematical concepts and topics within the standards. This type of balanced approach to lesson design naturally surfaces patterns and connections between concepts, tools, strategies, and real-world applications. Each lesson has a distinct structure made up of four primary components.

The time spent on each component in a daily lesson should vary between lessons and is guided by the rigor emphasized in the standard the lesson is addressing (figures 4.1 and 4.2). For example, if the word *fluently* is used within the text of a standard, a lesson involving that standard will often have more time devoted to Fluency Practice and Concept Development than to Application Problem. If the word *understand* is used in the text of a standard, then Concept Development is more likely to be weighted heavily. In the same way, the phrase *real-world problems* in the text of a standard will lead to a lesson that concentrates more on application problems. The Student Debrief component concludes the lesson with yet another carefully orchestrated opportunity for students to engage in one or more mathematical practice standards. It also provides time for reflection and consolidation of understanding.

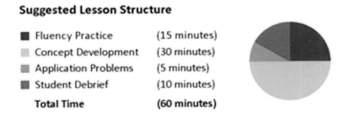

Figure 4.1   Suggested Lesson Structure

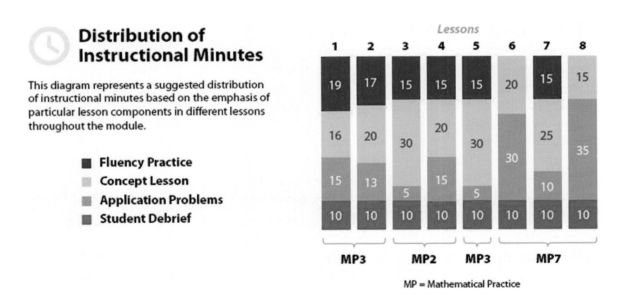

Figure 4.2   Distribution of Instructional Minutes

The time devoted to each of the four components of a lesson can be viewed at a glance using the Distribution of Instructional Minutes chart from the Module Overview. The actual order of Fluency Practice, Application Problem, Concept Development, and Student Debrief in each lesson is determined by the objective. In general, however, fluency is first because animated, adrenaline-rich work gets students ready to learn for the Application Problem and Concept Development. Solving a word problem before the Concept Development serves a variety of purposes, for example, giving a new concept a meaningful context or reviewing important understandings necessary for the new concept. The Student Debrief wraps up the ideas learned for the day and is the metacognitive component of the lesson structure (see its description later in this chapter).

The lesson structure we have just set out, consisting of four major components, is not the way to meet the demands for quality instruction. There are good reasons to change the structure at times. We use this suggested lesson structure for the most part but do at times reposition or omit a component, for example, positioning the Application Problem to follow the Concept Development, omitting it entirely, or omitting the fluency for a day. More significant reorganizations do occur during explorations. The Instructional Shifts require that the three components of rigor be taught with equal intensity. Although this does not mean an equal amount of time for each component every day, any alternative lesson structure needs to meet the high expectations demanded by the standards for all three components of rigor in the major work of each grade.

FLUENCY PRACTICE

Fluency is designed to promote automaticity by engaging students in practice in ways that excite and intrigue them as well as get their adrenaline flowing. Automaticity is critical so that students avoid using up too many of their attention resources with lower-level skills when they are addressing higher-level problems. Automaticity prepares students with the computational foundation to enable deep understanding in flexible ways.

We suggest that for the first three weeks of school, teachers include *at minimum* 10 minutes of daily fluency work. This is generally high-paced and energetic work, celebrating improvement and focusing on recognizing patterns and connections within the material. Early in the year, we want students to see their skills grow significantly on both the individual and class levels. Like opening a basketball practice with team drills and exercises, both personal and group improvements are exciting and prepare the players for application in the game setting.

A *Story of Units* offers fluency activities that teachers may either select and use or study and then create their own. Fluency activities for each lesson are intentionally organized so that activities revisit previously learned material to develop automaticity, anticipate future concepts, and strategically preview or build skills for the day's concept development. It is important to provide ample opportunities to review familiar fluencies as needed, as well as to begin developing automaticity with new ones. The suggestions may or may not be ideal for the students in a given class. As teachers work with the materials, they should adjust them to fit their students' needs.

Like drills in sports, the value of structured fluency practice should be immediately recognizable to students. Becoming proficient and staying proficient at math can be compared to doing the same in sports: use it or lose it.

CONCEPT DEVELOPMENT

Intentional sequencing of standards and topics across a grade ensures that students have the requisite understanding to fully access new learning goals and integrate them into their developing schemas. The conceptual development portion of a lesson articulates the standards and topics through a deliberate progression of material, from concrete to pictorial to abstract. This structure complements and supports an increasingly complex understanding of concepts.

Of course, not every lesson can move in this exact order. Sometimes the concrete level has been covered in a prior grade level. Sometimes the lesson moves from the abstract to the pictorial or concrete. For example, in "Draw a picture of 4 + 4 + 4," and "With your number disks [or bundles], show me 248 + 100," students begin with the abstract number problem and illustrate the idea pictorially or concretely.

The goal is always to strengthen students' understanding of numbers rather than to teach manipulatives. The concrete is important when conceptual understanding is weak. Manipulatives are expensive in terms of instructional minutes. However, omitting them can sometimes result in elongating the learning process if students have failed to miss a critical connection. When necessary, it is better to take the time to reestablish meaning at the concrete and pictorial levels and move as efficiently as possible to the abstract.

In A *Story of Units*, Concept Development constitutes the major portion of instruction and generally comprises at least twenty minutes of the total lesson time. It is the primary lesson component in which new learning is introduced. Concept Development elaborates on the "how-to" of delivery through models, sample vignettes, and dialogue, all meant to give teachers a snapshot of what the classroom might look and sound like at each step of the way. Teachers' word choices may be different from those in the vignettes, and they should use what works from the suggested talking points, along with their knowledge of their students' needs, as they write their own.

APPLICATION PROBLEMS

A *Story of Units* models a design that helps students understand how to choose and apply the correct mathematics concept to solve real-world problems. To achieve this, lessons use tools and models, problems that cause students to think quantitatively and creatively, and patterns that repeat so frequently that students come to see them as connected to their environment and other disciplines.

There are clearly different possible choices for delivery of instruction when engaging in problem solving. The beginning of the year should be characterized by establishing routines that encourage hard, intelligent work through guided practice rather than exploration. This practice serves to model the behaviors that students will need to work independently later. It is also wise to clearly establish a very different tone of work on application problems from that of the "quick answers" of fluency—for example, "We just did some fast math. Now let's slow down and take more time with these problems."

The more students participate in reasoning through problems with a systematic approach, the more they internalize those behaviors and thought processes. In A *Story of Units*, lessons provide application problems that directly relate to Concept Development. Students are encouraged to solve these problems using the following steps of read-draw-write (RDW):

1. **Read the problem.**
2. **Draw and label.**
3. **Write a number sentence and a word sentence.**

While moving through the RDW process, students ask themselves questions: *What do I see? Can I draw something? What conclusions can I make from my drawing?*

STUDENT DEBRIEF

In A *Story of Units*, the Student Debrief closes the lesson, but generally lessons should allow time for reflection and consolidation of understanding. This component in the *Eureka Math* curriculum models how a teacher might approach lesson closure.

Rather than stating the objective of the lesson to the students at its beginning, we wait until the dynamic action of the lesson has taken place. Then we reflect back on it with the students to analyze the learning that occurred. We want *them* to articulate the focus of the lesson.

In the Student Debrief, we develop students' metacognition by helping them make connections between parts of the lesson, concepts, strategies, and tools on their own. We draw out or introduce key vocabulary by helping students appropriately name the learning they describe.

The goal is for students to see and hear multiple perspectives from their classmates and mentally construct a multifaceted image of the concepts they are learning. Through questions that help make these connections explicit and dialogue that directly engages students in the Standards for Mathematical Practice, they articulate those observations so that the lesson's objective becomes clear to them.

Like the other lesson components, the Student Debrief includes suggested lists of questions to invite the reflection and active processing of the totality of the lesson. The purpose of these talking points is to guide teachers' planning for eliciting higher-order thinking by students. Rather than ask all of the questions provided, teachers should use those that resonate most as they consider what will best support students in articulating the focus from the lesson's multiple perspectives.

Sharing and analyzing high-quality student work is a consistent feature of the vignettes in this section. This technique encourages students to engage in the mathematical practices, which they come to value and respect as much as or more than speed in calculation. What the teacher values, the students will too; sharing and analyzing high-quality work gives teachers the opportunity to model and then demand authentic student work and dialogue.

Conversation constitutes a primary medium through which learning occurs in the Student Debrief. Teachers can prepare students by establishing routines for talking early in the year. For example, pair sharing is an invaluable structure to build for this and other components of the lesson. During the debrief, teachers should circulate as students share, noting which partnerships are bearing fruit and which need support. They might join struggling communicators for a moment to give them sentence stems. Regardless of the scaffolding techniques that a teacher decides to use, all students should be clear enough on the lesson's focus to either give a good example or make a statement about it.

Exit Tickets close the Student Debrief component of each lesson. These short, formative assessments are meant to provide quick glimpses of the day's major learning for students and teacher. Through this routine, students grow accustomed to showing accountability for each day's learning and produce valuable data for the teacher that become an indispensable planning tool.

STANDARDS FOR MATHEMATICAL PRACTICE

The Standards for Mathematical Practice are seamlessly woven into each lesson through various components of delivery that require the level of thinking and behaviors that the practices embody. The following examples from *A Story of Units* illustrate how teachers might integrate mathematical practices into daily lessons:

- Carefully crafted fluency activities engage students in looking for and making use of structure, as well as looking for and expressing regularity in repeated reasoning.

- The RDW sequence on which problem solving is based provides opportunities for students to select appropriate tools, model word problems using mathematics, and reason abstractly and quantitatively.

- Concept Development consistently invites students to make sense of problems and persevere in solving them as they grapple with new learning through increasingly complex concrete, pictorial, and abstract applications.

- Each lesson's Student Debrief, as well as ongoing debriefing embedded within each lesson component, requires students to construct arguments and critique the reasoning of others. Questioning and dialogue throughout the lessons ensure that students are not only engaging in the standards, but also that they are explicitly aware of, and reflecting on, those behaviors.

SAMPLE LESSON

In order to clearly illustrate the approach to lesson structure described above, a sample lesson follows. This is Lesson 7 from Grade 4 Module 5 whose objective is to use the area model and multiplication to show the equivalence of two fractions. Although Concept Development often follows Fluency Practice, this lesson provides an example of another lesson component, Application Problem, as the second component of the lesson.

Lesson 7

Objective: Use the area model and multiplication to show the equivalence of two fractions.

Suggested Lesson Structure

■ Fluency Practice	(12 minutes)
▨ Application Problem	(4 minutes)
▢ Concept Development	(34 minutes)
■ Student Debrief	(10 minutes)
Total Time	**(60 minutes)**

Fluency Practice (12 minutes)

▪ Break Apart Fractions **4.NF.3**	(4 minutes)
▪ Count by Equivalent Fractions **3.NF.3**	(4 minutes)
▪ Draw Equivalent Fractions **4.NF.1**	(4 minutes)

Break Apart Fractions (4 minutes)

Materials: (S) Personal white boards

Note: This fluency activity reviews G4–M5–Lessons 1–3.

T: (Project a tape diagram of 3 fifths with the whole labeled.) Name the fraction of 1 whole that's shaded.

S: $\frac{3}{5}$.

T: (Write $\frac{3}{5}$ = ___.) Say the fraction.

S: 3 fifths.

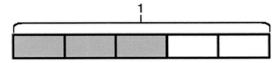

Figure 4.3

T: On your boards, write $\frac{3}{5}$ as a repeated addition sentence using unit fractions.

S: (Write $\frac{3}{5}=\frac{1}{5}+\frac{1}{5}+\frac{1}{5}$.)

T: (Write $\frac{3}{5}=\frac{1}{5}+\frac{1}{5}+\frac{1}{5}=\underline{\quad}\times\frac{1}{5}$.) On your boards, complete the number sentence.

S: (Write $\frac{3}{5}=\frac{1}{5}+\frac{1}{5}+\frac{1}{5}=3\times\frac{1}{5}$.)

Continue process for the following possible sequence: $\frac{5}{6}=\frac{1}{6}+\frac{1}{6}+\frac{1}{6}+\frac{1}{6}+\frac{1}{6}=5\times\frac{1}{6}$ and

$$\frac{5}{8}=\frac{1}{8}+\frac{1}{8}+\frac{1}{8}+\frac{1}{8}+\frac{1}{8}=5\times\frac{1}{8}.$$

Count by Equivalent Fractions (4 minutes)

Materials: (S) Personal white boards

Note: This fluency activity prepares students for lessons throughout this module.

T: Count from 0 to 10 by ones.

S: 0, 1, 2, 3, 4, 5, 6, 7, 8, 9, 10.

T: Count by 1 fourths to 10 fourths. Start at 0 fourths. (Write as students count.)

$\frac{0}{4}$	$\frac{1}{4}$	$\frac{2}{4}$	$\frac{3}{4}$	$\frac{4}{4}$	$\frac{5}{4}$	$\frac{6}{4}$	$\frac{7}{4}$	$\frac{8}{4}$	$\frac{9}{4}$	$\frac{10}{4}$
0	$\frac{1}{4}$	$\frac{2}{4}$	$\frac{3}{4}$	1	$\frac{5}{4}$	$\frac{6}{4}$	$\frac{7}{4}$	2	$\frac{9}{4}$	$\frac{10}{4}$

S: $\frac{0}{4},\frac{1}{4},\frac{2}{4},\frac{3}{4},\frac{4}{4},\frac{5}{4},\frac{6}{4},\frac{7}{4},\frac{8}{4},\frac{9}{4},\frac{10}{4}$.

T: 4 fourths is the same as 1 of what unit?

S: 1 one.

T: (Beneath 4 fourths, write 1.) 2 wholes is the same as how many fourths?

S: 8 fourths.

T: (Beneath $\frac{8}{4}$, write 2.) Let's count to 10 fourths again, but this time, say the whole numbers when you come to a whole number. Start at 0.

S: $0,\frac{1}{4},\frac{2}{4},\frac{3}{4},1,\frac{5}{4},\frac{6}{4},\frac{7}{4},2,\frac{9}{4},\frac{10}{4}$.

Repeat process, counting by thirds to 10 thirds.

Draw Equivalent Fractions (4 minutes)

Materials: (S) Personal white boards

Note: This fluency activity reviews G4–M5–Lesson 6.

T: (Write $\frac{2}{3}$.) Say the fraction.

S: $\frac{2}{3}$.

T: On your boards, draw an area model to show $\frac{2}{3}$.

S: (Draw a model partitioned into 3 equal units. Shade 2 units.)

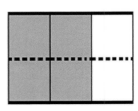

$\frac{2}{3}=\frac{4}{6}$

Figure 4.3 (Continued)

T: (Write $\frac{2}{3} = \frac{4}{}$.) Draw a dotted horizontal line to find the equivalent fraction.

S: (Draw a dotted horizontal line, breaking 3 units into 6 smaller units. Write $\frac{2}{3} = \frac{4}{6}$.)

Continue process for the following possible sequence: $\frac{2}{3} = \frac{6}{}$, $\frac{3}{4} = \frac{6}{}$, $\frac{2}{5} = \frac{4}{}$, and $\frac{4}{5} = \frac{12}{}$.

Application Problem (4 minutes)

Model an equivalent fraction for $\frac{4}{7}$ using an area model.

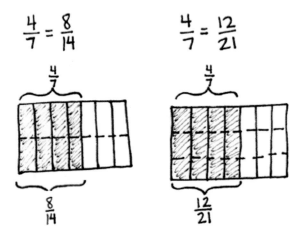

NOTES ON
MULTIPLE MEANS OF
REPRESENTATION:

Students working below grade level and others may benefit from explicit instruction as they decompose unit fractions. When doubling the number of units, instruct students to draw one horizontal dotted line. When tripling, draw two lines, and so on.

Note: This Application Problem reviews G4–M5–Lesson 6 and leads into today's lesson as students find equivalent fractions using multiplication.

Concept Development (34 minutes)

Materials: (S) Personal white boards

Problem 1: Determine that multiplying the numerator and denominator by *n* results in an equivalent fraction.

T: Draw an area model representing 1 whole partitioned into thirds. Shade and record $\frac{1}{3}$ below the area model. Draw 1 horizontal line across the area model.

S: (Partition area model.)

T: What happened to the size of the fractional units?

MP.7

S: The units got smaller. The unit became half the size.

T: What happened to the number of units in the whole?

S: There were 3; now there are 6. We doubled the total number of units.

T: What happened to the number of selected units when we drew the dotted line?

S: There was 1 unit selected, and now there are 2! It doubled, too!

T: That's right. We can record the doubling of units with multiplication: $\frac{1}{3} = \frac{1 \times 2}{3 \times 2} = \frac{2}{6}$.

S: Hey, I remember from third grade that $\frac{1}{3}$ is the same as $\frac{2}{6}$.

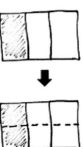

Figure 4.3 (Continued)

T: Yes, they are equivalent fractions.

T: Why didn't doubling the number of selected units make the fraction larger?

S: We didn't change the amount of the fraction, just the size. Yeah, so the size of the units became half as big.

T: Draw an area model representing 1 whole partitioned with a vertical line into 2 halves.

T: Shade and record $\frac{1}{2}$ below the area model. If we want to rewrite $\frac{1}{2}$ using 4 times as many units, what should we do?

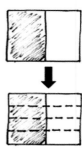

S: Draw horizontal dotted lines, three of them. Then, we can write a number sentence using multiplication. This time it's 4 times as many, so we will multiply the top number and the bottom number by 4.

T: Show me. (Allow time for students to partition the area model.) What happened to the size of the fractional unit?

S: The size of the fractional unit got smaller.

T: What happened to the number of units in the whole?

S: There are 4 times as many. They quadrupled.

T: What happened to the number of selected units?

S: There was 1, and now there are 4. The number of selected units quadrupled!

T: Has the size of the selected units changed?

S: There are more smaller unit fractions instead of one bigger unit fraction, but the area is still the same.

T: What can you conclude about $\frac{1}{2}$ and $\frac{4}{8}$?

S: They are equal!

T: Let's show that using multiplication: $\frac{1}{2} = \frac{1 \times 4}{2 \times 4} = \frac{4}{8}$. $\left(\frac{4 \text{ times as many selected units}}{4 \text{ times as many units in the whole}} \right)$

T: When we quadrupled the number of units, the number of selected units quadrupled. When we doubled the number of units, the number of selected units doubled. What do you predict would happen to the shaded fraction if we tripled the units?

S: The number of units within the shaded fraction would triple, too.

Problem 2: Given an area model, determine an equivalent fraction for the area selected.

T: (Display area model showing $\frac{1}{4}$.) Work with your partner to determine an equivalent fraction to $\frac{1}{4}$.

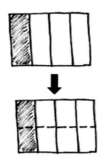

S: Let's draw one horizontal line. That will double the number of units. We can draw two horizontal lines. That will triple the number of units and make them smaller, too. If we multiply the top and bottom numbers by 4, we could quadruple the number of units. Each one will be a quarter the size, too.

Circulate to listen for student understanding and to monitor their work. Reconvene to examine one or more equivalent fractions.

T: Some groups drew one horizontal line. (Demonstrate.) Tell your partner what happened to the size of the units.

S: The units got smaller.

T: Tell your partner what happened to the number of units.

S: There are twice as many units.

Figure 4.3   (Continued)

T: Let's record that: $\frac{1}{4} = \frac{1 \times 2}{4 \times 2} = \frac{2}{8}$.

T: What is the relationship of the **numerators**, the top numbers, in the equivalent fractions?

S: The numerator in $\frac{2}{8}$ is double the numerator in $\frac{1}{4}$ because we doubled the number of selected units. Since the size of the selected units are half as big, we doubled the numerator.

T: What is the relationship of the **denominators**, the bottom numbers, in the equivalent fractions?

S: The denominator in $\frac{2}{8}$ is double the denominator in $\frac{1}{4}$ because we doubled the number of units. Since the size of the units are half as big, we doubled the denominator.

Problem 3: Express an equivalent fraction using multiplication and verify by drawing an area model.

T: Discuss with your partner how to find another way to name $\frac{1}{3}$ without drawing an area model first.

S: Let's triple the number of units in the whole. So, we have to multiply the numerator and the denominator by 3. Or, we could double the top number and double the bottom number.

T: Now verify that the fraction you found is equivalent by drawing an area model.

S: (Work.)

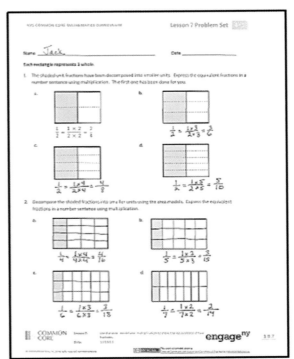

Problem Set (10 minutes)

Students should do their personal best to complete the Problem Set within the allotted 10 minutes. For some classes, it may be appropriate to modify the assignment by specifying which problems they work on first. Some problems do not specify a method for solving. Students solve these problems using the RDW approach used for Application Problems.

Student Debrief (10 minutes)

Lesson Objective: Use the area model and multiplication to show the equivalence of two fractions.

The Student Debrief is intended to invite reflection and active processing of the total lesson experience.

Invite students to review their solutions for the Problem Set. They should check work by comparing answers with a partner before going over answers as a class. Look for misconceptions or misunderstandings that can be addressed in the Debrief. Guide students in a conversation to debrief the Problem Set and process the lesson.

Figure 4.3   (Continued)

You may choose to use any combination of the questions below to lead the discussion.

- **What pattern did you notice for Problems 1(a–d)?**

- Discuss and compare with your partner your answers to Problems 2(e) and 2(f).

- In Problem 2, the unit fractions have different **denominators.** Discuss with your partner how the size of a unit fraction is related to the denominator.

- The **numerator** identifies the number of units selected. Can the numerator be larger than the denominator?

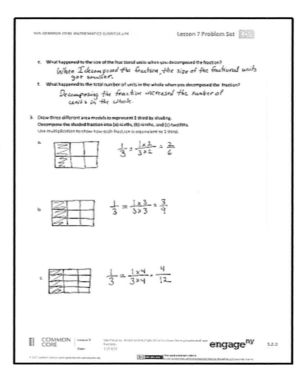

Exit Ticket (3 minutes)

After the Student Debrief, instruct students to complete the Exit Ticket. A review of their work will help you assess the students' understanding of the concepts that were presented in the lesson today and plan more effectively for future lessons. You may read the questions aloud to the students.

Figure 4.3 (Continued)

APPROACH TO ASSESSMENT

Assessments provide an opportunity for students to show their learning accomplishments in addition to offering them a pathway to monitor their progress, celebrate successes, examine mistakes, uncover misconceptions, and engage in self-reflection and analysis. A central goal of the assessment system as a whole is to make students aware of their strengths and weaknesses and to give them opportunities to try again, do better, and, in doing so, enjoy the experience of seeing their intelligent, hard work pay off as their skill and understanding increase. Furthermore, the data collected as a result of the assessments represent an invaluable tool in the hands of teachers and provide them with specific data about student understanding to direct their instruction.

In *A Story of Units*, assessment becomes a regular part of the class routine in the form of daily, mid-module, and end-of-module appraisal. Both the mid-module tasks and the end-of-module tasks are designed to allow quick scoring that make it possible for teachers to implement instructionally relevant, actionable feedback to students and to monitor student progress to determine the effectiveness of their instruction and make any needed adjustments. These mid-module and end-of-module tasks should be used in combination with instructionally embedded tasks, teacher-developed quizzes, and other formative assessment strategies in order to realize the full benefits of data-driven instruction.

DAILY FORMATIVE ASSESSMENTS

Problem Sets

As part of Concept Development, students may be asked to work on a Problem Set, either independently or with teacher guidance. They can be checked in class as part of the lesson. The Problem Sets often include fluency pertaining to the Concept Development, as well as conceptual and application word problems. The primary goal of the Problem Set is for students to apply the conceptual understandings learned during the lesson. Students work intently for a specified period of time, but the number of problems completed during this time will vary from student to student.

Exit Tickets

Exit Tickets are a critical element of the lesson structure. These quick assessments contain specific questions about what students learned that day. The purpose of the Exit Ticket is twofold: to teach students to grow accustomed to being held individually accountable for the work they have done after one day's instruction and to provide the teacher with valuable evidence of the efficacy of that day's work—which is indispensable for planning purposes.

Homework

Similar in content and format to the Problem Sets, Homework gives students additional practice on the skills they learn in class each day. The idea is not to introduce brand-new concepts or ideas, but to build student confidence with the material learned in class. Having already worked similar problems in class, the Homework gives students a chance to check their understanding and confirm that they can do the problems independently.

MID-MODULE ASSESSMENT TASK

A Mid-Module Assessment Task is provided for each module, specifically tailored to address approximately the first half of the learning objectives for which the module is designed. Careful articulation in a rubric provides guidance in understanding common preconceptions or misconceptions of students for discrete portions of knowledge or skill on their way to proficiency for each standard and to prepare them for PARCC assessments. Typically these tasks are one class period in length, and students complete them independently, without assistance. The problems should be new to the students and are not preceded by analogous problems. Teachers may use these tasks formatively or summatively.

END-OF-MODULE ASSESSMENT TASK

A summative End-of-Module Assessment Task is also provided for each module. These tasks are specifically designed based on the standards addressed in order to gauge students' full range of understanding of the module as a whole and to prepare them for PARCC assessments. Some items test understanding of specific standards, while others are synthesis items that assess either understanding of the broader concept addressed in the module or the ability to solve problems by combining knowledge, skills, and understanding. Like the mid-module tasks, these tasks are one class period in length and independently completed by the student without assistance. They also should be new to the students and not preceded by analogous problems.

Problems on these Mid-Module and End-of-Module Assessment Tasks are closely tied to the learning that takes place throughout the module. They build in complexity as the Problems Sets do in the Lessons.

RIGOR IN THE ASSESSMENTS

Each assessment encourages students to demonstrate procedural skill and conceptual understanding. Application problems, including multistep word problems, are always part of the assessments. Constructed response questions typically pose complex tasks that require students to explain their process for solving a problem. For these problems, answers alone are insufficient. Students must also be able to thoroughly explain their thought processes. Possible student work may include tape diagrams, number sentences, area models, and paragraphs. In any case, the rubrics for these items include elements on judging the thoroughness and correctness of the student's explanation.

CHAPTER 5

Approach to Differentiated Instruction

Teachers are confronted daily with meeting the needs of diverse learners in their classrooms, and differentiating instruction provides a means for meeting this challenge. This chapter explains how A *Story of Units* integrates Universal Design for Learning (UDL). Marginal notes to the teacher in lessons inform teachers about how to adapt activities to better meet the needs of various student groups.

The new standards require that "all students must have the opportunity to learn and meet the same high standards if they are to access the knowledge and skills necessary in their post-school lives." The writers of A *Story of Units* agree and feel strongly that accommodations cannot be just an extra set of resources for particular students. Instead, scaffolding must be folded into the curriculum in such a way that it is part of its very DNA. Said another way, faithful adherence to the modules is the primary scaffolding tool.

The modules that make up A *Story of Units* propose that the components of excellent math instruction do not change based on the audience. That said, specific resources within this curriculum highlight strategies that can provide critical access for all students.

Researched-based UDL has provided a structure for thinking about how to meet the needs of diverse learners. Broadly, that structure asks teachers to consider multiple means of representation, multiple means of action and expression, and multiple means of engagement. Charts at the end of this section offer suggested scaffolds, using this framework, for English language learners, students with disabilities, students performing above grade level, and students performing below grade level. UDL offers ideal settings for multiple entry points for students and minimizes instructional barriers to learning. Many of the suggestions on the chart are applicable to other students and overlapping populations.

In addition, individual lessons contain marginal notes to teachers (in text boxes) highlighting specific UDL information about scaffolds that might be employed with particular intentionality when working with students. These tips are strategically placed in the lesson where teachers might use the strategy to the best advantage.

It is important to note that the scaffolds and accommodations integrated into A *Story of Units* might change how learners access information and demonstrate learning; they do not substantially alter the instructional level, content, or performance criteria. Rather, they provide teachers with choices in how students access content and demonstrate their knowledge and ability.

We encourage teachers to pay particular attention to the manner in which knowledge is sequenced in A *Story of Units* and to capitalize on that sequence when working with special student populations. Most lessons contain a suggested teaching sequence that moves from simple to complex, starting, for example, with an introductory problem for a math topic and building up inductively to the general case encompassing multifaceted ideas. By breaking down problems from simple to complex, teachers can locate specific steps that students are struggling with or stretch out problems for students who desire a challenge.

Throughout A *Story of Units*, teachers are encouraged to give classwork using a *time* frame rather than a *task* frame. In other words, within a given time frame, all students are expected to do their personal best, working at their maximum potential: "Students, you have ten minutes to work independently." Bonus questions are always ready for accelerated students. The teacher circulates and monitors the work, error-correcting effectively and wisely. Some students complete more work in the time frame than others. Neither above- nor below-grade level students are overly praised or penalized. Personal success is what we are striving for.

Another vitally important component for meeting the needs of all students is the constant flow of data from student work. A *Story of Units* provides daily tracking through exit tickets for each lesson, as well as Mid- and End-of-Module Assessment Tasks to determine student understanding at benchmark points. These tasks should accompany teacher-made test items in a comprehensive assessment plan. Such data flow keeps teaching practice firmly grounded in student learning and makes incremental forward movement possible. A culture of precise error correction in the classroom breeds a comfort with data that is nonpunitive and honest. When feedback is provided with emotional neutrality, students understand that making mistakes is part of the learning process: "Students, for the next five minutes, I will be meeting with Brenda, Mehmet, and Jeremy. They did not remember to rename the remainder in the tens place as 10 ones in their long division on Problem 7." Conducting such sessions then provides the teacher the opportunity to quickly assess if students need to start at a simpler level or just need more monitored practice now that their eyes are open to their mistakes.

Good mathematics instruction, like any successful coaching, involves demonstration, modeling, and a lot of intelligent practice. In math, just as in sports, skill is acquired incrementally; as the student acquires greater skill, more complexity is added to the work, and the student's proficiency grows. The careful sequencing of the mathematics and the many scaffolds that have been designed into A *Story of Units* make it an excellent curriculum for meeting the needs of all students, including those with special and unique learning modes.

SCAFFOLDS FOR ENGLISH LANGUAGE LEARNERS

English language learners (ELLs) provide a variety of experiences that can add to the classroom environment. Their differences do not translate directly to shortfalls in knowledge base but rather present an opportunity to enrich the teaching and learning. The following chart provides a bank of suggestions within the UDL framework to aid ELLs. Variations on these accommodations are elaborated within lessons, demonstrating how and when they might be used.

Provide Multiple Means of Representation	• Introduce essential terms and vocabulary prior the mathematics instruction. • Clarify, compare, and make connections to math words in discussion, particularly during and after practice. • Highlight critical vocabulary in discussion. For example, show a picture of *half*. • Couple teacher-talk with math-they-can-see, such as models. • Let students use models and gestures to calculate and explain. For example, a student searching to define *multiplication* may model groups of 6 with drawings or concrete objects and write the number sentence to match. • Teach students how to ask questions (such as, "Do you agree?" and "Why do you think so?") to extend think-pair-share conversations. Model and post conversation starters, such as, "I agree because …" "Can you explain how you solved it?" "I noticed that …" "Your solution is different from [the same as] mine because …" "My mistake was to …" • Connect language (such as *tens*) with concrete and pictorial experiences (such as money and fingers).
Provide Multiple Means of Action and Expression	• Know, use, and make the most of student cultural and home experiences. Build on the student's background knowledge. • Check for understanding frequently (e.g., "Show me what you are thinking.") to benefit those who may shy away from asking questions. • Couple teacher-talk with illustrative gestures. Vary your voice to guide comprehension. Speak dynamically with expression. Make eye-to-eye contact, and speak slowly and distinctly. • Vary the grouping in the classroom, such as sometimes using small group instruction to help ELLs learn to negotiate vocabulary with classmates and other times using native language support to allow a student to find full proficiency of the mathematics first. • Provide sufficient wait time to allow the students to process the meanings in the different languages. • Listen intently in order to uncover the math content in the students' speech. • Keep teacher-talk clear and concise. • Point to visuals while speaking, using your hands to clearly indicate the image that corresponds to your words. • Get students up and moving, coupling language with motion such as, "Say *right angle*, and show me a right angle with your legs." "Make groups of 5 right now!" • Celebrate improvement. Intentionally highlight student math success frequently.
Provide Multiple Means of Engagement	• Provide a variety of ways to respond: oral, choral, student boards, concrete models (e.g., fingers), pictorial models (e.g., ten-frame), pair share, small group share. • Treat everyday and first language and experiences as resources, not as obstacles. Be aware of gerunds, such as *denominator* in English and *denominador* in Spanish. • Provide oral options for assessment rather than multiple choice. • Cultivate a math discourse of synthesis, analysis, and evaluation rather than simplified language. • Support oral or written response with sentence frames, such as, "_____ is ____ hundreds,___ tens, and ____ ones." • Ask questions to probe what students mean as they attempt expression in a second language. • Scaffold questioning to guide connections, analysis, and mastery. • Let students choose the language they prefer for arithmetic computation and discourse.

SCAFFOLDS FOR STUDENTS WITH DISABILITIES

Individualized Education Programs (IEPs) or Section 504 Accommodation Plans should be the first source of information for designing instruction for students with disabilities. The following chart provides an additional bank of suggestions within the UDL framework for strategies to use with these students in your class. Variations on these scaffolds are elaborated at particular points within lessons with text boxes at appropriate points, demonstrating how and when they might be used.

Provide Multiple Means of Representation	• Teach from simple to complex, moving from concrete to representation to abstract at the student's pace.

• Teach from simple to complex, moving from concrete to representation to abstract at the student's pace.
• Clarify, compare, and make connections to math words in discussion, particularly during and after practice.
• Partner key words with visuals (e.g., a photo of *ticket*) and gestures (e.g., for *paid*). Connect language (such as *tens*) with concrete and pictorial experiences (such as money and fingers). Couple teacher-talk with math-they-can-see, such as models. Let students use models and gestures to calculate and explain. For example, a student searching to define *multiplication* may model groups of 6 with drawings or concrete objects and write the number sentence to match.
• Teach students how to ask questions (such as, "Do you agree?" and "Why do you think so?") to extend think-pair-share conversations. Model and post conversation starters, such as: "I agree because …" "Can you explain how you solved it?" "I noticed that …" "Your solution is different from [the same as] mine because …" "My mistake was to …"
• Couple number sentences with models. For example, for equivalent fraction sprint, present 6/8 with

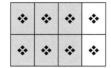

• Enlarge print for visually impaired learners.
• Use student boards to work on one calculation at a time.
• Invest in or make math picture dictionaries or word walls.

Provide Multiple Means of Action and Expression

• Provide a variety of ways to respond: oral, choral, student boards, concrete models (e.g., fingers), pictorial models (e.g., ten-frame), pair share, and small group share. For example, use student boards to adjust partner share for hearing-impaired students. Partners can jot questions and answers to one another on boards. Use vibrations or visual signs (such as a clap rather than a snap or saying, "Show") to elicit responses from hearing-impaired students.
• Vary choral response with written response (number sentences and models) on student boards to ease linguistic barriers. Support oral or written response with sentence frames, such as "_____ is _____ hundreds, _____ tens, and _____ ones."
• Adjust oral fluency games by using student and teacher boards or hand signals, such as showing the sum with fingers. Use visual signals or vibrations to elicit responses, for example, a hand pointed down means to count backward in Happy Counting (a fluency exercise).
• Adjust wait time for interpreters of hearing-impaired students.
• Select numbers and tasks that are just right for learners.
• Model each step of the algorithm before students begin.
• Give students a chance to practice the next day's sprint (fluency exercise) beforehand (e.g., at home).
• Give students a few extra minutes to process the information before giving the signal to respond.
• Assess by multiple means, including "show and tell" rather than written.
• Elaborate on the problem-solving process. Read word problems aloud. Post a visual display of the problem-solving process. Have students check off or highlight each step as they work. Talk through the problem-solving process step by step to demonstrate the thinking process. Before students solve, ask questions for comprehension, such as, "What unit are we counting? What happened to the units in the story?" Teach students to use self-questioning techniques, such as, *Does my answer make sense?*
• Concentrate on goals for accomplishment within a time frame as opposed to a task frame. Extend the time for the task. Guide students to evaluate process and practice. Have students ask themselves, *How did I improve? What did I do well?*
• Focus on students' mathematical reasoning (i.e., their ability to make comparisons, describe patterns, generalize, explain conclusions, specify claims, and use models), not their accuracy in language.

Provide Multiple Means of Engagement	• Make eye-to-eye contact, and keep teacher-talk clear and concise. Speak clearly when checking answers for sprints and problems. • Check frequently for understanding (e.g., *show*). Listen intently in order to uncover the math content in the students' speech. Use nonverbal signals, such as thumbs-up. Assign a buddy or a group to clarify directions or process. • Teach in small chunks so students get a lot of practice with one step at a time. • Know, use, and make the most of Deaf culture and sign language. • Use songs, rhymes, or rhythms to help students remember key concepts, such as, "Add your ones up first/Make a bundle if you can!" • Point to visuals and captions while speaking, using your hands to clearly indicate the image that corresponds to your words. • Incorporate activity. Get students up and moving, coupling language with motion, such as, "Say *right angle*, and show me a right angle with your legs," and "Make groups of 5 right now!" Make the most of the fun exercises for activities like sprints and fluencies. Conduct simple oral games, such as Happy Counting. Celebrate improvement. Intentionally highlight student math success frequently. • Follow predictable routines to allow students to focus on content rather than behavior. • Allow everyday and first language to express math understanding. • Reteach the same concept with a variety of fluency games. • Allow students to lead group and pair-share activities. • Provide learning aids, such as calculators and computers, to help students focus on conceptual understanding.

SCAFFOLDS FOR STUDENTS PERFORMING BELOW GRADE LEVEL

The following chart provides a bank of suggestions within the UDL framework for accommodating students who are below grade level in your class. Variations on these accommodations are elaborated within lessons, demonstrating how and when they might be used.

Provide Multiple Means of Representation	• Model problem-solving sets with drawings and graphic organizers (e.g., bar or tape diagram), giving many examples and visual displays. • Guide students as they select and practice using their own graphic organizers and models to solve. • Use direct instruction for vocabulary with visual or concrete representations. • Use explicit directions with steps and procedures enumerated. Guide students through initial practice promoting gradual independence: "I do, we do, you do." • Use alternative methods of delivery of instruction, such as recordings and videos, that can be accessed independently or repeated if necessary. • Scaffold complex concepts, and provide leveled problems for multiple entry points.
Provide Multiple Means of Action and Expression	• First use manipulatives or real objects (such as dollar bills); then make the transition from concrete to pictorial to abstract. • Have students restate their learning for the day. Ask for a different representation in the restatement: "Would you restate that answer in a different way or show me by using a diagram?" • Encourage students to explain their thinking and strategy for the solution. • Choose numbers and tasks that are just right for learners but teach the same concepts. • Adjust numbers in calculations to suit the learner's levels. For example, change 429 divided by 2 to 400 divided by 2 or 4 divided by 2.

Provide Multiple Means of Engagement	• Clearly model steps, procedures, and questions to ask when solving. • Cultivate peer-assisted learning interventions for instruction (e.g., dictation) and practice, particularly for computation work (e.g., peer modeling). Have students work together to solve and then check their solutions. • Teach students to ask themselves questions as they solve: *Do I know the meaning of all the words in this problem?; What is being asked? Do I have all of the information I need? What do I do first? What is the order to solve this problem? What calculations do I need to make?* • Practice routine to ensure smooth transitions. • Set goals with students regarding the type of math work students should complete in 60 seconds. • Set goals with the students regarding next steps and what to focus on next.

SCAFFOLDS FOR STUDENTS PERFORMING ABOVE GRADE LEVEL

The following chart provides a bank of suggestions within the UDL framework for accommodating students who are above grade level in your class. Variations on these accommodations are elaborated within lessons, demonstrating how and when they might be used.

Provide Multiple Means of Representation	• Teach students how to ask questions (such as, "Do you agree?" and "Why do you think so?") to extend think-pair-share conversations. Model and post conversation starters, such as, "I agree because …" "Can you explain how you solved it?" "I noticed that …" "Your solution is different from [the same as] mine because …" "My mistake was to …" • Incorporate written reflection, evaluation, and synthesis. • Allow creativity in expression and modeling solutions.
Provide Multiple Means of Action and Expression	• Encourage students to explain their reasoning both orally and in writing. • Extend exploration of math topics by means of challenging games, puzzles, and brain teasers. Offer choices of independent or group assignments for early finishers. • Encourage students to notice and explore patterns and to identify rules and relationships in math. Have students share their observations in discussion and writing (e.g., journaling). • Foster their curiosity about numbers and mathematical ideas. Facilitate research and exploration through discussion, experiments, Internet searches, trips, and other means. • Have students compete in a secondary simultaneous competition, such as skip counting by 75s, while peers are completing the sprint. • Let students choose their mode of response: written, oral, concrete, pictorial, or abstract. • Increase the pace. Offer two word problems to solve rather than one. Adjust the difficulty level by increasing the number of steps (e.g., change a one-step problem to a two-step problem), enhancing the operation (e.g., addition to multiplication), increasing numbers to millions, or decreasing numbers to decimals or fractions. • Let students compose their own word problems to show their mastery and extension of the content.
Provide Multiple Means of Engagement	• Push student comprehension into higher levels of Bloom's Taxonomy with questions such as, "What would happen if …?" "Can you propose an alternative?" "How would you evaluate …?" "What choice would you have made?" Ask "why?" and "what if?" questions. • Celebrate improvement in completion time (e.g., Sprint A completed in 45 seconds and Sprint B completed in 30 seconds). • Make the most of the fun exercises for practicing skip counting. • Accept and elicit student ideas and suggestions for ways to extend games. • Cultivate student persistence in problem solving, and do not overlook their need for guidance and support.

CHAPTER 6

Grade-Level Module Summary and Unpacking of Standards

Although the standards delineate what students should learn at each grade level, teachers must still fill in the blanks when it comes to translating this information for use in their daily classroom practice. Questions often remain about how concepts should be connected and where parameters should be set. The content of each grade level in A *Story of Units* is contained in five to eight modules that span an academic year.

This chapter presents key information from the modules to provide an overview of the content and explain the mathematical progression. The standards are translated for teachers and a fuller picture is drawn of the teaching and learning that should take place through the school year. Each module has these sections:

An Overview of the module

Focus Grade-Level Standards

Foundational Standards

Focus Standards for Mathematical Practice

Topic Overview narratives, coherence links, and lesson objectives

The Module Overview provides a broad overview for the entire module and includes information on the sequencing of the topics. The Topic Overviews unpack the standards by providing additional details about the skills and concepts students should master at the lesson level. Further unpacking of the standards continues as the lesson objectives illuminate what students should know and be able to do to demonstrate mastery. This information, taken together for all modules, tells a story of the mathematics that students should learn for this grade level.

MODULE 1: PLACE VALUE, ROUNDING, AND ALGORITHMS FOR ADDITION AND SUBTRACTION

OVERVIEW

In this 25-day module, students extend their work with whole numbers. They begin with large numbers using familiar units of hundreds and thousands and develop their understanding of millions by building knowledge of the pattern of *times ten* in the base-ten system on the place value chart (4.NBT.1). They recognize that each sequence of three digits is read as hundreds, tens, and ones, followed by the naming of the corresponding base thousand unit (thousand, million, billion).[1]

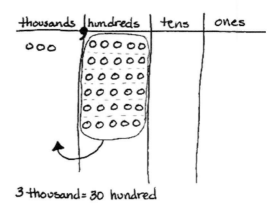

3 thousand = 30 hundred

The place value chart is fundamental in Topic A. Building on their previous knowledge of bundling, students learn that 10 hundreds can be composed into 1 thousand, and therefore 30 hundreds can be composed into 3 thousands because a digit's value is ten times what it would be one place to its right (4.NBT.1). Conversely, students learn to recognize that in a number such as 7,777 each 7 has a value that is 10 times the value of its neighbor to the immediate right; for example, 1 thousand can be decomposed into 10 hundreds, and therefore 7 thousands can be decomposed into 70 hundreds.

Similarly, multiplying by 10 will shift digits one place to the left, and dividing by 10 will shift digits one place to the right.

$$3,000 = 300 \times 10 \qquad 3,000 \div 10 = 300$$

In Topic B, students use place value as a basis for comparison of whole numbers. Although this is not a new topic, it becomes more complex because the numbers are larger. For example, it becomes clear that 34,156 is 3 thousand greater than 31,156.

$$34,156 > 31,156$$

Comparison leads directly into rounding, where students apply and extend their skill with isolating units. Students mastered rounding to the nearest ten and hundred with three-digit numbers in Grade 3. Now, in Grade 4, they move into Topic C and learn to round to any place value (4.NBT.3) initially using the vertical number line, though ultimately moving away from the visual model altogether. Topic C also includes word problems where students apply rounding to real-life situations.

In Grade 4, students become fluent with the standard algorithms for addition and subtraction. In Topics D and E, students focus on single like-unit calculations (e.g., ones with ones, thousands with thousands), at times requiring the composition of greater units when adding (10 hundreds are composed into 1 thousand) and decomposition into smaller units when subtracting (1 thousand is decomposed into 10 hundreds) (4.NBT.4). Throughout these topics, students apply their algorithmic knowledge to solve word problems. Also, students use a variable to represent the unknown quantity.

The module culminates with multistep word problems in Topic F (4.OA.3). Students use tape diagrams throughout the topic to model additive compare problems like the one exemplified below. These diagrams facilitate deeper comprehension and serve as a way to support the reasonableness of an answer.

A goat produces 5,212 gallons of milk a year. A cow produces 17,279 gallons a year. How much more milk does the goat need to produce to make the same amount of milk as a cow?

17,279 – 5,212 = _____

The goat needs to produce _____ more gallons of milk a year.

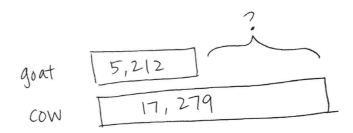

The Mid-Module Assessment follows Topic C. The End-of-Module Assessment follows Topic F.

FOCUS GRADE-LEVEL STANDARDS

Use the four operations with whole numbers to solve problems.[2]

4.OA.3 Solve multistep word problems posed with whole numbers and having whole-number answers using the four operations, including problems in which remainders must be interpreted. Represent these problems using equations with a letter standing for the unknown quantity. Assess the reasonableness of answers using mental computation and estimation strategies including rounding.

Generalize place value understanding for multi-digit whole numbers. (Grade 4 expectations are limited to whole numbers less than or equal to 1,000,000.)

4.NBT.1 Recognize that in a multi-digit whole number, a digit in one place represents ten times what it represents in the place to its right. *For example, recognize that 700 ÷ 70 = 10 by applying concepts of place value and division.*

4.NBT.2 Read and write multi-digit whole numbers using base-ten numerals, number names, and expanded form. Compare two multi-digit numbers based on meanings of the digits in each place, using >, =, and < symbols to record the results of comparisons.

4.NBT.3 Use place value understanding to round multi-digit whole numbers to any place.

Use place value understanding and properties of operations to perform multi-digit arithmetic.[3]

4.NBT.4 Fluently add and subtract multi-digit whole numbers using the standard algorithm.

FOUNDATIONAL STANDARDS

3.OA.8 Solve two-step word problems using the four operations. Represent these problems using equations with a letter standing for the unknown quantity. Assess the reasonableness of answers using mental computation and estimation strategies including rounding.[4]

3.NBT.1 Use place value understanding to round whole numbers to the nearest 10 or 100.

3.NBT.2 Fluently add and subtract within 1,000 using strategies and algorithms based on place value, properties of operations, and/or the relationship between addition and subtraction.

FOCUS STANDARDS FOR MATHEMATICAL PRACTICE

MP.1 *Make sense of problems and persevere in solving them.* Students use the place value chart to draw diagrams of the relationship between a digit's value and what it would be one place to its right, for instance, by representing 3 thousands as 30 hundreds. Students also use the place value chart to compare very large numbers.

MP.2 *Reason abstractly and quantitatively.* Students make sense of quantities and their relationships as they use both special strategies and the standard addition algorithm to add and subtract multi-digit numbers. They also decontextualize when they represent problems symbolically and contextualize when they consider the value of the units used and understand the meaning of the quantities as they compute.

MP.3 *Construct viable arguments and critique the reasoning of others.* Students construct arguments as they use the place value chart and model single- and multistep problems. Students also use the standard algorithm as a general strategy to add and subtract multi-digit numbers when a special strategy is not suitable.

MP.5 *Use appropriate tools strategically.* Students decide on the appropriateness of using special strategies or the standard algorithm when adding and subtracting multi-digit numbers.

MP.6 *Attend to precision.* Students use the place value chart to represent digits and their values as they compose and decompose base-ten units.

MODULE TOPIC SUMMARIES

Topic A: Place Value of Multi-Digit Whole Numbers

In Topic A, students build the place value chart to 1 million and learn the relationship between each place value as 10 times the value of the place to the right. Students manipulate numbers to see this relationship, such as 30 hundreds can be composed as 3 thousands. Conversely, students decompose numbers to see that 7 thousands is the same as 70 hundreds. As students build the place value chart into thousands and up to 1 million, the sequence of 3 digits is emphasized. They become familiar with the base thousand unit names up to 1 billion. Students fluently write numbers in multiple formats: as digits, in unit form, as words, and in expanded form up to 1 million.

Focus Standard:	4.NBT.1	Recognize that in a multi-digit whole number, a digit in one place represents ten times what it represents in the place to its right. *For example, recognize that 700 ÷ 70 = 10 by applying concepts of place value and division.*
	4.NBT.2	Read and write multi-digit whole numbers using base-ten numerals, number names, and expanded form. Compare two multi-digit numbers based on meanings of the digits in each place, using >, =, and < symbols to record the results of comparisons.
Instructional Days:	4	
Coherence		
Links from:	G3–M2	Place Value and Problem Solving with Units of Measure
Links to:	G5–M1	Place Value and Decimal Fractions

Objective 1: Interpret a multiplication equation as a comparison.
(Lesson 1)

Objective 2: Recognize that a digit represents 10 times the value of what it represents in the place to its right.
(Lesson 2)

Objective 3: Name numbers within 1 million by building understanding of the place value chart and placement of commas for naming base thousand units.
(Lesson 3)

Objective 4: Read and write multi-digit numbers using base-ten numerals, number names, and expanded form.
(Lesson 4)

Topic B: Comparing Multi-Digit Whole Numbers

In Topic B, students use place value to compare whole numbers. Initially using the place value chart, students will compare the value of each digit to surmise which number is of greater value. Moving away from dependency on models and toward fluency with numbers, students compare numbers by observing across the entire number and noticing value differences. For example, in comparing 12,566 to 19,534, it is evident that 19 thousand is greater than 12 thousand because of the meaning of the digits in the thousands. Students continue with number fluency by finding what is 1, 10, or 100 thousand more or less than a given number.

Focus Standard:	4.NBT.2	Read and write multi-digit whole numbers using base-ten numerals, number names, and expanded form. Compare two multi-digit numbers based on meanings of the digits in each place, using >, =, and < symbols to record the results of comparisons.
Instructional Days:	2	
Coherence		
Links from:	G2–M3	Place Value, Counting, and Comparison of Numbers to 1,000
Links to:	G5–M1	Place Value and Decimal Fractions

Objective 1: Compare numbers based on the meanings of the digits, using >, <, or = to record the comparison.
(Lesson 5)

Objective 2: Find 1, 10, and 100 thousand more and less than a given number.
(Lesson 6)

Topic C: Rounding Multi-Digit Whole Numbers

In Topic C, students round to any place using the vertical number line and approximation. The vertical number line allows students to line up place values of the numbers they are comparing. In Grade 3, students rounded to the nearest 10 or 100 using place value understanding; now they extend this understanding by rounding to the nearest thousand, ten thousand, and hundred thousand. Uniformity in the base-ten system easily transfers understanding from the Grade 3 (3.NBT.1) to the Grade 4 (4.NBT.3) standard. Rounding to the leftmost unit is easiest for students, but Grade 4 students learn the advantages to rounding to any place value, which increases accuracy. Students move from dependency on the number line and learn to approximate the number to a particular unit. To round 34,108 to the nearest thousand, students find the nearest multiple, 34,000 or 35,000, by seeing if 34,108 is more than or less than halfway between the multiples. The final concept of Topic C presents complex and real-world examples of rounding, including instances where the number requires rounding down but the context requires rounding up.

Focus Standard:	4.NBT.3	Use place value understanding to round multi-digit whole numbers to any place.
Instructional Days:	4	
Coherence		
Links from:	G3–M2	Place Value and Problem Solving with Units of Measure
Links to:	G5–M1	Place Value and Decimal Fractions

Objective 1: Round multi-digit numbers to the thousands place using the vertical number line.
(Lesson 7)

Objective 2: Round multi-digit numbers to any place using the vertical number line.
(Lesson 8)

Objective 3: Use place value understanding to round multi-digit numbers to any place value.
(Lesson 9)

Objective 4: Use place value understanding to round multi-digit numbers to any place value using real-world applications.
(Lesson 10)

Topic D: Multi-Digit Whole-Number Addition

Moving away from special strategies for addition, students develop fluency with the standard addition algorithm (4.NBT.4). They compose larger units to add like base-ten units, such as composing 10 hundreds to make 1 thousand and working across the numbers unit by unit (ones with ones, thousands with thousands). Recording of the regrouping occurs on the line under the addends, as shown to the right. For example, students do not record the 0 in the ones column and the 1 above the tens column; instead they record 10, writing the 1 under the tens column and a 0 in the ones column. Students practice and apply the algorithm within the context of word problems and assess the reasonableness of their answers using rounding (4.OA.3). When using tape diagrams to model word problems, they use a variable to represent the unknown quantity.

$$755{,}206$$
$$+\ \ 89{,}814$$
$$\overline{845{,}020}$$

Focus Standard:	4.OA.3	Solve multistep word problems posed with whole numbers and having whole-number answers using the four operations, including problems in which remainders must be interpreted. Represent these problems using equations with a letter standing for the unknown quantity. Assess the reasonableness of answers using mental computation and estimation strategies including rounding.
	4.NBT.4	Fluently add and subtract multi-digit whole numbers using the standard algorithm.
Instructional Days:	2	
Coherence		
Links from:	G3–M2	Place Value and Problem Solving with Units of Measure
Links to:	G5–M1	Place Value and Decimal Fractions

Objective 1: Use place value understanding to fluently add multi-digit whole numbers using the standard addition algorithm and apply the algorithm to solve word problems using tape diagrams.
(Lesson 11)

Objective 2: Solve multistep word problems using the standard addition algorithm modeled with tape diagrams and assess the reasonableness of answers using rounding.
(Lesson 12)

Topic E: Multi-Digit Whole-Number Subtraction

Following the introduction of the standard algorithm for addition in Topic D, the standard algorithm for subtraction replaces special strategies for subtraction in Topic E. Moving slowly from smaller to larger minuends, students practice decomposing larger units into smaller units. First, only one decomposition is introduced, where one zero may appear in the minuend. Students continue to decompose all necessary digits before performing the algorithm, allowing subtraction from left to right or, as taught in the lessons, from right to left. Students gain fluency in the algorithm to subtract numbers from 1 million, allowing for multiple decompositions (4.NBT.4).

The topic concludes with practicing the standard subtraction algorithm in the context of two-step word problems where students have to assess the reasonableness of their answers by rounding (4.OA.3). When using tape diagrams to model word problems, students use a variable to represent the unknown quantity.

Focus Standard:	4.OA.3	Solve multistep word problems posed with whole numbers and having whole-number answers using the four operations, including problems in which remainders must be interpreted. Represent these problems using equations with a letter standing for the unknown quantity. Assess the reasonableness of answers using mental computation and estimation strategies including rounding.
	4.NBT.4	Fluently add and subtract multi-digit whole numbers using the standard algorithm.
Instructional Days:	4	
Coherence		
Links from:	G3–M2	Place Value and Problem Solving with Units of Measure
Links to:	G5–M1	Place Value and Decimal Fractions

Objective 1: Use place value understanding to decompose to smaller units once using the standard subtraction algorithm, and apply the algorithm to solve word problems using tape diagrams.
(Lesson 13)

Objective 2: Use place value understanding to decompose to smaller units up to three times using the standard subtraction algorithm, and apply the algorithm to solve word problems using tape diagrams.
(Lesson 14)

Objective 3: Use place value understanding to fluently decompose to smaller units multiple times in any place using the standard subtraction algorithm, and apply the algorithm to solve word problems using tape diagrams.
(Lesson 15)

Objective 4: Solve two-step word problems using the standard subtraction algorithm fluently modeled with tape diagrams and assess the reasonableness of answers using rounding.
(Lesson 16)

Topic F: Addition and Subtraction Word Problems

Module 1 culminates with multistep addition and subtraction word problems in Topic F (4.OA.3). In these lessons, the format for the Concept Development is different from the traditional vignette. Instead of following instruction, the Problem Set facilitates the problems and discussion of the Concept Development. Throughout the module, students use tape diagrams to model word problems and solve additive comparative word problems. Students also continue using a variable to represent an unknown quantity. To culminate the module, students are given tape diagrams or equations and are encouraged to use their own creativity and the mathematics they learned during this module to write their word problems to solve using place value understanding and the algorithms for addition and subtraction. The module facilitates deeper comprehension and supports the reasonableness in an answer. Solving multistep word problems using multiplication and division is addressed in later modules.

Focus Standard:	4.OA.3	Solve multistep word problems posed with whole numbers and having whole-number answers using the four operations, including problems in which remainders must be interpreted. Represent these problems using equations with a letter standing for the unknown quantity. Assess the reasonableness of answers using mental computation and estimation strategies including rounding.
Instructional Days:	3	
Coherence		
Links from:	G3–M2	Place Value and Problem Solving with Units of Measure
Links to:	G5–M1	Place Value and Decimal Fractions

Objective 1: Solve additive compare word problems modeled with tape diagrams.
(Lesson 17)

Objective 2: Solve multistep word problems modeled with tape diagrams and assess the reasonableness of answers using rounding.
(Lesson 18)

Objective 3: Create and solve multistep word problems from given tape diagrams and equations.
(Lesson 19)

MODULE 2: UNIT CONVERSIONS AND PROBLEM SOLVING WITH METRIC MEASUREMENT

OVERVIEW

The idea of a mixed unit shows up in many varied contexts. Students have become accustomed to, for instance, thinking of 250 as the mixed units of 2 hundreds 5 tens. Mixed units are also used in the context of 2 hr 5 min, \$2.50, 2 km 5 m, 2' 5", and $2\frac{5}{8}$ (hours and minutes, dollars and cents, kilometers and meters, feet and inches, ones and eighths). While the context and the units may vary greatly, there are many common threads present in any mixed-unit calculation. Consider the connections and similarities between the following equalities:

	2,437	→	2 thousands	437 ones	=	2,437 ones
2 km 437 m	2,437 m	→	2 kilometers	437 meters	=	2,437 meters
2 kg 437 g	2,437 g	→	2 kilograms	437 grams	=	2,437 grams
2 L 437 mL	2,437 mL	→	2 liters	437 milliliters	=	2,437 milliliters

This 7-day module is paramount in setting the foundation for developing fluency with the manipulation of place value units, a skill on which Module 3 greatly depends. In order to explore the process of working with mixed units, Module 2 focuses on length, mass, and capacity in the metric system,[5] where place value serves as a natural guide for moving between larger and smaller units.

In Topic A, students review place value concepts while building fluency to decompose or convert from larger to smaller units (4.MD.1). They learn the relative sizes of measurement units, building off prior knowledge of grams and kilograms from Grade 3 (3.MD.2) and meters and centimeters from Grade 2 (2.MD.3). As students progress through the topics, they reason about correct unit sizes and use diagrams such as number lines with measurement scales to represent problems. Conversions between the units are recorded in a two-column table. Single-step problems involving addition and subtraction of metric units provide an opportunity to practice mental math calculations as well as solve using the addition and subtraction algorithms established in Module 1. Students reason by choosing to convert between mixed and single units before or after the computation (4.MD.2). By connecting their familiarity of metric units and place value, the module moves swiftly through each unit of conversion, spending only one day on each type. This initial understanding of unit conversions leads to further application and practice throughout subsequent modules, such as when multiplying and dividing metric units.

In Topic B, students again build off their measurement work from previous grade levels, solidify their understanding of the relationship between metric units and the place value chart, and apply unit conversions to solve and reason about multistep word problems (4.MD.2). Applying the skills learned in Module 1, students discover and explore the relationship between place value and conversions. The beauty of both our place value and measurement systems is the efficiency and precision permitted by the use of units of different sizes to express a given quantity. As students solve word problems by adding and subtracting metric units, their ability to reason in parts and wholes is taken to the next level. This is important preparation for multi-digit operations and for manipulating fractional units in future modules. Tape diagrams and number lines serve as models throughout the module to support the application of the standard algorithm to word problems.

FOCUS GRADE-LEVEL STANDARDS

Solve problems involving measurement and conversion of measurements from a larger unit to a smaller unit.[6]

4.MD.1[7] Know relative sizes of measurement units within one system of units including km, m, cm; kg, g; lb, oz.; l, ml; hr, min, sec. Within a single system of measurement, express measurements in a larger unit in terms of a smaller unit. Record measurement equivalents in a two-column table. _For example, know that 1 ft is 12 times as long as 1 in. Express the length of a 4 ft snake as 48 in. Generate a conversion table for feet and inches listing the number pairs_ (1, 12), (2, 24), (3, 36), ...

4.MD.2[8] Use the four operations to solve word problems involving distances, intervals of time, liquid volumes, masses of objects, and money, including problems involving simple fractions or decimals and problems that require expressing measurements given in a larger unit in terms of a smaller unit. Represent measurement quantities using diagrams such as number line diagrams that feature a measurement scale.

FOUNDATIONAL STANDARDS

2.NBT.1 Understand that the three digits of a three-digit number represent amounts of hundreds, tens, and ones; e.g., 706 equals 7 hundreds, 0 tens, and 6 ones. Understand the following as special cases:

    a.   100 can be thought of as a bundle of ten tens—called a "hundred."

3.MD.2 Measure and estimate liquid volumes and masses of objects using standard units of grams (g), kilograms (kg), and liters (l). (Excludes compound units such as cm^3 and finding the geometric volume of a container.) Add, subtract, multiply, or divide to solve one-step word problems involving masses or volumes that are given in the same units, e.g., by using drawings (such as a beaker with a measurement scale) to represent the problem. (Excludes multiplicative comparison problems, i.e., problems involving notions of "times as much.")

4.OA.3 Solve multistep word problems posed with whole numbers and having whole-number answers using the four operations, including problems in which remainders must be interpreted. Represent these problems using equations with a letter standing for the unknown quantity. Assess the reasonableness of answers using mental computation and estimation strategies including rounding.

4.NBT.4 Fluently add and subtract multi-digit whole numbers using the standard algorithm.

FOCUS STANDARDS FOR MATHEMATICAL PRACTICE

MP.1 _Make sense of problems and persevere in solving them._ Students use place value knowledge to convert larger units to smaller units before adding and subtracting. They are able to fluently add and subtract metric units of length, weight, and capacity using the standard algorithm. Tape diagrams and number lines conceptualize a problem before it is solved and are used to find the reasonableness of an answer.

MP.7 *Look for and make use of structure.* Students use knowledge of place value and mixed units to find similarities and patterns when converting from a larger to a smaller unit. Making use of parts and wholes allows for seamless conversion. They recognize that 1 thousand equals 1,000 ones relates to 1 kilometer equals 1,000 meters. Using this pattern, they might extend thinking to convert smaller to larger units when making a conversion chart.

MP.8 *Look for and express regularity in repeated reasoning.* Students find that metric unit conversions share a relationship on the place value chart. For example, 1,000 ones equals 1 thousand, 1,000 g equals 1 kg, 1,000 ml equals 1 l, and 1,000 m equals 1 km. Knowing and using these conversions and similarities allows for quick and easy conversion and calculation.

MODULE TOPIC SUMMARIES

Topic A: Metric Unit Conversions

In order to explore the process of working with mixed units, Module 2 focuses on length, mass, and capacity in the metric system,[9] where place value serves as a natural guide for moving between larger and smaller units. In Topic A, students review place value concepts while building fluency to decompose or convert from larger to smaller units (4.MD.1). They learn the relative sizes of measurement units, building off prior knowledge of grams and kilograms from Grade 3 (3.MD.2) and meters and centimeters from Grade 2 (2.MD.3). Conversions between the units are recorded in a two-column table beginning in Lesson 1. Recording the unit conversions in a table allows students to see the ease of converting from a smaller unit to a larger unit (e.g., 200 centimeters is the same as 2 meters because 1 meter is equal to 100 centimeters). As students progress through Lessons 1–3, they reason about

$$2 \text{ km } 608 \text{ m } + 3 \text{ km } 412 \text{ m}$$

Algorithms:

2 km 608 m
+ 3 km 412 m
─────────────
5 km 1020 m
1 km 20m

6 km 20 m = 6,020 m

or

2,608 m
+ 3,412 m
─────────────
6,020 m = 6 km 20m

Simplifying Strategies:

2 km + 3 km = 5 km
608 m + 412 m = 600 m + 420 m
  600   8   = 1,020 m

5 km + 1 km 20m = 6 km 20 m

or

2,608 m + 3,412 m
 2,000 600 8   3,000 400 12

5,000 + 1,000 + 20 = 6,020 m

correct unit sizes and use diagrams, such as number lines with measurement scales, to represent problems. Single-step problems involving addition and subtraction of metric units provide an opportunity to practice simplifying strategies as well as to solve using the addition and subtraction algorithm established in Module 1 (4.NBT.4) (see previous page). Students practice reasoning by choosing to convert mixed units to a single unit before or after the computation (4.MD.2).

Word problems provide a context in which to apply the conversions and include the addition and subtraction of mixed units. Connecting students' familiarity of metric units and place value, the module moves swiftly through each unit of conversion, spending only one day on each type. This initial understanding of unit conversions will allow further application and practice throughout subsequent modules, such as when multiplying and dividing metric units.

Focus Standard:	4.MD.1[10]	Know relative sizes of measurement units within one system of units including km, m, cm; kg, g; lb, oz.; l, ml; hr, min, sec. Within a single system of measurement, express measurements in a larger unit in terms of a smaller unit. Record measurement equivalents in a two-column table. *For example, know that 1 ft is 12 times as long as 1 in. Express the length of a 4 ft snake as 48 in. Generate a conversion table for feet and inches listing the number pairs (1, 12), (2, 24), (3, 36), ...*
	4.MD.2[11]	Use the four operations to solve word problems involving distances, intervals of time, liquid volumes, masses of objects, and money, including problems involving simple fractions or decimals, and problems that require expressing measurements given in a larger unit in terms of a smaller unit. Represent measurement quantities using diagrams such as number line diagrams that feature a measurement scale.
Instructional Days:	3	
Coherence		
Links from:	G2–M2	Addition and Subtraction of Length Units
Links to:	G5–M1	Place Value and Decimal Fractions
	G5–M2	Multi-Digit Whole-Number and Decimal Fraction Operations

Objective 1: Express metric length measurements in terms of a smaller unit; model and solve addition and subtraction word problems involving metric length.
(Lesson 1)

Objective 2: Express metric mass measurements in terms of a smaller unit; model and solve addition and subtraction word problems involving metric mass.
(Lesson 2)

Objective 3: Express metric capacity measurements in terms of a smaller unit; model and solve addition and subtraction word problems involving metric capacity.
(Lesson 3)

Topic B: Application of Metric Unit Conversions

In Topic B, students again build off of their measurement work from previous grade levels, solidify their understanding of the relationship between metric units and the place value chart, and apply unit conversions to solve and reason about multistep word problems (4.MD.2). Applying the skills learned in Module 1, students discover and explore the relationship between place value and conversions. The beauty of our place value and measurement systems is the efficiency and precision permitted by the use of different size units to express a given quantity.

Lesson 4 extracts the connection of metric measurement conversions to place value by making statements such as, "1 kilometer is 1,000 times as much as 1 meter" and by comparing mixed units of measure. In Lesson 5, as students solve two- and three-step word problems by adding and subtracting metric units, their ability to reason in parts and wholes is taken to the next level. This is important preparation for multi-digit operations and for manipulating fractional units in future modules.

Throughout Topic B, tape diagrams and number lines serve as models to support the application of the standard algorithm to word problems. Students solve problems by converting between units and by using simplifying strategies or algorithms (4.MD.1).

Focus Standard:	4.MD.1[12]	Know relative sizes of measurement units within one system of units including km, m, cm; kg, g; lb, oz.; l, ml; hr, min, sec. Within a single system of measurement, express measurements in a larger unit in terms of a smaller unit. Record measurement equivalents in a two-column table. *For example, know that 1 ft is 12 times as long as 1 in. Express the length of a 4 ft snake as 48 in. Generate a conversion table for feet and inches listing the number pairs (1, 12), (2, 24), (3, 36), …*
	4.MD.2[13]	Use the four operations to solve word problems involving distances, intervals of time, liquid volumes, masses of objects, and money, including problems involving simple fractions or decimals, and problems that require expressing measurements given in a larger unit in terms of a smaller unit. Represent measurement quantities using diagrams such as number line diagrams that feature a measurement scale.
Instructional Days:	2	
Coherence		
Links from:	G2–M2	Addition and Subtraction of Length Units
Links to:	G5–M1	Place Value and Decimal Fractions
	G5–M2	Multi-Digit Whole-Number and Decimal Fraction Operations

Objective 1: Know and relate metric units to place value units in order to express measurements in different units.
(Lesson 4)

Objective 2: Use addition and subtraction to solve multistep word problems involving length, mass, and capacity.
(Lesson 5)

MODULE 3: MULTI-DIGIT MULTIPLICATION AND DIVISION

OVERVIEW

In this 43-day module, students use place value understanding and visual representations to solve multiplication and division problems with multi-digit numbers. As a key area of focus for Grade 4, this module moves slowly but comprehensively to develop students' ability to reason about the methods and models chosen to solve problems with multi-digit factors and dividends.

Students begin in Topic A by investigating the formulas for area and perimeter. They then solve multiplicative comparison problems including the language of *times as much* with a focus on problems using area and perimeter as a context (e.g., "A field is 9 feet wide.

It is 4 times as long as it is wide. What is the perimeter of the field?"). Students create diagrams to represent these problems as well as write equations with symbols for the unknown quantities (4.OA.1). This is foundational for understanding multiplication as scaling in Grade 5 and sets the stage for proportional reasoning in Grade 6. This Grade 4 module, beginning with area and perimeter, allows for new and interesting word problems as students learn to calculate with larger numbers and interpret more complex problems (4.OA.2, 4.OA.3, 4.MD.3).

In Topic B, students use number disks to multiply single-digit numbers by multiples of 10, 100, and 1,000 and two-digit multiples of 10 by two-digit multiples of 10 (4.NBT.5). Reasoning between arrays and written numerical work allows students to see the role of place value units in multiplication (as pictured below). Students also practice the language of units to prepare them for multiplication of a single-digit factor by a factor with up to four digits and multiplication of 2 two-digit factors.

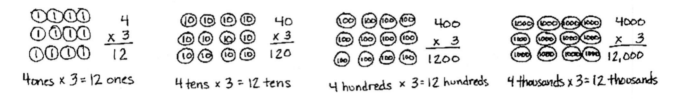

In preparation for two-digit by two-digit multiplication, students practice the new complexity of multiplying 2 two-digit multiples of 10. For example, students have multiplied 20 by 10 on the place value chart and know that it shifts the value one place to the left: $10 \times 20 = 200$. To multiply 20 by 30, the associative property allows for simply tripling the product, $3 \times (10 \times 20)$, or multiplying the units, 3 tens $\times$ 2 tens = 6 hundreds, alternatively, $(3 \times 10) \times (2 \times 10) = (3 \times 2) \times (10 \times 10)$. Introducing this concept early in the module allows students to practice during fluency so that by the time it is embedded within the two-digit by two-digit multiplication in Topic H, understanding and skill are in place.

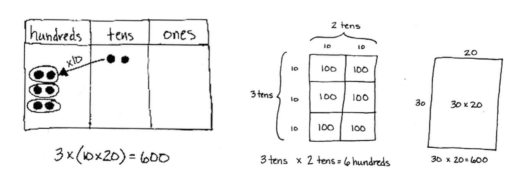

Building on their work in Topic B, students begin in Topic C decomposing numbers into base-ten units in order to find products of single-digit by multi-digit numbers. Students use the distributive property and multiply using number disks to model. Practice with number disks is used for two-, three-, and four-digit by one-digit multiplication problems with recordings as partial products. Students bridge partial products to the recording of multiplication via the standard algorithm.[14] Finally, the partial products method, the standard algorithm, and the area model are compared and connected by the distributive property (4.NBT.5):

$$1,423 \times 3$$

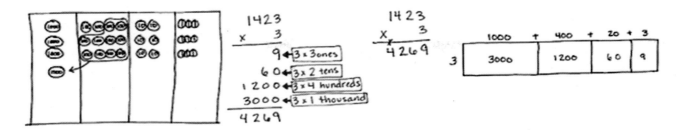

Topic D gives students the opportunity to apply their new multiplication skills to solve multistep word problems (4.OA.3, 4.NBT.5) and multiplicative comparison problems (4.OA.2). Students write equations from statements within the problems (4.OA.1) and use a combination of addition, subtraction, and multiplication to solve.

In Topic E, students synthesize their Grade 3 knowledge of division types (*group size unknown* and *number of groups unknown*) with their new, deeper understanding of place value.

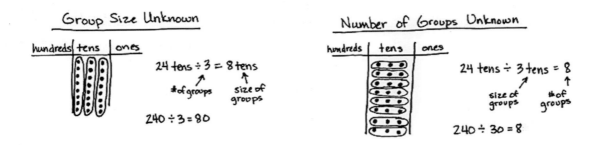

Students focus on interpreting the remainder within division problems in both word problems and within long division (4.OA.3). A remainder of 1, as exemplified below, represents a leftover flower in the first situation and a remainder of 1 ten in the second situation.[15]

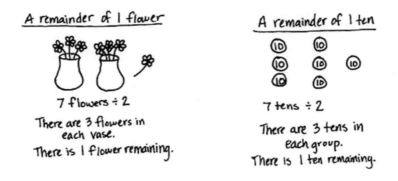

While we have no reason to subdivide a remaining flower, there are good reasons to subdivide a remaining ten. Students apply this simple idea to divide two-digit numbers unit by unit: dividing the tens units first, finding the remainder (the number of tens unable to be divided), and decomposing remaining tens into ones to then be divided. Students represent division with single-digit divisors using arrays and the area model before practicing with place value disks. The standard division algorithm[16] is practiced using place value knowledge, decomposing unit by unit. Finally, students use the area model to solve division problems, first with and then without remainders (4.NBT.6).

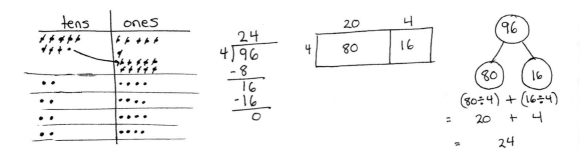

In Topic F, armed with an understanding of remainders, students explore factors, multiples, and prime and composite numbers within 100 (4.OA.4), gaining valuable insights into patterns of divisibility as they test for primes and find factors and multiples. This prepares them for Topic G's work with multi-digit dividends.

Topic G extends the practice of division with three- and four-digit dividends using place value understanding. A connection to Topic B is made initially with dividing multiples of 10, 100, and 1,000 by single-digit numbers. Number disks support students visually as they decompose each unit before dividing. Students then practice using the standard algorithm to record long division. They solve word problems and make connections to the area model as they did with two-digit dividends (4.NBT.6, 4.OA.3).

Finally, the module closes as students multiply two-digit by two-digit numbers. Students use their place value understanding and understanding of the area model to empower them to multiply by larger numbers, as pictured to the right. Topic H culminates at the most abstract level by explicitly connecting the partial products appearing in the area model to the distributive property and recording the calculation vertically (4.NBT.5). Students see that partial products written vertically are the same as those obtained via the distributive property: 4 twenty-sixes + 30 twenty-sixes = 104 + 780 = 884.

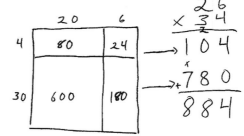

As students progress through this module, they learn to apply the multiplication and division algorithms because of their in-depth experience with the place value system and multiple conceptual models. This helps to prepare them for fluency with the multiplication algorithm in Grade 5 and the division algorithm in Grade 6. Students in Grade 4 are encouraged to continue using models to solve when appropriate.

FOCUS GRADE-LEVEL STANDARDS

Use the four operations with whole numbers to solve problems.

4.OA.1 Interpret a multiplication equation as a comparison, e.g., interpret 35 = 5 × 7 as a statement that 35 is 5 times as many as 7 and 7 times as many as 5. Represent verbal statements of multiplicative comparisons as multiplication equations.

4.OA.2 Multiply or divide to solve word problems involving multiplicative comparison, e.g., by using drawings and equations with a symbol for the unknown number to represent the problem, distinguishing multiplicative comparison from additive comparison. (See Standards Glossary, Table 2.)

4.OA.3 Solve multistep word problems posed with whole numbers and having whole-number answers using the four operations, including problems in which remainders must be interpreted. Represent these problems using equations with a letter standing for the unknown quantity. Assess the reasonableness of answers using mental computation and estimation strategies including rounding.

Gain familiarity with factors and multiples.

4.OA.4 Find all factor pairs for a whole number in the range 1–100. Recognize that a whole number is a multiple of each of its factors. Determine whether a given whole number in the range 1–100 is a multiple of a given one-digit number. Determine whether a given whole number in the range 1–100 is prime or composite.

Use place value understanding and properties of operations to perform multi-digit arithmetic.[17]

4.NBT.5 Multiply a whole number of up to four digits by a one-digit whole number, and multiply two two-digit numbers, using strategies based on place value and the properties of operations. Illustrate and explain the calculation by using equations, rectangular arrays, and/or area models.

4.NBT.6 Find whole-number quotients and remainders with up to four-digit dividends and one-digit divisors, using strategies based on place value, the properties of operations, and/or the relationship between multiplication and division. Illustrate and explain the calculation by using equations, rectangular arrays, and/or area models.

Solve problems involving measurement and conversion of measurements from a larger unit to a smaller unit.[18]

4.MD.3 Apply the area and perimeter formulas for rectangles in real world and mathematical problems. For example, find the width of a rectangular room given the area of the flooring and the length, by viewing the area formula as a multiplication equation with an unknown factor.

FOUNDATIONAL STANDARDS

Represent and solve problems involving multiplication and division.

3.OA.3 Use multiplication and division within 100 to solve word problems in situations involving equal groups, arrays, and measurement quantities, e.g., by using drawings and equations with a symbol for the unknown number to represent the problem. (See Standards Glossary, Table 2.)

3.OA.4 Determine the unknown whole number in a multiplication or division equation relating three whole numbers. *For example, determine the unknown number that makes the equation true in each of the equations* $8 \times ? = 48$, $5 = \_ \div 3$, $6 \times 6 = ?$

Understand properties of multiplication and the relationship between multiplication and division.

3.OA.5 Apply properties of operations as strategies to multiply and divide. (Students need not use formal terms for these properties.) *Examples: If* $6 \times 4 = 24$ *is known, then* $4 \times 6 = 24$ *is also* known. (*Commutative property of multiplication.*) 3 × 5 × 2 *can be found by* 3 × 5 = 15, *then* 15 × 2 = 30, *or by* 5 × 2 = 10, *then* 3 × 10 = 30. (*Associative property of multiplication.*) *Knowing that* 8 × 5 = 40 *and* 8 × 2 = 16, *one can find* 8 × 7 *as* 8 × (5 + 2) = (8 × 5) + (8 × 2) = 40 + 16 = 56. (*Distributive property.*)

3.OA.6 Understand division as an unknown-factor problem. *For example, find* 32 ÷ 8 *by finding the number that makes* 32 *when multiplied by* 8.

Multiply and divide within 100.

3.OA.7 Fluently multiply and divide within 100, using strategies such as the relationship between multiplication and division (e.g., knowing that 8 × 5 = 40, one knows 40 ÷ 5 = 8) or properties of operations. By the end of Grade 3, know from memory all products of two one-digit numbers.

Solve problems involving the four operations, and identify and explain patterns in arithmetic.

3.OA.8 Solve two-step word problems using the four operations. Represent these problems using equations with a letter standing for the unknown quantity. Assess the reasonableness of answers using mental computation and estimation strategies including rounding. (This standard is limited to problems posed with whole numbers and having whole number answers; students should know how to perform operations in the conventional order when there are no parentheses to specify a particular order, i.e., Order of Operations.)

Use place value understanding and properties of operations to perform multi-digit arithmetic.

3.NBT.3 Multiply one-digit whole numbers by multiples of 10 in the range 10–90 (e.g., 9 × 80, 5 × 60) using strategies based on place value and properties of operations.

Geometric measurement: understand concepts of area and relate area to multiplication and to addition.

3.MD.7 Relate area to the operations of multiplication and addition.

Geometric measurement: recognize perimeter as an attribute of plane figures and distinguish between linear and area measures.

3.MD.8 Solve real world and mathematical problems involving perimeters of polygons, including finding the perimeter given the side lengths, finding an unknown side length, and exhibiting rectangles with the same perimeter and different areas or with the same area and different perimeters.

FOCUS STANDARDS FOR MATHEMATICAL PRACTICE

MP.2 *Reason abstractly and quantitatively.* Students solve multistep word problems using the four operations by writing equations with a letter standing in for the unknown quantity.

MP.4 *Model with mathematics.* Students apply their understanding of place value to create area models and rectangular arrays when performing multi-digit multiplication and division. They use these models to illustrate and explain calculations.

MP.5 *Use appropriate tools strategically.* Students use mental computation and estimation strategies to assess the reasonableness of their answers when solving multistep word problems. They draw and label bar and area models to solve problems as part of the RDW process. In addition, students select an appropriate place value strategy when solving multiplication and division problems.

MP.8 *Look for and express regularity in repeated reasoning.* Students express the regularity they notice in repeated reasoning when they apply place value strategies in solving multiplication and division problems. They move systematically through the place values, decomposing or composing units as necessary, applying the same reasoning to each successive unit.

MODULE TOPIC SUMMARIES

Topic A: Multiplicative Comparison Word Problems

Students begin in Topic A by investigating the formulas for area and perimeter. In Lesson 1, they use those formulas to solve for area and perimeter and to find the measurements of unknown lengths and widths. In Lessons 2 and 3, they use their understanding of the area and perimeter formulas to solve multiplicative comparison problems including the language of *times as much* with a focus on problems using area and perimeter as a context (e.g., "A field is 9 feet wide. It is 4 times as long as it is wide. What is the perimeter of the field?"). Students create diagrams to represent these problems as well as write equations with symbols for the unknown quantities.

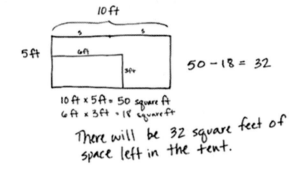

Problem 2: The width of David's tent is 5 feet. The length is twice the width. David's rectangular air mattress measures 3 feet by 6 feet. If David puts the air mattress in the tent, how many square feet of floor space will be available for the rest of his things?

Multiplicative comparison is foundational for understanding multiplication as *scaling* in Grade 5 and sets the stage for proportional reasoning in Grade 6. Students determine, using *times as much*, the length of one side of a rectangle as compared to its width. This Grade 4 module, beginning with area and perimeter, allows for new and interesting word problems as students learn to calculate with larger numbers and interpret more complex problems (4.OA.2, 4.MD.3).

Focus Standard:	4.OA.1	Interpret a multiplication equation as a comparison, e.g., interpret 35 = 5 × 7 as a statement that 35 is 5 times as many as 7 and 7 times as many as 5. Represent verbal statements of multiplicative comparisons as multiplication equations.
	4.OA.2	Multiply or divide to solve word problems involving multiplicative comparison, e.g., by using drawings and equations with a symbol for the unknown number to represent the problem, distinguishing multiplicative comparison from additive comparison. (See Standards Glossary, Table 2.)
	4.MD.3	Apply the area and perimeter formulas for rectangles in real world and mathematical problems. For example, find the width of a rectangular room given the area of the flooring and the length, by viewing the area formula as a multiplication equation with an unknown factor.
Instructional Days:	3	
Coherence		
Links from:	G3–M4	Multiplication and Area
	G3–M7	Geometry and Measurement Word Problems
Links to:	G5–M5	Addition and Multiplication with Volume and Area

Objective 1: Investigate and use the formulas for area and perimeter of rectangles.
(Lesson 1)

Objective 2: Solve multiplicative comparison word problems by applying the area and perimeter formulas.
(Lesson 2)

Objective 3: Demonstrate understanding of area and perimeter formulas by solving multistep real-world problems.
(Lesson 3)

Topic B: Multiplication by 10, 100, and 1,000

In Topic B, students examine multiplication patterns when multiplying by 10, 100, and 1,000. Reasoning between arrays and written numerical work allows students to see the role of place value units in multiplication (as pictured below). Students also practice the language of units to prepare them for multiplication of a single-digit factor by a factor with up to four digits. Teachers also continue using the phrase "_____ is _____ times as much as _____" (e.g., "120 is 3 times as much as 40"). This carries forward multiplicative comparison from Topic A, in the context of area, to Topic B, in the context of both calculations and word problems.

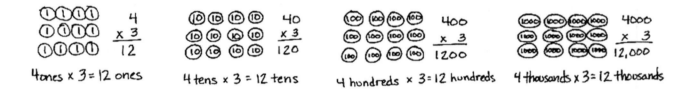

In preparation for two-digit by two-digit multiplication, students practice the new complexity of multiplying 2 two-digit multiples of 10. For example, students have multiplied 20 by 10 on the place value chart and know that it shifts the value one place to the left: $10 \times 20 = 200$. To multiply 20 by 30, the associative property allows for simply tripling the product, $3 \times (10 \times 20)$, or multiplying the units, 3 tens × 2 tens = 6 hundreds, alternatively, $(3 \times 10) \times (2 \times 10) = (3 \times 2) \times (10 \times 10)$.

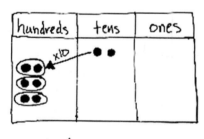

Introducing this early in the module allows students to practice this multiplication during fluency so that by the time it is embedded within the two-digit by two-digit multiplication in Topic H, they have developed both understanding and procedural fluency. Specifically, the lessons in this topic build understanding in the following way. In Lesson 4, students interpret and represent patterns when multiplying by 10, 100, and 1,000 in arrays and numerically. Next, in Lesson 5, students draw disks to multiply single-digit numbers by multiples of 10, 100, and 1,000. Finally, in Lesson 6, students use disks to multiply two-digit multiples of 10 by two-digit multiples of 10 (4.NBT.5) with the area model.

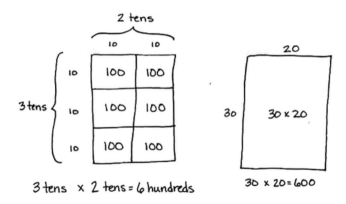

3 tens × 2 tens = 6 hundreds   30 × 20 = 600

Focus Standard:	4.NBT.5	Multiply a whole number of up to four digits by a one-digit whole number, and multiply two two-digit numbers, using strategies based on place value and the properties of operations. Illustrate and explain the calculation by using equations, rectangular arrays, and/or area models.
Instructional Days:	3	
Coherence		
Links from:	G3–M1	Properties of Multiplication and Division and Problem Solving with Units of 2–5 and 10
Links to:	G5–M1	Place Value and Decimal Fractions

Objective 1: Interpret and represent patterns when multiplying by 10, 100, and 1,000 in arrays and numerically.
(Lesson 4)

Objective 2: Multiply multiples of 10, 100, and 1,000 by single digits, recognizing patterns.
(Lesson 5)

Objective 3: Multiply two-digit multiples of 10 by two-digit multiples of 10 with the area model.
(Lesson 6)

Topic C: Multiplication of up to Four Digits by Single-Digit Numbers

Building on their work in Topic B, students begin in Topic C decomposing numbers into base-ten units in order to find products of single-digit by multi-digit numbers. Students practice multiplying using models, using the standard algorithm, and in the context of word problems, including multiplicative comparison problems. In Lessons 7 and 8, students use place value disks to represent the multiplication of two-, three-, and four-digit numbers by a one-digit whole number. Lessons 9 and 10 move students to the abstract level as they multiply three- and four-digit numbers by one-digit numbers using the standard algorithm. Finally, in Lesson 11, they compare and connect partial products, the standard algorithm, and the area model via the distributive property (4.NBT.5).

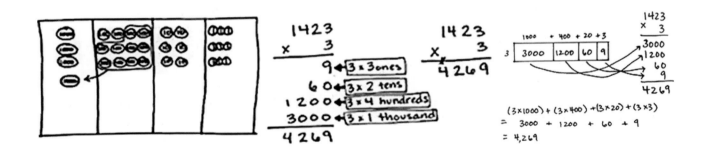

These calculations are then contextualized within multiplicative comparison word problems—for example:

Jackson's younger brother, Sam, ran 1,423 meters. Jackson ran 3 times as far. How far did Jackson run?

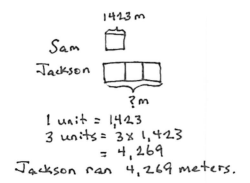

Focus Standard:	4.NBT.5	Multiply a whole number of up to four digits by a one-digit whole number, and multiply two two-digit numbers, using strategies based on place value and the properties of operations. Illustrate and explain the calculation by using equations, rectangular arrays, and/or area models.
Instructional Days:	5	
Coherence		
Links from:	G3–M1	Properties of Multiplication and Division and Problem Solving with Units of 2–5 and 10
	G3–M3	Multiplication and Division with Units of 0, 1, 6–9, and Multiples of 10
Links to:	G5–M2	Multi-Digit Whole-Number and Decimal Fraction Operations

Objective 1: Use place value disks to represent two-digit by one-digit multiplication.
(Lesson 7)

Objective 2: Extend the use of place value disks to represent three- and four-digit by one-digit multiplication.
(Lesson 8)

Objective 3: Multiply three- and four-digit numbers by one-digit numbers applying the standard algorithm.
(Lessons 9–10)

Objective 4: Connect the area model and the partial products method to the standard algorithm.
(Lesson 11)

Topic D: Multiplication Word Problems

Topic D gives students the opportunity to apply their new multiplication skills to solve multistep word problems (4.OA.3) and multiplicative comparison problems (4.OA.2). In Lesson 12, students extend their work with multiplicative comparison from Topic A to solve real-world problems. Students use a combination of addition, subtraction, and multiplication to solve multistep problems in Lesson 13.

Problem 4: In one month, Charlie read 814 pages. In the same month his mom read 4 times as many pages as Charlie, and that was 143 pages more than Charlie's dad read. What was the total number of pages read by Charlie and his parents?

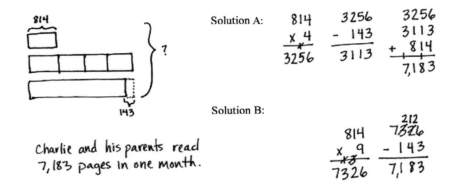

Charlie and his parents read 7,183 pages in one month.

Focus Standard:	4.OA.1	Interpret a multiplication equation as a comparison, e.g., interpret 35 = 5 × 7 as a statement that 35 is 5 times as many as 7 and 7 times as many as 5. Represent verbal statements of multiplicative comparisons as multiplication equations.
	4.OA.2	Multiply or divide to solve word problems involving multiplicative comparison, e.g., by using drawings and equations with a symbol for the unknown number to represent the problem, distinguishing multiplicative comparison from additive comparison. (See Standards Glossary, Table 2.)
	4.OA.3	Solve multistep word problems posed with whole numbers and having whole-number answers using the four operations, including problems in which remainders must be interpreted. Represent these problems using equations with a letter standing for the unknown quantity. Assess the reasonableness of answers using mental computation and estimation strategies including rounding.
	4.NBT.5	Multiply a whole number of up to four digits by a one-digit whole number, and multiply two two-digit numbers, using strategies based on place value and the properties of operations. Illustrate and explain the calculation by using equations, rectangular arrays, and/or area models.
Instructional Days:	2	
Coherence		
Links from:	G3–M1	Properties of Multiplication and Division and Problem Solving with Units of 2–5 and 10
	G3–M3	Multiplication and Division with Units of 0, 1, 6–9, and Multiples of 10
Links to:	G5–M2	Multi-Digit Whole-Number and Decimal Fraction Operations

Objective 1: Solve two-step word problems, including multiplicative comparison. (Lesson 12)

Objective 2: Use multiplication, addition, or subtraction to solve multistep word problems. (Lesson 13)

Topic E: Division of Tens and Ones with Successive Remainders

In Topic E, students synthesize their Grade 3 knowledge of division types (*group size unknown* and *number of groups unknown*) with their new, deeper understanding of place value.

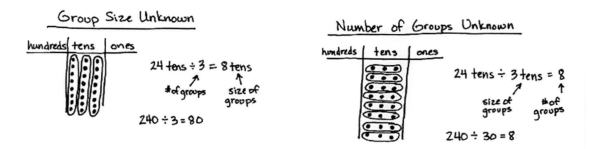

Students focus on interpreting the remainder within division problems both in word problems and within long division (4.OA.3). A remainder of one, as exemplified below, represents a leftover flower in the first situation and a remainder of 1 ten in the second situation.[19]

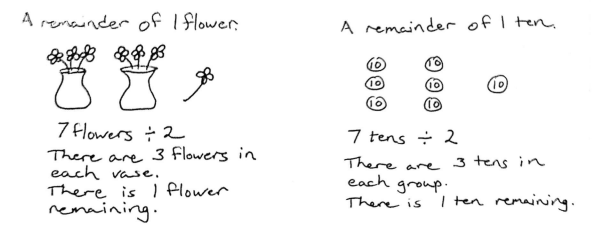

While we have no reason to subdivide a remaining flower, there are good reasons to subdivide a remaining ten. Students apply this simple idea to divide two-digit numbers unit by unit: dividing the tens units first, finding the remainder (the number of tens unable to be divided), and decomposing remaining tens into ones to then be divided.

Lesson 14 begins Topic E by having students solve division word problems with remainders. In Lesson 15, students deepen their understanding of division by solving problems with remainders using both arrays and the area model. Students practice dividing two-digit dividends with a remainder in the ones place using number disks in Lesson 16 and continue that modeling in Lesson 17 in which the remainder in the tens place is decomposed into ones. The long division algorithm[20] is introduced in Lesson 16 by directly relating the steps of the algorithm to the steps involved when dividing using number disks. Introducing the algorithm in this manner helps students to understand how place value plays a role in the steps of the algorithm. The same process of relating the standard algorithm to the concrete representation of division continues in Lesson 17. Lesson 18 moves students to the abstract level by requiring them to solve division problems numerically without drawing. In Lesson 19, students explain the successive remainders of the algorithm by using place value understanding and number disks. Finally, in Lessons 20 and 21, students use the area model to solve division problems and then compare the standard algorithm to the area model (4.NBT.6). Lesson 20 focuses on division problems without remainders, while Lesson 21 involves remainders.

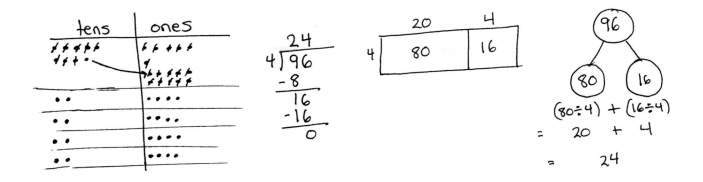

Quotients and remainders are independent of each other, but both must be included to give a complete response. A quotient and a remainder cannot be recorded after an equal sign because the symbol R or the words *with a remainder of* are invalid in an equation. Therefore, a quotient and a remainder can be written as a statement such as, "Seven divided by two is three with a remainder of one," or "The quotient is three and the remainder is one." It is mathematically correct to record the quotient and the remainder together at the top of the long division algorithm.

Focus Standard:	4.NBT.6	Find whole-number quotients and remainders with up to four-digit dividends and one-digit divisors, using strategies based on place value, the properties of operations, and/or the relationship between multiplication and division. Illustrate and explain the calculation by using equations, rectangular arrays, and/or area models.
Instructional Days:	8	
Coherence		
Links from:	G3–M1	Properties of Multiplication and Division and Problem Solving with Units of 2–5 and 10
	G3–M3	Multiplication and Division with Units of 0, 1, 6–9, and Multiples of 10
Links to:	G5–M2	Multi-Digit Whole-Number and Decimal Fraction Operations

Objective 1: Solve division word problems with remainders.
(Lesson 14)

Objective 2: Understand and solve division problems with a remainder using the array and area models.
(Lesson 15)

Objective 3: Understand and solve two-digit dividend division problems with a remainder in the ones place by using number disks.
(Lesson 16)

Objective 4: Represent and solve division problems requiring decomposing a remainder in the tens.
(Lesson 17)

Objective 5: Find whole number quotients and remainders.
(Lesson 18)

Objective 6: Explain remainders by using place value understanding and models.
(Lesson 19)

Objective 7: Solve division problems without remainders using the area model. (Lesson 20)

Objective 8: Solve division problems with remainders using the area model. (Lesson 21)

Topic F: Reasoning with Divisibility

In Topic F, armed with an understanding of remainders, students explore factors, multiples, and prime and composite numbers within 100 (4.OA.4). They gain valuable insights into patterns of divisibility as they test for primes and find factors and multiples, at times using their new skill of dividing double-digit dividends. This prepares them for Topic G's work with dividends of up to four digits.

Lesson 22 has students find factor pairs for numbers to 100 and then use their understanding of factors to determine whether numbers are prime or composite. In Lesson 23, students use division to examine numbers to 100 for factors and make observations about patterns they observe, for example, "When 2 is a factor, the numbers are even." Lesson 24 transitions the work with factors into a study of multiples, encouraging students to notice that the set of multiples of a number is infinite while the set of factors is finite. In Lesson 25, the sieve of Eratosthenes uses multiples to enable students to identify and explore the properties of prime and composite numbers to 100.

Focus Standard:	4.OA.4	Find all factor pairs for a whole number in the range 1–100. Recognize that a whole number is a multiple of each of its factors. Determine whether a given whole number in the range 1–100 is a multiple of a given one-digit number. Determine whether a given whole number in the range 1–100 is prime or composite.
Instructional Days:	4	
Coherence		
Links from:	G3–M1	Properties of Multiplication and Division and Problem Solving with Units of 2–5 and 10
	G3–M3	Multiplication and Division with Units of 0, 1, 6–9, and Multiples of 10
Links to:	G5–M2	Multi-Digit Whole-Number and Decimal Fraction Operations
	G5–M3	Addition and Subtraction of Fractions

Objective 1: Find factor pairs for numbers to 100, and use understanding of factors to define prime and composite. (Lesson 22)

Objective 2: Use division and the associative property to test for factors and observe patterns. (Lesson 23)

Objective 3: Determine whether a whole number is a multiple of another number. (Lesson 24)

Objective 4: Explore properties of prime and composite numbers to 100 by using multiples. (Lesson 25)

Topic G: Division of Thousands, Hundreds, Tens, and Ones

Topic G extends to division with three- and four-digit dividends using place value understanding. Students begin the topic by connecting multiplication of 10, 100, and 1,000 by single-digit numbers from Topic B to division of multiples of 10, 100, and 1,000 in Lesson 26. Using unit language, students find their division facts allow them to divide much larger numbers.

$$12 \text{ ones} \div 4 = 3 \text{ ones} \qquad 12 \text{ tens} \div 4 = 3 \text{ tens} \qquad 12 \text{ hundreds} \div 4 = 3 \text{ hundreds}$$
$$12 \div 4 = 3 \qquad\qquad 120 \div 4 = 30 \qquad\qquad 1200 \div 4 = 300$$

In Lesson 27, number disks support students visually as they decompose each unit before dividing. This lesson contains a first-use script on the steps of solving long division using number disks and the algorithm in tandem (4.NBT.6).

Students then move to the abstract level in Lessons 28 and 29, recording long division with place value understanding–first of three-digit, then four-digit numbers using small divisors. In Lesson 30, students practice dividing when there are zeros in the dividend or in the quotient.

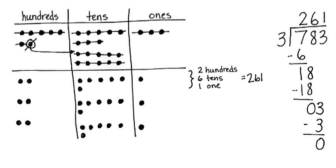

Lessons 31 and 32 give students opportunities to apply their understanding of division by solving word problems (4.OA.3). In Lesson 31, students identify word problems as *number of groups unknown* or *group size unknown*, modeled using tape diagrams. Lesson 32 applies their place value understanding of solving long division using larger divisors of 6, 7, 8, and 9. Concluding this topic, Lesson 33 has students make connections between the area model and the standard algorithm for long division.

Focus Standard:	4.OA.3	Solve multistep word problems posed with whole numbers and having whole-number answers using the four operations, including problems in which remainders must be interpreted. Represent these problems using equations with a letter standing for the unknown quantity. Assess the reasonableness of answers using mental computation and estimation strategies including rounding.
	4.NBT.6	Find whole-number quotients and remainders with up to four-digit dividends and one-digit divisors, using strategies based on place value, the properties of operations, and/or the relationship between multiplication and division. Illustrate and explain the calculation by using equations, rectangular arrays, and/or area models.

Instructional Days:	8	
Coherence		
Links from:	G3–M1	Properties of Multiplication and Division and Problem Solving with Units of 2–5 and 10
	G3–M3	Multiplication and Division with Units of 0, 1, 6–9, and Multiples of 10
Links to:	G5–M2	Multi-Digit Whole-Number and Decimal Fraction Operations

Objective 1: Divide multiples of 10, 100, and 1,000 by single-digit numbers.
(Lesson 26)

Objective 2: Represent and solve division problems with up to a three-digit dividend numerically and with number disks requiring decomposing a remainder in the hundreds place.
(Lesson 27)

Objective 3: Represent and solve three-digit dividend division with divisors of 2, 3, 4, and 5 numerically.
(Lesson 28)

Objective 4: Represent numerically four-digit dividend division with divisors of 2, 3, 4, and 5, decomposing a remainder up to three times.
(Lesson 29)

Objective 5: Solve division problems with a zero in the dividend or in the quotient.
(Lesson 30)

Objective 6: Interpret division word problems as either *number of groups unknown* or *group size unknown.*
(Lesson 31)

Objective 7: Interpret and find whole number quotients and remainders to solve one-step division word problems with larger divisors of 6, 7, 8, and 9.
(Lesson 32)

Objective 8: Explain the connection of the area model of division to the long division algorithm for three- and four-digit dividends.
(Lesson 33)

Topic H: Multiplication of Two-Digit by Two-Digit Numbers

Module 3 closes with Topic H as students multiply two-digit by two-digit numbers.

Lesson 34 begins this topic by having students use the area model to represent and solve the multiplication of two-digit multiples of 10 by two-digit numbers using a place value chart. Practice with this model helps to prepare students for two-digit by two-digit multiplication and builds the understanding of multiplying units of 10. In Lesson 35, students extend their learning to represent and solve the same types of problems using area models and partial products.

In Lesson 36, students make connections to the distributive property and use both the area model and four partial products to solve problems. Lesson 37 deepens students' understanding of multi-digit multiplication by transitioning from four partial products with representation of the area model to two partial products with representation of the area model and then to two partial products without representation of the area model.

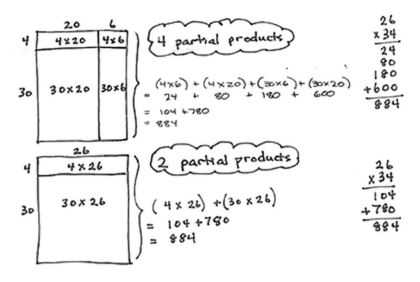

Topic H culminates at the most abstract level with Lesson 38 as students are introduced to the multiplication algorithm for two-digit by two-digit numbers. Knowledge from Lessons 34 to 37 provides a firm foundation for understanding the process of the algorithm as students make connections from the area model to partial products to the standard algorithm (4.NBT.5). Students see that partial products written vertically are the same as those obtained via the distributive property: 4 twenty-sixes + 30 twenty-sixes = 104 + 780 = 884.

Focus Standard:	4.NBT.5	Multiply a whole number of up to four digits by a one-digit whole number, and multiply two two-digit numbers, using strategies based on place value and the properties of operations. Illustrate and explain the calculation by using equations, rectangular arrays, and/or area models.
Instructional Days:	5	
Coherence		
Links from:	G3–M1	Properties of Multiplication and Division and Problem Solving with Units of 2–5 and 10
	G3–M3	Multiplication and Division with Units of 0, 1, 6–9, and Multiples of 10
Links to:	G5–M2	Multi-Digit Whole-Number and Decimal Fraction Operations

Objective 1: Multiply two-digit multiples of 10 by two-digit numbers using a place value chart. (Lesson 34)

Objective 2: Multiply two-digit multiples of 10 by two-digit numbers using the area model. (Lesson 35)

Objective 3: Multiply two-digit by two-digit numbers using four partial products. (Lesson 36)

Objective 4: Transition from four partial products to the standard algorithm for two-digit by two-digit multiplication. (Lessons 37 and 38)

MODULE 4: ANGLE MEASURE AND PLANE FIGURES

OVERVIEW

This 20-day module introduces points, lines, line segments, rays, and angles, as well as the relationships among them. Students construct, recognize, and define these geometric objects before using their new knowledge and understanding to classify figures and solve problems. With angle measure playing a key role in their work throughout the module, students learn how to create and measure angles, as well as create and solve equations to find unknown angle measures. In these problems where the unknown angle is represented by a letter, students explore both measuring the unknown angle with a protractor and reasoning through solving an equation. This connection between the measurement tool and the numerical work lays an important foundation for success with middle school geometry and algebra. Through decomposition and composition activities as well as an exploration of symmetry, students recognize specific attributes present in two-dimensional figures. They further develop their understanding of these attributes as they classify two-dimensional figures based on them.

Topic A begins with students drawing points, lines, line segments, and rays and identifying these in various contexts and within familiar figures. Students recognize that two rays sharing a common endpoint form an angle (4.MD.5). They next create right angles through a paper folding activity, identify right angles in their environment, and see that one angle can be greater (obtuse) or less (acute) than a right angle. Next, students use their understanding of angles to explore relationships between pairs of lines as they define, draw, and recognize intersecting, perpendicular, and parallel lines (4.G.1).

In Topic B, students explore the definition of degree measure, beginning with a circular protractor. By dividing the circumference of a circle into 360 equal parts, they recognize one part as representing 1 degree (4.MD.5). Through exploration, students realize that although the size of a circle may change, an angle spans an arc representing a constant fraction of the circumference. By carefully distinguishing the attribute of degree measure from that of length measure, the common misconception that degrees are a measure of length is avoided. Armed with their understanding of the degree as a unit of measure, students use various protractors to measure angles to the nearest degree and sketch angles of a given measure (4.MD.6). The idea that an angle measures the amount of "turning" in a particular direction is explored as students recognize familiar angles in varied contexts (4.G.1, 4.MD.5).

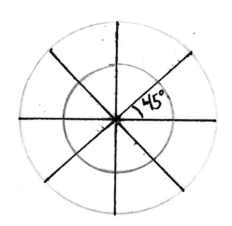

Topic C begins by decomposing 360 degrees using pattern blocks, allowing students to see that a group of angles meeting at a point with no spaces or overlaps adds up to 360 degrees. With this new understanding, students now discover that the combined measure of two adjacent angles on a line is 180 degrees (supplementary angles), the combined measure of two angles meeting to form a right angle is 90 degrees (complementary angles), and vertically opposite angles have the same measure. They use these properties to solve unknown-angle problems (4.MD.7).

An introduction to symmetry opens Topic D as students recognize lines of symmetry for two-dimensional figures, identify line-symmetric figures, and draw lines of symmetry (4.G.3). Given one half of a line-symmetric figure and the line of symmetry, students draw the other half of the figure. This leads to their work with triangles. Students are introduced to the precise definition of a triangle and then classify triangles based on angle measure and side length (4.G.2). For isosceles triangles, a line of symmetry is identified, and a folding activity demonstrates that base angles are equal. Folding an equilateral triangle highlights multiple lines of symmetry and establishes that all interior angles are equal. Students construct triangles given a set of classifying criteria (e.g., create a triangle that is both right and isosceles). Finally, they explore the definitions of familiar quadrilaterals and classify them based on their attributes, including angle measure and parallel and perpendicular lines (4.G.2). This work builds on reasoning that the students learned in Grade 3 about the attributes of shapes and lays a foundation for hierarchical classification of two-dimensional figures in Grade 5. The topic concludes as students compare and analyze two-dimensional figures according to their properties and use grid paper to construct two-dimensional figures given a set of criteria.

The Mid-Module Assessment follows Topic B. The End-of-Module Assessment follows Topic D.

FOCUS GRADE-LEVEL STANDARDS

Geometric measurement: understand concepts of angle and measure angles.

4.MD.5 Recognize angles as geometric shapes that are formed whenever two rays share a common endpoint, and understand concepts of angle measurement:

    a. An angle is measured with reference to a circle with its center at the common endpoint of the rays, by considering the fraction of the circular arc between the points where the two rays intersect the circle. An angle that turns through 1/360 of a circle is called a "one-degree angle," and can be used to measure angles.

    b. An angle that turns through n one-degree angles is said to have an angle measure of n degrees.

4.MD.6 Measure angles in whole-number degrees using a protractor. Sketch angles of specified measure.

4.MD.7 Recognize angle measure as additive. When an angle is decomposed into non-overlapping parts, the angle measure of the whole is the sum of the angle measures of the parts. Solve addition and subtraction problems to find unknown angles on a diagram in real world and mathematical problems, e.g., by using an equation with a symbol for the unknown angle measure.

Draw and identify lines and angles, and classify shapes by properties of their lines and angles.

4.G.1 Draw points, lines, line segments, rays, angles (right, acute, obtuse), and perpendicular and parallel lines. Identify these in two-dimensional figures.

4.G.2 Classify two-dimensional figures based on the presence or absence of parallel or perpendicular lines, or the presence or absence of angles of a specified size. Recognize right triangles as a category, and identify right triangles.

4.G.3 Recognize a line of symmetry for a two-dimensional figure as a line across the figure such that the figure can be folded along the line into matching parts. Identify line-symmetric figures and draw lines of symmetry.

FOUNDATIONAL STANDARDS

3.OA.8 Solve two-step word problems using the four operations. Represent these problems using equations with a letter standing in for the unknown quantity. Assess the reasonableness of answers using mental computation and estimation strategies including rounding. (This standard is limited to problems posed with whole numbers and having whole number answers; students should know how to perform operations in the conventional order when there are no parentheses to specify a particular order, i.e., Order of Operations.)

3.G.1 Understand that shapes in different categories (e.g., rhombuses, rectangles, and others) may share attributes (e.g., having four sides), and that the shared attributes can define a larger category (e.g., quadrilaterals). Recognize rhombuses, rectangles, and squares as examples of quadrilaterals, and draw examples of quadrilaterals that do not belong to any of these subcategories.

FOCUS STANDARDS FOR MATHEMATICAL PRACTICE

MP.2 *Reason abstractly and quantitatively.* Students represent angle measures within equations, and when determining the measure of an unknown angle, they represent the unknown angle with a letter or symbol in both the diagram and the equation. They reason about the properties of groups of figures during classification activities.

MP.3 *Construct viable arguments and critique the reasoning of others.* Knowing and using the relationships between adjacent and vertical angles, students construct an argument for identifying the angle measures of all four angles generated by two intersecting lines when given the measure of one angle. Students explore the concepts of parallelism and perpendicularity on different types of grids with activities that require justifying whether completing specific tasks is possible on different grids.

MP.5 *Use appropriate tools strategically.* Students choose to use protractors when measuring and sketching angles, drawing perpendicular lines, and precisely constructing two-dimensional figures with specific angle measurements. They use set squares and straightedges to construct parallel lines. They also choose to use straightedges for sketching lines, line segments, and rays.

MP.6 *Attend to precision.* Students use clear and precise vocabulary. They learn, for example, to cross-classify triangles by both angle size and side length (e.g., naming a shape as a right, isosceles triangle). They use set squares and straightedges to construct parallel lines and become sufficiently familiar with a protractor to decide which set of numbers to use when measuring an angle whose orientation is such that it opens from either direction or when the angle measures more than 180 degrees.

MODULE TOPIC SUMMARIES

Topic A: Lines and Angles

Topic A begins with students drawing points, lines, line segments, and rays, and identifying these in various contexts and familiar figures. As they continue, they recognize that two rays sharing a common endpoint form an angle. In Lesson 2, students create right angles through a paper folding activity and identify right angles in their environment by comparison with the right angle they have made. They also draw acute, right, and obtuse angles. This represents their first experience with angle comparison and the idea that one angle's measure can be greater (obtuse) or less (acute) than that of a right angle.

Next, students use their understanding of angles to explore relationships between pairs of lines, defining and recognizing intersecting, perpendicular, and parallel lines. In Lesson 3, their knowledge of right angles leads them to identify and define, as well as construct, perpendicular lines. Students learn in Lesson 4 that lines that never intersect also have a special relationship and are called *parallel*. Students use, in conjunction with a straightedge, the right angle template that they created in Lesson 2 to construct parallel lines (4.G.1). Activities using different grids give students the opportunity to explore the concepts of perpendicularity and parallelism.

Focus Standard:	4.G.1	Draw points, lines, line segments, rays, angles (right, acute, obtuse), and perpendicular and parallel lines. Identify these in two-dimensional figures.
Instructional Days:	4	
Coherence		
Links from:	G2–M8	Time, Shapes, and Fractions as Equal Parts of Shapes
Links to:	G5–M5	Addition and Multiplication with Volume and Area

Objective 1: Identify and draw points, lines, line segments, rays, and angles and recognize them in various contexts and familiar figures.
(Lesson 1)

Objective 2: Use right angles to determine whether angles are equal to, greater than, or less than right angles. Draw right, obtuse, and acute angles.
(Lesson 2)

Objective 3: Identify, define, and draw perpendicular lines.
(Lesson 3)

Objective 4: Identify, define, and draw parallel lines.
(Lesson 4)

Topic B: Angle Measurement

In Topic B, students explore the definition of degree measure. Beginning in Lesson 5 with a circular protractor, students divide the circumference of a circle into 360 equal parts, treating each part as representing 1 degree (4.MD.5). Students apply this understanding as they discover that a right angle measures 90 degrees and, in turn, that the angles they know as acute measure less than 90 degrees, and obtuse angles measure more than 90 degrees. The idea that an angle measures the amount of "turning" in a particular direction is explored, giving students the opportunity to recognize familiar angles in varied positions (4.G.1, 4.MD.5).

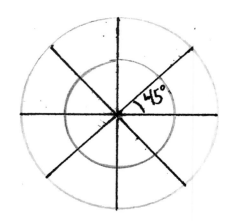

Through experimentation with circles of various sizes and angles constructed to varying specifications in Lesson 6, students discover that although the size of a circle may change, an angle spans an arc representing a constant fraction of the circumference. This reasoning forms the basis for the understanding that degree measure is not a measure of length. For example, as shown at right, the 45° angle spans ⅛ of the circumference of the circle, whether we choose the small circle or the large one.

Armed with this understanding of the degree as a unit of measure, students use various protractors in Lesson 7, including standard 180° protractors, to measure angles to the nearest degree and construct angles of a given measure (4.MD.6).

The topic wraps up in Lesson 8 as students further explore angle measure as an amount of turning. This provides a link to Grade 3 work with fractions, as students reason that a $\frac{1}{4}$ turn is a right angle and measures 90°, a $\frac{1}{2}$ turn measures 180°, and a $\frac{3}{4}$ turn measures 270°. They go on to identify these angles in their environment.

Focus Standard:	4.MD.5	Recognize angles as geometric shapes that are formed whenever two rays share a common endpoint, and understand concepts of angle measurement: a. An angle is measured with reference to a circle with its center at the common endpoint of the rays, by considering the fraction of the circular arc between the points where the two rays intersect the circle. An angle that turns through 1/360 of a circle is called a "one-degree angle," and can be used to measure angles. b. An angle that turns through *n* one-degree angles is said to have an angle measure of *n* degrees.
	4.MD.6	Measure angles in whole-number degrees using a protractor. Sketch angles of specified measure.
Instructional Days:	4	
Coherence		
Links from:	G2–M8	Time, Shapes, and Fractions as Equal Parts of Shapes

Objective 1: Use a circular protractor to understand a 1 degree angle as $\frac{1}{360}$ of a turn. Explore benchmark angles using the protractor.
(Lesson 5)

Objective 2: Use varied protractors to distinguish angle measure from length measurement.
(Lesson 6)

Objective 3: Measure and draw angles. Sketch given angle measures and verify with a protractor.
(Lesson 7)

Objective 4: Identify and measure angles as turns and recognize them in various contexts.
(Lesson 8)

Topic C: Problem Solving with the Addition of Angle Measures

In Topic C, students use concrete examples to discover the additive nature of angle measure. Working with pattern blocks in Lesson 9, they see that the measures of all of the angles at a point, with no overlaps or gaps, add up to 360 degrees, and they use this fact to find the measure of the pattern blocks' angles.

In Lesson 10, students use what they know about the additive nature of angle measure to reason about the relationships between pairs of adjacent angles. They discover that the measures of two angles on a straight line add up to 180 degrees (supplementary angles) and that the measures of two angles meeting to form a right angle add up to 90 degrees (complementary angles).

In Lesson 11, students extend their learning by determining the measures of unknown angles for adjacent angles that add up to 360 degrees. In addition, through their work with angles on a line, students go on to discover that vertical angles have the same measure.

In both Lessons 10 and 11, students write addition and subtraction equations to solve unknown angle problems. They solve these problems using a variety of pictorial and numerical strategies, combined with the use of a protractor to verify answers (4.MD.7).

Focus Standard:	4.MD.7	Recognize angle measure as additive. When an angle is decomposed into non-overlapping parts, the angle measure of the whole is the sum of the angle measures of the parts. Solve addition and subtraction problems to find unknown angles on a diagram in real world and mathematical problems, e.g., by using an equation with a symbol for the unknown angle measure.
Instructional Days:	3	
Coherence		
Links from:	G3–M7	Geometry and Measurement Word Problems

Objective 1: Decompose angles using pattern blocks.
(Lesson 9)

Objective 2: Use the addition of adjacent angle measures to solve problems using a symbol for the unknown angle measure.
(Lessons 10 and 11)

Topic D: Two-Dimensional Figures and Symmetry

An introduction to symmetry opens Topic D. In Lesson 12, students recognize lines of symmetry for two-dimensional figures, identify line-symmetric figures, and draw lines of symmetry. Given half of a figure and a line of symmetry, they draw the missing half. The topic then builds on students' prior knowledge of two-dimensional figures and allows them time to explore their properties. Throughout this culminating topic of the module, students use all of their prior knowledge of line and angle measure to classify and construct two-dimensional figures (4.G.2, 4.G.3).

In Lesson 13, students are introduced to the precise definition of a triangle and further their understanding of right, acute, and obtuse angles by identifying them in triangles.

They then classify triangles as right, acute, or obtuse based on angle measurements. Through a paper folding activity with a right triangle, students see that the non-right angles of a right triangle are complementary. They also learn that triangles can be classified as equilateral, isosceles, or scalene based on side lengths. For isosceles triangles, lines of symmetry are identified, and a folding activity demonstrates that base angles are equal. Folding an equilateral triangle highlights multiple lines of symmetry and proves not only that all sides are equal in length but also that all interior angles have the same measure. Students apply their understanding of triangle classification in Lesson 14 as they construct triangles given a set of classifying criteria (e.g., create a triangle that is both right and isosceles).

As the topic progresses into Lesson 15, students explore the definitions of familiar quadrilaterals and reason about their attributes, including angle measure and parallel and perpendicular lines. This work builds on Grade 3 reasoning about the attributes of shapes and lays a foundation for hierarchical classification of two-dimensional figures in Grade 5. In Lesson 16, students compare and analyze two-dimensional figures according to their properties and use grid paper to construct two-dimensional figures given a set of criteria.

Focus Standard:	4.G.1	Draw points, lines, line segments, rays, angles (right, acute, obtuse), and perpendicular and parallel lines. Identify these in two-dimensional figures.
	4.G.2	Classify two-dimensional figures based on the presence or absence of parallel or perpendicular lines, or the presence or absence of angles of a specified size. Recognize right triangles as a category, and identify right triangles.
	4.G.3	Recognize a line of symmetry for a two-dimensional figure as a line across the figure such that the figure can be folded along the line into matching parts. Identify line-symmetric figures and draw lines of symmetry.
Instructional Days:	5	
Coherence		
Links from:	G3–M7	Geometry and Measurement Word Problems
Links to:	G5–M5	Addition and Multiplication with Volume and Area

Objective 1: Recognize lines of symmetry for given two-dimensional figures; identify line-symmetric figures and draw lines of symmetry.
(Lesson 12)

Objective 2: Analyze and classify triangles based on side length, angle measure, or both.
(Lesson 13)

Objective 3: Define and construct triangles from given criteria. Explore symmetry in triangles.
(Lesson 14)

Objective 4: Classify quadrilaterals based on parallel and perpendicular lines and the presence or absence of angles of a specified size.
(Lesson 15)

Objective 5: Reason about attributes to construct quadrilaterals on square or triangular grid paper.
(Lesson 16)

MODULE 5: FRACTION EQUIVALENCE, ORDERING, AND OPERATIONS

OVERVIEW

In this 45-day module, students build on their Grade 3 work with unit fractions as they explore fraction equivalence and extend this understanding to mixed numbers. This leads to the comparison of fractions and mixed numbers and the representation of both in a variety of models. Benchmark fractions play an important part in students' ability to generalize and reason about relative fraction and mixed-number sizes. Students then have the opportunity to apply what they know to be true for whole number operations to the new concepts of fraction and mixed-number operations.

Students begin Topic A by decomposing fractions and creating tape diagrams to represent them as sums of fractions with the same denominator in different ways (e.g., $\frac{3}{5} = \frac{1}{5} + \frac{1}{5} + \frac{1}{5} = \frac{1}{5} + \frac{2}{5}$) (4.NF.3b). They go on to see that representing a fraction as the repeated addition of a unit fraction is the same as multiplying that unit fraction by a whole number. This is already a familiar fact in other contexts. For example, just as 3 twos = 2 + 2 + 2 = 3 × 2, so does $\frac{3}{4} = \frac{1}{4} + \frac{1}{4} + \frac{1}{4} = 3 \times \frac{1}{4}$.

The introduction of multiplication as a record of the decomposition of a fraction (4.NF.4a) early in the module allows students to become familiar with the notation before they work with more complex problems. As students continue working with decomposition, they represent familiar unit fractions as the sum of smaller unit fractions. A folded paper activity allows them to see that when the number of fractional parts in a whole increases, the size of the pieces decreases. They go on to investigate this concept with the use of tape diagrams and area models. Reasoning enables them to explain why two different fractions can represent the same portion of a whole (4.NF.1).

$$\frac{1}{3} = \frac{1}{6} + \frac{1}{6} = \frac{2}{6}$$

$$\frac{2}{3} = \left(\frac{1}{6} + \frac{1}{6}\right) + \left(\frac{1}{6} + \frac{1}{6}\right) = \frac{4}{6}$$

In Topic B, students use tape diagrams and area models to analyze their work from earlier in the module and begin using multiplication to create an equivalent fraction comprising smaller units, for example, $\frac{2}{3} = \frac{2 \times 4}{3 \times 4} = \frac{8}{12}$ (4.NF.1). Based on the use of multiplication, they reason that division can be used to create a fraction comprising larger units (or a single unit) that is equivalent to a given fraction, for example, $\frac{8}{12} = \frac{8 \div 4}{12 \div 4} = \frac{2}{3}$. Their work is justified using area models and tape diagrams and, conversely, multiplication is used to test for and verify equivalence. Students use the tape diagram to transition to modeling equivalence on the number line. They see that by

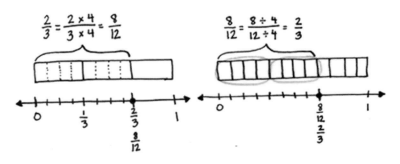

multiplying, any unit fraction length can be partitioned into n equal lengths and that doing so multiplies both the total number of fractional units (the denominator) and the number of selected units (the numerator) by n. They also see that there are times when fractional units can be grouped together, or divided, into larger fractional units. When that occurs, both the total number of fractional units and the number of selected units are divided by the same number.

In Grade 3, students compared fractions using fraction strips and number lines with the same denominators. In Topic C, they expand on comparing fractions by reasoning about fractions with unlike denominators. Students use the relationship between the numerator and denominator of a fraction to compare to a known benchmark (e.g., 0, $\frac{1}{2}$, or 1) on the number line. Alternatively, they compare using the same numerators. They find that the fraction with the greater denominator is the lesser fraction, since the size of the fractional unit is smaller as the whole is decomposed into more equal parts, for example, $\frac{1}{5} > \frac{1}{10}$ and therefore $\frac{3}{5} > \frac{3}{10}$. Throughout, their reasoning is supported using tape diagrams and number lines in cases where one numerator or denominator is a factor of the other, such as $\frac{1}{5}$ and $\frac{1}{10}$ or $\frac{2}{3}$ and $\frac{5}{6}$. When the units are unrelated, students use area models and multiplication, the general method pictured below to the left, whereby two fractions are expressed in terms of the same denominators. Students also reason that comparing fractions can be done only when referring to the same whole, and they record their comparisons using the comparison symbols <, >, and = (4.NF.2).

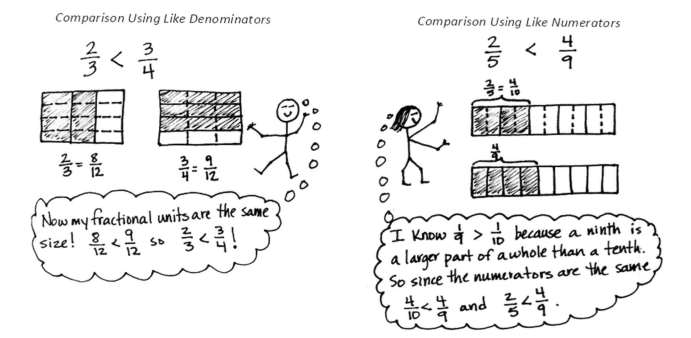

In Topic D, students apply their understanding of whole number addition (the combining of like units) and subtraction (finding an unknown part) to work with fractions (4.NF.3a). They see through visual models that if the units are the same, computation can be performed immediately, for example, 2 bananas + 3 bananas = 5 bananas and 2 eighths + 3 eighths = 5 eighths. They see that when they are subtracting fractions from one whole, the whole is decomposed into the same units as the part being subtracted, for example, $1 - \frac{3}{5} = \frac{5}{5} - \frac{3}{5} = \frac{2}{5}$.

Students practice adding more than two fractions and model fractions in word problems using tape diagrams (4.NF.3d). As an extension of the Grade 4 standards, students apply their knowledge of decomposition from earlier topics to add fractions with related units using tape diagrams and area models to support their numerical work. To find the sum of $\frac{1}{2}$ and $\frac{1}{4}$, for example, one simply decomposes 1 half into 2 smaller equal units, fourths, just as in Topics A and B. Now the addition can be completed: $\frac{2}{4} + \frac{1}{4} = \frac{3}{4}$. Though not assessed, this work is warranted because in Module 6, students will be asked to add tenths and hundredths when working with decimal fractions and decimal notation.

At the start of Topic E, students use decomposition and visual models to add and subtract fractions less than 1 to or from whole numbers (e.g., $4 + \frac{3}{4} = 4\frac{3}{4}$ and $4 - \frac{3}{4} = (3 + 1) - \frac{3}{4}$). They use addition and multiplication to build fractions greater than 1 and represent them on the number line.

Students then use these visual models and decompositions to reason about the various forms in which a fraction greater than or equal to 1 may be presented: as both fractions and mixed numbers. They practice converting (4.NF.1) between these forms and come to understand the usefulness of each form in different situations. Through this understanding, the common misconception that every improper fraction must be converted to a mixed number is avoided. Next, students compare fractions greater than 1, building on their rounding skills and using their understanding of benchmarks to reason about which of two fractions is greater (4.NF.2). This activity continues to build understanding of the relationship between the numerator and denominator of a fraction. Students progress to finding and using like denominators or numerators to compare and order mixed numbers. They apply their skills of comparing numbers greater than 1 by solving word problems (4.NF.3d) requiring the interpretation of data presented in line plots (4.MD.4). Students use addition and subtraction strategies to solve the problems, as well as decomposition and modeling to compare numbers in the data sets.

In Topic F, students estimate sums and differences of mixed numbers, rounding before performing the actual operation to determine what a reasonable outcome will be. They go on to use decomposition to add and subtract mixed numbers (4.NF.3c). This work builds on their understanding of a mixed number being the sum of a whole number and a fraction.

$$3\frac{2}{5} + 2\frac{4}{5} = 3 + \frac{2}{5} + 2\frac{4}{5} = 3 + 2 + \frac{2}{5} + \frac{4}{5}$$

I can add the parts in any order without changing the sum.

Using unit form, students add and subtract like units first (e.g., ones and ones, fourths and fourths). They use decomposition, shown with number bonds, in mixed-number addition to make one from fractional units before finding the sum. When subtracting, students learn to decompose the minuend or the subtrahend when there are not enough fractional units to subtract from. Alternatively, students can rename the subtrahend, giving more units to the fractional units, which connects to whole number subtraction when renaming 9 tens 2 ones as 8 tens 12 ones.

$3\frac{1}{5} - \frac{3}{5} = 2\frac{1}{5} + \frac{2}{5} = 2\frac{3}{5}$

$2\frac{1}{5}$ | 1 — Take one out to subtract from one!

$3\frac{1}{5} - \frac{3}{5} = 3 - \frac{2}{5} = 2\frac{3}{5}$

$\frac{1}{5}$ $\frac{2}{5}$ — Just like subtracting from one!

$3\frac{1}{5} - \frac{3}{5} = 2\frac{6}{5} - \frac{3}{5} = 2\frac{3}{5}$

$2\frac{6}{5}$ — Rename to make more fifths!

In Topic G, students build on the concept of representing repeated addition as multiplication, applying this familiar concept to work with fractions (4.NF.4a, 4.NF.4b). They use the associative property and their understanding of decomposition. Just as with whole numbers, the unit remains unchanged—for example,

$$4 \times \frac{3}{5} = 4 \times \left(3 \times \frac{1}{5}\right) = (4 \times 3) \times \frac{1}{5} = \frac{4 \times 3}{5} = \frac{12}{5}$$

This understanding connects to students' work with place value and whole numbers. Students go on to explore the use of the distributive property to multiply a whole number by a mixed number. They recognize that they are multiplying each part of a mixed number by the whole number and use efficient strategies to do so. The topic closes with solving multiplicative comparison word problems involving fractions (4.NF.4c), as well as problems involving the interpretation of data presented on a line plot (4.MD.4).

$5 \times 3\frac{3}{4} = 5 \times \left(3 + \frac{3}{4}\right)$

$= (5 \times 3) + \left(5 \times \frac{3}{4}\right)$

$= 15 + \frac{15}{4}$

$= 15 + 3\frac{3}{4}$

$= 18\frac{3}{4}$

The final topic comprises an exploration lesson where students find the sum of all like denominators from $\frac{0}{n}$ to $\frac{n}{n}$. For example, they might find the sum of all fifths from $\frac{0}{5}$ to $\frac{5}{5}$. Students discover they can make pairs with a sum of 1 to add more efficiently, e.g., $\frac{0}{5} + \frac{5}{5}, \frac{1}{5} + \frac{4}{5}, \frac{2}{5} + \frac{3}{5}$. They then extend this to find sums of eighths, tenths, and twelfths, observing patterns when finding the sum of odd and even denominators (4.OA.5).

The Mid-Module Assessment follows Topic D, and the End-of-Module Assessment follows Topic H.

FOCUS GRADE-LEVEL STANDARDS

Generate and analyze patterns.

4.OA.5 Generate a number or shape pattern that follows a given rule. Identify apparent features of the pattern that were not explicit in the rule itself. *For example, given the rule "Add 3" and the starting number 1, generate terms in the resulting sequence and observe that the terms appear to alternate between odd and even numbers. Explain informally why the numbers will continue to alternate in this way.*

Extend understanding of fraction equivalence and ordering.

4.NF.1 Explain why a fraction a/b is equivalent to a fraction $(n \times a)/(n \times b)$ by using visual fraction models, with attention to how the number and size of the parts differ even though the two fractions themselves are the same size. Use this principle to recognize and generate equivalent fractions.

4.NF.2 Compare two fractions with different numerators and different denominators, e.g., by creating common denominators or numerators, or by comparing to a benchmark fraction such as 1/2. Recognize that comparisons are valid only when the two fractions refer to the same whole. Record the results of comparisons with symbols >, =, or <, and justify the conclusions, e.g., by using a visual fraction model.

Build fractions from unit fractions by applying and extending previous understandings of operations on whole numbers.

4.NF.3 Understand a fraction a/b with $a > 1$ as a sum of fractions $1/b$.

    a.   Understand addition and subtraction of fractions as joining and separating parts referring to the same whole.

    b.   Decompose a fraction into a sum of fractions with the same denominator in more than one way, recording each decomposition by an equation. Justify decompositions, e.g., by using a visual fraction model. *Examples:* $3/8 = 1/8 + 1/8 + 1/8$; $3/8 = 1/8 + 2/8$; $2\,1/8 = 1 + 1 + 1/8 = 8/8 + 8/8 + 1/8$.

    c.   Add and subtract mixed numbers with like denominators, e.g., by replacing each mixed number with an equivalent fraction, and/or by using properties of operations and the relationship between addition and subtraction.

    d.   Solve word problems involving addition and subtraction of fractions referring to the same whole and having like denominators, e.g., by using visual fraction models and equations to represent the problem.

4.NF.4 Apply and extend previous understandings of multiplication to multiply a fraction by a whole number.

    a.   Understand a fraction a/b as a multiple of $1/b$. For example, use a visual fraction model to represent 5/4 as the product $5 \times (1/4)$, recording the conclusion by the equation $5/4 = 5 \times (1/4)$.

    b.   Understand a multiple of a/b as a multiple of $1/b$, and use this understanding to multiply a fraction by a whole number. *For example, use a visual fraction model to express $3 \times (2/5)$ as $6 \times (1/5)$, recognizing this product as 6/5. (In general, $n \times (a/b) = (n \times a)/b$.)*

    c.   Solve word problems involving multiplication of a fraction by a whole number, e.g., by using visual fraction models and equations to represent the problem. *For example, if each person at a party will eat 3/8 of a pound of roast beef, and there will be 5 people at the party, how many pounds of roast beef will be needed? Between what two whole numbers does your answer lie?*

Represent and interpret data.

4.MD.4 Make a line plot to display a data set of measurements in fractions of a unit (1/2, 1/4, 1/8). Solve problems involving addition and subtraction of fractions by using information presented in line plots. *For example, from a line plot find and interpret the difference in length between the longest and shortest specimens in an insect collection.*

FOUNDATIONAL STANDARDS

3.NF.1 Understand a fraction $1/b$ as the quantity formed by 1 part when a whole is partitioned into b equal parts; understand a fraction a/b as the quantity formed by a parts of size $1/b$.

3.NF.2 Understand a fraction as a number on the number line; represent fractions on a number line diagram.

   a. Represent a fraction $1/b$ on a number line diagram by defining the interval from 0 to 1 as the whole and partitioning it into b equal parts. Recognize that each part has size $1/b$ and that the endpoint of the part based at 0 locates the number $1/b$ on the number line.

   b. Represent a fraction a/b on a number line diagram by marking off a lengths of $1/b$ from 0. Recognize that the resulting interval has size a/b and that its endpoint locates the number a/b on the number line.

3.NF.3 Explain equivalence of fractions in special cases, and compare fractions by reasoning about their size.

   a. Understand two fractions as equivalent (equal) if they are the same size, or the same point on a number line.

   b. Recognize and generate simple equivalent fractions, e.g., $1/2 = 2/4$, $4/6 = 2/3$). Explain why the fractions are equivalent, e.g., by using a visual fraction model.

   c. Express whole numbers as fractions, and recognize fractions that are equivalent to whole numbers. *Examples: Express 3 in the form $3 = 3/1$; recognize that $6/1 = 6$; locate $4/4$ and 1 at the same point of a number line diagram.*

   d. Compare two fractions with the same numerator or the same denominator by reasoning about their size. Recognize that comparisons are valid only when the two fractions refer to the same whole. Record the results of comparisons with the symbols >, =, or <, and justify the conclusions, e.g., by using a visual fraction model.

3.G.2 Partition shapes into parts with equal areas. Express the area of each part as a unit fraction of the whole. For example, partition a shape into 4 parts with equal area, and describe the area of each part as $1/4$ of the area of the shape.

FOCUS STANDARDS FOR MATHEMATICAL PRACTICE

MP.2 *Reason abstractly and quantitatively.* Students will reason both abstractly and quantitatively throughout this module. They will draw area models, number lines, and tape diagrams to represent fractional quantities as well as word problems.

MP.3 *Construct viable arguments and critique the reasoning of others.* Much of the work in this module is centered on multiple ways to solve fraction and mixed-number problems. Students explore various strategies and participate in many *turn and talk* and *explain to your partner* activities. In doing so, they construct arguments to defend their choice of strategy, as well as think about and critique the reasoning of others.

MP.4 *Model with mathematics.* Throughout this module, students represent fractions with various models. They use area models to investigate and prove equivalence and the number line to compare and order fractions as well as model addition and subtraction of fractions. Students also use models in problem solving as they create line plots to display given sets of fractional data and solve problems requiring the interpretation of data presented in line plots.

MP.7 *Look for and make use of structure.* As they progress through this fraction module, students look for and use patterns and connections that will help them build understanding of new concepts. They relate and apply what they know about operations with whole numbers to operations with fractions.

MODULE TOPIC SUMMARIES

Topic A: Decomposition and Fraction Equivalence

Topic A builds on Grade 3 work with unit fractions. Students explore fraction equivalence through the decomposition of nonunit fractions into unit fractions, as well as the decomposition of unit fractions into smaller unit fractions. They represent these decompositions, and prove equivalence, using visual models.

$$1 = \frac{1}{3} + \frac{1}{3} + \frac{1}{3}$$
$$= \frac{2}{3} + \frac{1}{3}$$
$$= \frac{3}{3}$$

In Lessons 1 and 2, students decompose fractions as unit fractions, drawing tape diagrams to represent them as sums of fractions with the same denominator in different ways, e.g., $\frac{3}{5} = \frac{1}{5} + \frac{1}{5} + \frac{1}{5} = \frac{1}{5} + \frac{2}{5}$.

$$\frac{2}{3} = \frac{1}{3} + \frac{1}{3}$$
$$= 2 \times \frac{1}{3}$$

In Lesson 3, students see that representing a fraction as the repeated addition of a unit fraction is the same as multiplying that unit fraction by a whole number. This is already a familiar fact in other contexts. For example,

$$\frac{4}{3} = \frac{3}{3} + \frac{1}{3}$$
$$= 4 \times \frac{1}{3}$$

$$3 \text{ bananas} = 1 \text{ banana} + 1 \text{ banana} + 1 \text{ banana} = 3 \times 1 \text{ banana},$$
$$3 \text{ twos} = 2 + 2 + 2 = 3 \times 2$$
$$3 \text{ fourths} = 1 \text{ fourth} + 1 \text{ fourth} + 1 \text{ fourth} = 3 \times 1 \text{ fourth},$$
$$\frac{3}{4} = \frac{1}{4} + \frac{1}{4} + \frac{1}{4} = 3 \times \frac{1}{4}$$

By introducing multiplication as a record of the decomposition of a fraction early in the module, students are accustomed to the notation by the time they work with more complex problems in Topic G.

Students continue with decomposition in Lesson 4, where they represent fractions, for example, $\frac{1}{2}$, $\frac{1}{3}$, and $\frac{2}{3}$, as the sum of smaller unit fractions. They fold a paper strip to see that the number of fractional parts in a whole increases, while the size of the pieces decreases.

Students investigate and verify this idea through a paper folding activity and record the results with tape diagrams, for example, $\frac{1}{2} = \frac{1}{4} + \frac{1}{4} = \left(\frac{1}{8} + \frac{1}{8}\right) + \left(\frac{1}{8} + \frac{1}{8}\right) = \frac{4}{8}$.

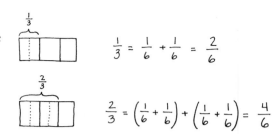

In Lesson 5, this idea is further investigated as students represent the decomposition of unit fractions in area models. In Lesson 6, students use the area model for a second day, this time to represent fractions with different numerators. They explain why two different fractions represent the same portion of a whole.

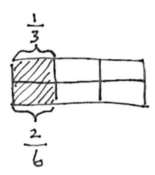
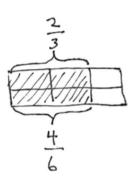

Focus Standard:	4.NF.3b	Understand a fraction a/b with $a > 1$ as a sum of fractions $1/b$.
		b. Decompose a fraction into a sum of fractions with the same denominator in more than one way, recording each decomposition by an equation. Justify decompositions, e.g., by using a visual fraction model. *Examples: 3/8 = 1/8 + 1/8 + 1/8; 3/8 = 1/8 + 2/8; 2 1/8 = 1 + 1 + 1/8 = 8/8 + 8/8 + 1/8.*
	4.NF.4a	Apply and extend previous understandings of multiplication to multiply a fraction by a whole number.
		a. Understand a fraction a/b as a multiple of 1/b. For example, use a visual fraction model to represent 5/4 as the product 5 × (1/4), recording the conclusion by the equation 5/4 = 5 × (1/4).
Instructional Days:	6	
Coherence		
Links from:	G3–M5	Fractions as Numbers on the Number Line
Links to:	G5–M3	Addition and Subtraction of Fractions

Objective 1: Decompose fractions as a sum of unit fractions using tape diagrams.
(Lessons 1 and 2)

Objective 2: Decompose nonunit fractions and represent them as a whole number times a unit fraction using tape diagrams.
(Lesson 3)

Objective 3: Decompose fractions into sums of smaller unit fractions using tape diagrams.
(Lesson 4)

Objective 4: Decompose unit fractions using area models to show equivalence.
(Lesson 5)

Objective 5: Decompose fractions using area models to show equivalence.
(Lesson 6)

Topic B: *Fraction Equivalence Using Multiplication and Division*

In Topic B, students start to generalize their work with fraction equivalence. In Lessons 7 and 8, students analyze their earlier work with tape diagrams and the area model in Lessons 3 through 5 to begin using multiplication to create an equivalent fraction comprising smaller units, for example, $\frac{2}{3} = \frac{2 \times 4}{3 \times 4} = \frac{8}{12}$. Conversely, students reason, in Lessons 9 and 10, that division can be used to create a fraction comprising larger units (or a single unit) that is equivalent to a given fraction, for example, $\frac{8}{12} = \frac{8 \div 4}{12 \div 4} = \frac{2}{3}$. The numerical work of Lessons 7 through 10 is introduced and supported using area models and tape diagrams.

In Lesson 11, students use tape diagrams to transition their knowledge of fraction equivalence to the number line. They see that any unit fraction length can be partitioned into n equal lengths. For example, each third in the interval from 0 to 1 may be partitioned into 4 equal parts. Doing so multiplies both the total number of fractional units (the denominator) and the number of selected units (the numerator) by 4. Students also see that in some cases, fractional units may be grouped together to form some number of larger fractional units. For example, when the interval from 0 to 1 is partitioned into twelfths, one may group 4 twelfths at a time to make thirds. In doing so, both the total number of fractional units and the number of selected units are divided by 4.

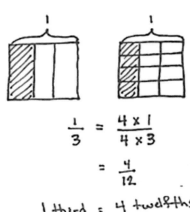

$$\frac{1}{3} = \frac{4 \times 1}{4 \times 3}$$

$$= \frac{4}{12}$$

1 third = 4 twelfths

Focus Standard:	4.NF.1	Explain why a fraction a/b is equivalent to a fraction $(n \times a)/(n \times b)$ by using visual fraction models, with attention to how the number and size of the parts differ even though the two fractions themselves are the same size. Use this principle to recognize and generate equivalent fractions.
Instructional Days:	5	
Coherence		
Links from:	G3–M5	Fractions as Numbers on the Number Line
Links to:	G5–M3	Addition and Subtraction of Fractions
	G5–M4	Multiplication and Division of Fractions and Decimal Fractions

Objective 1: Use the area model and multiplication to show the equivalence of two fractions.
(Lessons 7 and 8)

Objective 2: Use the area model and division to show the equivalence of two fractions.
(Lessons 9 and 10)

Objective 3: Explain fraction equivalence using a tape diagram and the number line, and relate that to the use of multiplication and division.
(Lesson 11)

Topic C: Fraction Comparison

In Topic C, students use benchmarks and common units to compare fractions with different numerators and different denominators. The use of benchmarks is the focus of Lessons 12 and 13 and is modeled using a number line. Students use the relationship between the numerator and denominator of a fraction to compare to a known benchmark (e.g., 0, $\frac{1}{2}$, or 1) and then use that information to compare the given fractions. For example, when comparing $\frac{4}{7}$ and $\frac{2}{5}$, students reason that 4 sevenths is more than 1 half, while 2 fifths is less than 1 half. They then conclude that 4 sevenths is greater than 2 fifths.

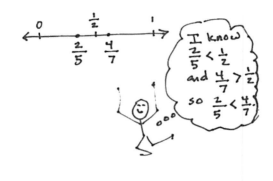

In Lesson 14, students reason that they can also use like numerators based on what they know about the size of the fractional units. They begin at a simple level by reasoning, for example, that 3 fifths is less than 3 fourths because fifths are smaller than fourths. They then see, too, that it is easy to make like numerators at times to compare, for example, $\frac{2}{5} < \frac{4}{9}$ because $\frac{2}{5} = \frac{4}{10}$, and $\frac{4}{10} < \frac{4}{9}$ because $\frac{1}{10} < \frac{1}{9}$. Using their experience from fractions in Grade 3, they know the larger the denominator of a unit fraction, the smaller the size of the fractional unit. Like numerators are modeled using tape diagrams directly above each other, where one fractional unit is partitioned into smaller unit fractions. The lesson then moves to comparing fractions with related denominators, such as $\frac{2}{3}$ and $\frac{5}{6}$, wherein one denominator is a factor of the other, using both tape diagrams and the number line.

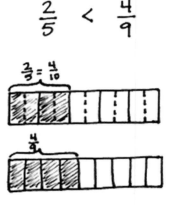

In Lesson 15, students compare fractions by using an area model to express two fractions, wherein one denominator is not a factor of the other, in terms of the same unit using multiplication, for example, $\frac{2}{3} < \frac{3}{4}$ because $\frac{2}{3} = \frac{2 \times 4}{3 \times 4} = \frac{8}{12}$ and $\frac{3}{4} = \frac{3 \times 3}{4 \times 3} = \frac{9}{12}$ and $\frac{8}{12} < \frac{9}{12}$. The area for $\frac{2}{3}$ is partitioned vertically, and the area for $\frac{3}{4}$ is partitioned horizontally.

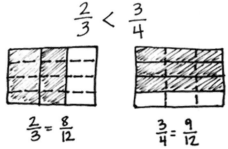

To find the equivalent fraction and create the same-size units, the areas are decomposed horizontally and vertically, respectively. Now the unit fractions are the same in each model or equation, and students can easily compare. The topic culminates with students comparing pairs of fractions and deciding which strategy is either necessary or efficient: reasoning using benchmarks and what they know about units; drawing a model such as number line, tape diagram, or area model; or the general method of finding like denominators through multiplication.

Focus Standard:	4.NF.2	Compare two fractions with different numerators and different denominators, e.g., by creating common denominators or numerators, or by comparing to a benchmark fraction such as 1/2. Recognize that comparisons are valid only when the two fractions refer to the same whole. Record the results of comparisons with symbols >, =, or <, and justify the conclusions, e.g., by using a visual fraction model.
Instructional Days:	4	
Coherence		
Links from:	G3–M5	Fractions as Numbers on the Number Line
Links to:	G5–M3	Addition and Subtraction of Fractions

Objective 1: Reason using benchmarks to compare two fractions on the number line. (Lessons 12 and 13)

Objective 2: Find common units or number of units to compare two fractions. (Lessons 14 and 15)

Topic D: Fraction Addition and Subtraction

Topic D bridges students' understanding of whole number addition and subtraction to fractions. Everything that they know to be true of addition and subtraction with whole numbers now applies to fractions. Addition is finding a total by combining like units. Subtraction is finding an unknown part. Implicit in the equations 3 + 2 = 5 and 2 = 5 – 3 is the assumption that the numbers are referring to the same units.

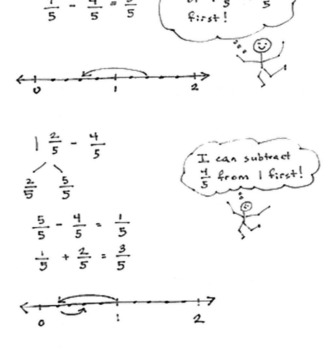

In Lessons 16 and 17, students generalize familiar facts about whole number addition and subtraction to work with fractions. Just as 3 apples – 2 apples = 1 apple, students note that 3 fourths – 2 fourths = 1 fourth. Just as 6 days + 3 days = 9 days = 1 week 2 days, students note that $\frac{6}{7}+\frac{3}{7}=\frac{9}{7}=\frac{7}{7}+\frac{2}{7}=1\frac{2}{7}$. In Lesson 17, students decompose a whole into a fraction having the same denominator as the subtrahend. For example, 1 – 4 fifths becomes 5 fifths – 4 fifths = 1 fifth, connecting with Topic B skills. They then see that when solving $1\frac{2}{5}-\frac{4}{5}$, they have a choice of subtracting $\frac{4}{5}$ from $\frac{7}{5}$ or from 1 (as pictured to the right). Students model with tape diagrams and number lines to understand and then verify their numerical work.

In Lesson 18, students add more than two fractions and see sums of more than one whole, such as $\frac{2}{8}+\frac{5}{8}+\frac{7}{8}+\frac{14}{8}$. As students move into problem solving in Lesson 19, they create tape diagrams or number lines to represent and solve fraction addition and subtraction word problems (see the example on the next page). These problems bridge students into work with mixed numbers, which follows the Mid-Module Assessment.

Mary mixed $\frac{3}{4}$ cup of wheat flour, $\frac{2}{4}$ cup of rice flour, and $\frac{1}{4}$ cup of oat flour for her bread dough. How many cups of flour did she put in her bread in all?

$$\frac{3}{4} + \frac{2}{4} + \frac{1}{4} = \frac{6}{4}$$

$$\frac{6}{4} = \frac{4}{4} + \frac{2}{4} = 1 + \frac{2}{4} = 1\frac{2}{4}$$

Mary used $\frac{6}{4}$ or $1\frac{2}{4}$ cups flour.

$$\frac{2}{6} + \frac{1}{6} = \frac{3}{6}$$

$$\frac{4}{6} + \frac{5}{6} = \frac{9}{6} = 1\frac{3}{6}$$

In Lessons 20 and 21, students add fractions with related units, where one denominator is a multiple (or factor) of the other. In order to add such fractions, a decomposition is necessary (see above right). Decomposing one unit into another is familiar territory: students have had ample practice composing and decomposing in Topics A and B, when working with place value units, converting units of measurement, and using the distributive property. For example, they have converted between equivalent measurement units (e.g., 100 cm = 1 m), and they have used such conversions to do arithmetic (e.g., 1 meter − 54 centimeters). With fractions, the concept is the same. To find the sum of $\frac{1}{2}$ and $\frac{1}{4}$, one simply renames (converts, decomposes) $\frac{1}{2}$ as $\frac{2}{4}$ and adds: $\frac{2}{4} + \frac{1}{4} = \frac{3}{4}$. All numerical work is accompanied by visual models that allow students to use and apply their skills and understandings. Number sentences involve the related units of 2, 4, and 8; 2 and 10; 3 and 6; and 5 and 10. The addition of fractions with related units is also foundational to decimal work when adding tenths and hundredths in Module 6. (Note that addition of fractions with related denominators will not be assessed.)

Focus Standard:	4.NF.3ad	Understand a fraction a/b with $a > 1$ as a sum of fractions $1/b$.
		a. Understand addition and subtraction of fractions as joining and separating parts referring to the same whole.
		d. Solve word problems involving addition and subtraction of fractions referring to the same whole and having like denominators, e.g., by using visual fraction models and equations to represent the problem.
Instructional Days:	6	
Coherence		
Links from:	G3–M5	Fractions as Numbers on the Number Line
Links to:	G5–M3	Addition and Subtraction of Fractions

Objective 1: Use visual models to add and subtract two fractions with the same units. (Lesson 16)

Objective 2: Use visual models to add and subtract two fractions with the same units, including subtraction from one whole.
(Lesson 17)

Objective 2: Add and subtract more than two fractions.
(Lesson 18)

Objective 3: Solve word problems involving addition and subtraction of fractions.
(Lesson 19)

Objective 4: Use visual models to add two fractions with related units using the denominators 2, 3, 4, 5, 6, 8, 10, and 12.
(Lessons 20 and 21)

Topic E: Extending Fraction Equivalence to Fractions Greater than 1

In Topic E, students study equivalence involving both ones and fractional units. In Lesson 22, they use decomposition and visual models to add and subtract fractions less than 1 to and from whole numbers, for example, $4 + \frac{3}{4} = 4\frac{3}{4}$ and $4 - \frac{3}{4} = (3+1) - \frac{3}{4}$, subtracting the fraction from 1 using a number bond and a number line.

Lesson 23 has students using addition and multiplication to build fractions greater than 1 and then representing them on the number line. Fractions can be expressed in both mixed units of a whole number and a fraction or simply as a fraction, as pictured below, for example, $7 \times \frac{1}{3} = \frac{3}{3} + \frac{3}{3} + \frac{1}{3} = 2 \times \frac{3}{3} + \frac{1}{3} = \frac{7}{3} = 2\frac{1}{3}$:

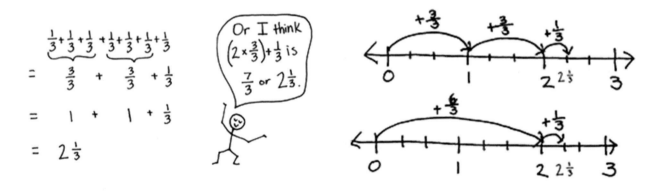

In Lessons 24 and 25, students use decompositions to reason about the various equivalent forms in which a fraction greater than or equal to 1 may be presented: both as fractions and as mixed numbers. In Lesson 24, they decompose, for example, 11 fourths into 8 fourths and 3 fourths, $\frac{11}{4} = \frac{8}{4} + \frac{3}{4}$, or they can think of it as $\frac{11}{4} = \frac{4}{4} + \frac{4}{4} + \frac{3}{4} = 2 \times \frac{4}{4} + \frac{3}{4} = 2\frac{3}{4}$. In Lesson 25, students are then able to decompose the 2 wholes into 8 fourths, so their original number can now be looked at as $\frac{8}{4} + \frac{3}{4}$ or $\frac{11}{4}$. In this way, they see that $2\frac{3}{4} = \frac{11}{4}$. This fact is reinforced when they plot $\frac{11}{4}$ on the number line and see that it is at the same point as $2\frac{3}{4}$. Unfortunately, the term *improper fraction* carries with it some baggage. As many have observed, there is nothing "improper" about an improper fraction. Nevertheless, as a mathematical term, it is useful for describing a particular form in which a fraction may be presented (i.e., a fraction is improper if the numerator is greater than or equal to the denominator). Students do need practice in converting between the various forms a fraction may take, but take care not to foster the misconception that every improper fraction *must* be converted to a mixed number.

Students compare fractions greater than 1 in Lessons 26 and 27. They begin by using their understanding of benchmarks to reason about which of two fractions is greater. This activity builds on students' rounding skills, having them identify the whole numbers and the halfway points between them on the number line. The relationship between the numerator and denominator of a fraction is a key concept here as students consider relationships to whole numbers; for example, a student might reason that $\frac{23}{8}$ is less than $\frac{29}{10}$ because $\frac{23}{8}$ is 1 eighth less than 3, but $\frac{29}{10}$ is 1 tenth less than 3. They know each fraction is 1 fractional unit away from 3 and since $\frac{1}{8} > \frac{1}{10}$, then $\frac{23}{8} < \frac{29}{10}$. Students progress to finding and using like denominators to compare and order mixed numbers. Once again, students must use reasoning skills as they determine that when they have two fractions with the same numerator, the larger fraction will have a larger unit (or smaller denominator). Conversely, when they have two fractions with the same denominator, the larger one will have the larger number of units (or larger numerator).

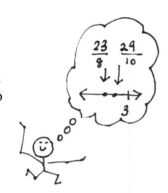

Lesson 28 wraps up the topic with word problems requiring the interpretation of data presented in line plots. Students create line plots to display a given data set that includes fraction and mixed-number values. To do this, they apply their skill in comparing mixed numbers through reasoning and the use of common numerators or denominators. For example, a data set might contain both $1\frac{5}{9}$ and $\frac{14}{9}$, giving students the opportunity to determine that they must be plotted at the same point. They also use addition and subtraction to solve the problems.

Focus Standard:	4.NF.1	Explain why a fraction a/b is equivalent to a fraction $(n \times a)/(n \times b)$ by using visual fraction models, with attention to how the number and size of the parts differ even though the two fractions themselves are the same size. Use this principle to recognize and generate equivalent fractions.
	4.NF.2	Compare two fractions with different numerators and different denominators, e.g., by creating common denominators or numerators, or by comparing to a benchmark fraction such as 1/2. Recognize that comparisons are valid only when the two fractions refer to the same whole. Record the results of comparisons with symbols >, =, or <, and justify the conclusions, e.g., by using a visual fraction model.
	4.NF.3	Understand a fraction a/b with $a > 1$ as a sum of fractions $1/b$.
		a. Understand addition and subtraction of fractions as joining and separating parts referring to the same whole.
		b. Decompose a fraction into a sum of fractions with the same denominator in more than one way, recording each decomposition by an equation. Justify decompositions, e.g., by using a visual fraction model. *Examples: 3/8 = 1/8 + 1/8 + 1/8; 3/8 = 1/8 + 2/8; 2 1/8 = 1 + 1 + 1/8 = 8/8 + 8/8 + 1/8.*
		c. Add and subtract mixed numbers with like denominators, e.g., by replacing each mixed number with an equivalent fraction, and/or by using properties of operations and the relationship between addition and subtraction.
		d. Solve word problems involving addition and subtraction of fractions referring to the same whole and having like denominators, e.g., by using visual fraction models and equations to represent the problem.
Instructional Days:	7	
Coherence		
Links from:	G3–M5	Fractions as Numbers on the Number Line
Links to:	G5–M3	Addition and Subtraction of Fractions
	G5–M4	Multiplication and Division of Fractions and Decimal Fractions

Objective 1: Add a fraction less than 1 to, or subtract a fraction less than 1 from, a whole number using decomposition and visual models.
(Lesson 22)

Objective 2: Add and multiply unit fractions to build fractions greater than 1 using visual models.
(Lesson 23)

Objective 3: Decompose and compose fractions greater than 1 to express them in various forms.
(Lessons 24 and 25)

Objective 4: Compare fractions greater than 1 by reasoning using benchmark fractions.
(Lesson 26)

Objective 5: Compare fractions greater than 1 by creating common numerators or denominators.
(Lesson 27)

Objective 6: Solve word problems with line plots.
(Lesson 28)

Topic F: Addition and Subtraction of Fractions by Decomposition

Topic F provides students with the opportunity to use their understandings of fraction addition and subtraction as they explore mixed-number addition and subtraction by decomposition.

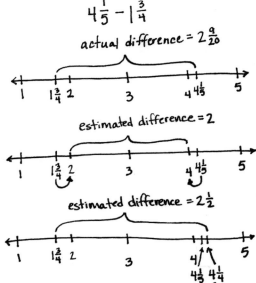

Lesson 29 focuses on the process of using benchmark numbers to estimate sums and differences of mixed numbers. Students once again call on their understanding of benchmark fractions as they determine, prior to performing the actual operation, what a reasonable outcome will be. One student might use benchmark whole numbers and reason, for example, that the difference between $4\frac{1}{5}$ and $1\frac{3}{4}$ is close to 2 because $4\frac{1}{5}$ is closer to 4 than 5, $1\frac{3}{4}$ is closer to 2 than 1, and the difference between 4 and 2 is 2. Another student might use familiar benchmark fractions and reason that the answer will be closer to $2\frac{1}{2}$ since $4\frac{1}{5}$ is about $\frac{1}{4}$ more than 4 and $1\frac{3}{4}$ is about $\frac{1}{4}$ less than 2, making the difference about a half more than 2 or $2\frac{1}{2}$.

In Lesson 30, students begin adding a mixed number to a fraction using unit form. They add like units, applying their Grade 1 and 2 understanding of completing a unit to add when the sum of the fractional units exceeds 1. Students ask, "How many more do we need to make one?" rather than, "How many more do we need to make ten?" as was the case in Grade 1. A number bond decomposes the fraction to make one and can be modeled on the number line or using the arrow way, as shown to the right. Alternatively, a number bond can be used after adding like units, when the sum results in a mixed number with a fraction greater than 1, to decompose the fraction greater than 1 into ones and fractional units.

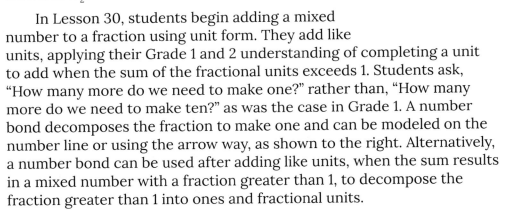

Directly applying what was learned in Lesson 30, Lesson 31 starts with adding like units, ones with ones and fourths with fourths, to add two mixed numbers. Students can, again, choose to make one before finding the sum or to decompose the sum to result in a proper mixed number.

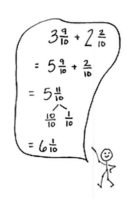

Lessons 32 and 33 follow the same sequence for subtraction. In Lesson 32, students simply subtract a fraction from a mixed number, using three main strategies both when there are and when there are not enough fractional units. They count back or up, subtract from 1, or take one out to subtract from 1. In Lesson 33, students apply these strategies after subtracting the ones first. They model subtraction of mixed numbers using a number line or the arrow way.

In Lesson 34, students learn another strategy for subtraction by decomposing the total into a mixed number and an improper fraction to either subtract a fraction or a mixed number.

Focus Standard:	4.NF.3cd	Understand a fraction a/b with $a > 1$ as a sum of fractions $1/b$.
		c. Add and subtract mixed numbers with like denominators, e.g., by replacing each mixed number with an equivalent fraction, and/or by using properties of operations and the relationship between addition and subtraction.
		d. Solve word problems involving addition and subtraction of fractions referring to the same whole and having like denominators, e.g., by using visual fraction models and equations to represent the problem.
	4.MD.4	Make a line plot to display a data set of measurements in fractions of a unit (1/2, 1/4, 1/8). Solve problems involving addition and subtraction of fractions by using information presented in line plots. For example, from a line plot find and interpret the difference in length between the longest and shortest specimens in an insect collection.

Instructional Days:	6	
Coherence		
Links from:	G3–M5	Fractions as Numbers on the Number Line
Links to:	G5–M3	Addition and Subtraction of Fractions

Objective 1: Estimate sums and differences using benchmark numbers.
(Lesson 29)

Objective 2: Add a mixed number and a fraction.
(Lesson 30)

Objective 3: Add mixed numbers.
(Lesson 31)

Objective 4: Subtract a fraction from a mixed number.
(Lesson 32)

Objective 5: Subtract a mixed number from a mixed number.
(Lesson 33)

Objective 6: Subtract mixed numbers.
(Lesson 34)

Topic G: Repeated Addition of Fractions as Multiplication

Topic G extends the concept of representing repeated addition as multiplication, applying this familiar concept to work with fractions.

Multiplying a whole number times a fraction was introduced in Topic A as students learned to decompose fractions, for example, $\frac{3}{5} = \frac{1}{5} + \frac{1}{5} + \frac{1}{5} = 3 \times \frac{1}{5}$. In Lessons 35 and 36, students use the associative property, as exemplified below, to multiply a whole number times a mixed number.

$$3 \text{ bananas} + 3 \text{ bananas} + 3 \text{ bananas} + 3 \text{ bananas}$$
$$= 4 \times 3 \text{ bananas}$$
$$= 4 \times (3 \times 1 \text{ bananas}) = (4 \times 3) \times 1 \text{ banana}$$
$$= 12 \text{ bananas}$$

$$3 \text{ fifths} + 3 \text{ fifths} + 3 \text{ fifths} + 3 \text{ fifths}$$
$$= 4 \times 3 \text{ fifths} = 4 \times (3 \text{ fifths}) = (4 \times 3) \text{ fifths}$$
$$= 12 \text{ fifths}$$

$$4 \times \frac{3}{5} 4 \times \left(3 \times \frac{1}{5}\right) = (4 \times 3) \times \frac{1}{5} = \frac{4 \times 3}{5} = \frac{12}{5}$$

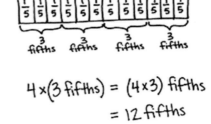

Students may never have considered before that 3 bananas = 3 × 1 banana, but it is an understanding that connects place value, whole number work, measurement conversions, and fractions—for example, 3 hundreds = 3 × 1 hundred, or 3 feet = 3 (1 foot); 1 foot = 12 inches, therefore, 3 feet = 3 × (12 inches) = (3 × 12) inches = 36 inches.

Students explore the use of the distributive property in Lessons 37 and 38 to multiply a whole number by a mixed number. They see the multiplication of each part of a mixed number by the whole number and use the appropriate strategies to do so. As students progress through each lesson, they are encouraged to record only as much as they need to keep track of the math. As shown below, there are multiple steps when using the distributive property, and students can get lost in those steps. Efficiency in solving is encouraged.

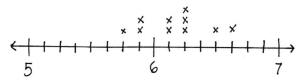

$$2 \times 3\tfrac{1}{5} = (2 \times 3) + (2 \times \tfrac{1}{5})$$
$$= 6 + \tfrac{2}{5} = 6\tfrac{2}{5}$$

$$4 \times 9\tfrac{3}{4} = 36 + \tfrac{12}{4}$$
$$= 36 + 3$$
$$= 39$$

$$5 \times 3\tfrac{3}{4} = 5 \times (3 + \tfrac{3}{4}) = (5 \times 3) + (5 \times \tfrac{3}{4}) = 15 + \tfrac{5 \times 3}{4} = 15 + \tfrac{15}{4} = 15 + 3\tfrac{3}{4} = 18\tfrac{3}{4}$$

In Lesson 39, students build their problem-solving skills by solving multiplicative comparison word problems involving mixed numbers, for example, "Jennifer bought 3 times as much meat on Saturday as she did on Monday. If she bought $1\tfrac{1}{2}$ pounds on Monday, how much did she buy on both days?" They create and use tape diagrams to represent these problems before using various strategies to solve them numerically.

Monday | $1\tfrac{1}{2}$ pounds |

Saturday | $1\tfrac{1}{2}$ pounds | $1\tfrac{1}{2}$ pounds | $1\tfrac{1}{2}$ pounds | ?

$$4 \times 1\tfrac{1}{2} = (4 \times 1) + (4 \times \tfrac{1}{2}) = 4 + \tfrac{4 \times 1}{2} = 4 + \tfrac{4}{2} = 4 + 2 = 6$$
Jennifer bought 6 pounds of meat.

In Lesson 40, students solve word problems involving multiplication of a fraction by a whole number and also work with data presented in line plots.

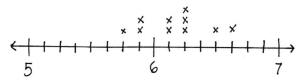

Focus Standard:	4.NF.4	Apply and extend previous understandings of multiplication to multiply a fraction by a whole number.

a. Understand a fraction a/b as a multiple of 1/b. For example, use a visual fraction model to represent 5/4 as the product 5 × (1/4), recording the conclusion by the equation 5/4 = 5 × (1/4).

b. Understand a multiple of a/b as a multiple of 1/b, and use this understanding to multiply a fraction by a whole number. For example, use a visual fraction model to express 3 × (2/5) as 6 × (1/5), recognizing this product as 6/5. (In general, n × (a/b) = (n × a)/b.)

c. Solve word problems involving multiplication of a fraction by a whole number, e.g., by using visual fraction models and equations to represent the problem. *For example, if each person at a party will eat 3/8 of a pound of roast beef, and there will be 5 people at the party, how many pounds of roast beef will be needed? Between what two whole numbers does your answer lie?*

	4.MD.4	Make a line plot to display a data set of measurements in fractions of a unit (1/2, 1/4, 1/8). Solve problems involving addition and subtraction of fractions by using information presented in line plots. *For example, from a line plot find and interpret the difference in length between the longest and shortest specimens in an insect collection.*
Instructional Days:	6	
Coherence		
Links from:	G3–M5	Fractions as Numbers on the Number Line
Links to:	G5–M3	Addition and Subtraction of Fractions
	G5–M4	Multiplication and Division of Fractions and Decimal Fractions

Objective 1: Represent the multiplication of n times a/b as $(n \times a)/b$ using the associative property and visual models.
(Lessons 35 and 36)

Objective 2: Find the product of a whole number and a mixed number using the distributive property.
(Lessons 37 and 38)

Objective 3: Solve multiplicative comparison word problems involving fractions.
(Lesson 39)

Objective 4: Solve word problems involving the multiplication of a whole number and a fraction including those involving line plots.
(Lesson 40)

Topic H: *Explore a Fraction Pattern*

This final topic is an exploration lesson in which students find the sum of all like denominators from $\frac{0}{n}$ to $\frac{n}{n}$. For example, they might find the sum of all fifths from $\frac{0}{5}$ to $\frac{5}{5}$. Students discover they can make pairs with a sum of 1 to add more efficiently, for example, $\frac{0}{5}+\frac{5}{5}, \frac{1}{5}+\frac{4}{5}, \frac{2}{5}+\frac{3}{5}$. As they make this discovery, they share and compare their strategies with partners. Through discussion of their strategies, they determine which are most efficient.

Next, students extend the use of their strategies to find sums of eighths, tenths, and twelfths, observing patterns when finding the sum of odd and even denominators (4.OA.5). Advanced students can be challenged to find the sum of all hundredths from 0 hundredths to 100 hundredths.

Focus Standard:	4.OA.5	Generate a number or shape pattern that follows a given rule. Identify apparent features of the pattern that were not explicit in the rule itself. *For example, given the rule "Add 3" and the starting number 1, generate terms in the resulting sequence and observe that the terms appear to alternate between odd and even numbers. Explain informally why the numbers will continue to alternate in this way.*
Instructional Days:	1	
Coherence		
Links from:	G3–M5	Fractions as Numbers on the Number Line
Links to:	G5–M3	Addition and Subtraction of Fractions

Objective 1: Find and use a pattern to calculate the sum of all fractional parts between 0 and 1. Share and critique peer strategies.
(Lesson 41)

MODULE 6: DECIMAL FRACTIONS

OVERVIEW

This 20-day module gives students their first opportunity to explore decimal numbers via their relationship to decimal fractions, expressing a given quantity in both fraction and decimal forms. Using the understanding of fractions developed throughout Module 5, students apply the same reasoning to decimal numbers, building a solid foundation for Grade 5 work with decimal operations. Previously referred to as whole numbers, all numbers written in the base-ten number system with place value units that are powers of 10 are henceforth referred to as decimal numbers, a set that now includes tenths and hundredths—for example, 1, 15, 248, 0.3, 3.02, and 24.345.

In Topic A, students use their understanding of fractions to explore tenths. At the opening of the topic, they use metric measurement to see tenths in relationship to different whole units: centimeters, meters, kilograms, and liters. Students explore, creating and identifying tenths of various wholes, as they draw lines of specified length, identify the weight of objects, and read the level of liquid measurements. Students connect these concrete experiences pictorially as tenths are represented on the number line and with tape diagrams as pictured to the right. Students express tenths as decimal fractions and are introduced to decimal notation. They write statements of equivalence in unit,

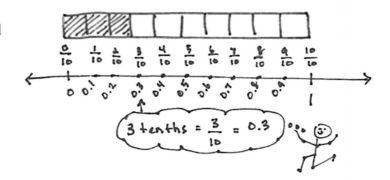

fraction, and decimal forms, for example, 3 tenths $= \frac{3}{10} = 0.3$ (4.NF.6). Next, students return to the use of metric measurement to investigate decimal fractions greater than 1. Using a centimeter ruler, they draw lines that measure, for example, $2\frac{4}{10}$ or $6\frac{8}{10}$ centimeters. Using the area model, students see that numbers containing a whole number and fractional part (i.e., mixed numbers) can also be expressed using decimal notation provided that the fractional part can be converted to a decimal number (4.NF.6). Students use place value disks to represent the value of each digit in a decimal number. Just as they wrote whole numbers in expanded form using multiplication, students write the value of a decimal number in expanded form using fractions and decimals, for example, 2 ones 4 tenths $= 2\frac{4}{10} = (2\times1)+\left(4\times\frac{1}{10}\right)$ and $2.4 = (2\times1)+(4\times0.1)$. In addition, students plot decimal numbers on the number line.

Students decompose tenths into 10 equal parts to create hundredths in Topic B. Through the decomposition of a meter, students identify 1 centimeter as 1 hundredth of a meter. As they count up by hundredths, they realize the equivalence of 10 hundredths and 1 tenth and go on to represent them as both decimal fractions and decimal numbers (4.NF.5). Students use area models, tape diagrams, and number disks on a place value chart to see and model the equivalence of numbers involving units of tenths and hundredths. They express the value of the number in both decimal and fraction expanded forms.

$$31\tfrac{46}{100} = (3\times10) + (1\times1) + \left(4\times\tfrac{1}{10}\right) + \left(6\times\tfrac{1}{100}\right)$$
$$31.46 = (3\times10) + (1\times1) + (4\times0.1) + (6\times0.01)$$

Close work with the place value chart helps students see that place value units are not symmetric about the decimal point—a common misconception that often leads students to mistakenly believe there is a "oneths" place. They explore the placement of decimal numbers to hundredths and recognize that the place value chart is symmetric about the ones column. This understanding

Symmetry with respect to the ones place

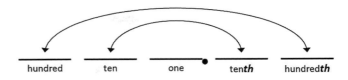

helps students recognize that even as we move to the units on the right side of the decimal on the place value chart, a column continues to represent a unit 10 times as large as that of the column to its right. This understanding builds on the place value work done in Module 1 and enables students to understand that 3.2, for example, might be modeled as 3 ones 2 tenths, 32 tenths, or 320 hundredths. Topic B concludes with students using their knowledge of fraction equivalence to work with decimal numbers expressed in unit form, fraction form, and decimal form (4.NF.6).

The focus of Topic C is comparison of decimal numbers (4.NF.7). To begin, students work with concrete representations of measurements. They see measurement of length on meter sticks, of mass using a scale, and of volume using graduated cylinders. In each case, students record the measurements on a place value chart and then compare them. They use their understanding of metric measurement and decimals to answer questions such as, "Which is greater? Less? Which is longer?

Rice Bag	ones (kilograms)	.	tenths	hundredths
A	O	.	1	O
B	O	.	6	5
C	O	.	7	
D	O	.	4	6

0.7 kg, 0.65 kg, 0.46 kg, 0.1 kg

Shorter? Which is heavier? Lighter?" Comparing the decimals in the context of measurement supports students' justification of their comparisons and grounds their reasoning, while at the same time setting them up for work with decimal comparison at a more concrete level. Next, students use area models and number lines to compare decimal numbers and use the <, >, and = symbols to record their comparisons. All of their work with comparisons at the pictorial level helps to eradicate the common misconception that is often made when students assume a greater number of hundredths must be greater than a lesser number of tenths. For example, when comparing 7 tenths and 27 hundredths, students recognize that 7 tenths is greater than 27 hundredths because, in any comparison, one must consider the *size of the units.* Students go on to arrange mixed groups of decimal fractions in unit, fraction, and decimal forms in order from greatest to least or least to greatest. They use their understanding of different ways of expressing equivalent values in order to arrange a set of decimal fractions as pictured below.

$\frac{37}{100} < 0.5 < 1$ and 22 hundredths $< 1\frac{4}{10} < 1.54$

Topic D introduces the addition of decimals by way of finding equivalent decimal fractions and adding fractions. Students add tenths and hundredths, recognizing that they must convert the addends to the same units (4.NF.5). The sum is then converted back into a decimal (4.NF.6). They use their knowledge of like denominators and understanding of fraction equivalence to do so. Students use the same process to add and subtract mixed numbers involving decimal units. They then apply their new learning to solve word problems involving metric measurements.

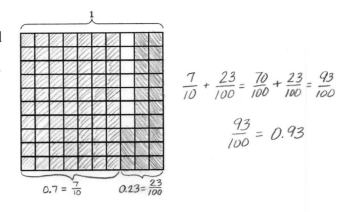

Students conclude their work with decimal fractions in Topic E by applying their knowledge to the real-world context of money. They recognize 1 penny as $\frac{1}{100}$ dollar, 1 dime as $\frac{1}{10}$ dollar, and 1 quarter as $\frac{25}{100}$ dollar. They apply their understanding of tenths and hundredths to write given amounts of money in both fraction

and decimal forms. To do this, students decompose a given amount of money into dollars, quarters, dimes, and pennies, and express the amount as a decimal fraction and decimal number. Students then add various numbers of coins and dollars using Grade 2 knowledge of the equivalence of 100 cents to 1 dollar. Addition and subtraction word problems are solved using unit form, adding dollars and cents. Multiplication and division word problems are solved using cents as the unit (4.MD.2). The final answer in each word problem is converted from cents into a decimal using a dollar symbol for the unit—for example:

Jack has 2 quarters and 7 dimes. Jim has 1 dollar, 3 quarters, and 6 pennies. How much money do they have together? Write your answer as a decimal.

Jack | 50¢ | 70¢ |

Jim | $1 | 75¢ | 6¢ |

They have $3.01 together.

1 dollar 20 cents + 1 dollar 81 cents

= 2 dollars 101 cents
          ⌃
        100 1

= 3 dollars 1 cent

= $3.01

FOCUS GRADE-LEVEL STANDARDS

Understand decimal notations for fractions, and compare decimal fractions.

4.NF.5 Express a fraction with denominator 10 as an equivalent fraction with denominator 100, and use this technique to add two fractions with respective denominators 10 and 100.

For example, express 3/10 as 30/100, and add 3/10 + 4/100 = 34/100. (Students who can generate equivalent fractions can develop strategies for adding fractions with unlike denominators in general. But addition and subtraction with unlike denominators in general is not a requirement at this grade.)

4.NF.6 Use decimal notation for fractions with denominators 10 or 100. *For example, rewrite 0.62 as 62/100; describe a length as 0.62 meters; locate 0.62 on a number line diagram.*

4.NF.7 Compare two decimals to hundredths by reasoning about their size. Recognize that comparisons are valid only when the two decimals refer to the same whole. Record the results of comparisons with the symbols >, =, or <, and justify the conclusions, e.g., by using a visual model.

Solve problems involving measurement and conversion of measurements from a larger unit to a smaller unit.[21]

4.MD.2 Use the four operations to solve word problems involving distances, intervals of time, liquid volumes, masses of objects, and money, including problems involving simple fractions or decimals, and problems that require expressing measurements given in a larger unit in terms of a smaller unit. Represent measurement quantities using diagrams such as number line diagrams that feature a measurement scale.

FOUNDATIONAL STANDARDS

2.MD.8 Solve word problems involving dollar bills, quarters, dimes, nickels, and pennies, using $ and ¢ symbols appropriately. *Example: If you have 2 dimes and 3 pennies, how many cents do you have?*

3.NBT.3 Multiply one-digit whole numbers by multiples of 10 in the range 10–90 (e.g., 9 × 80, 5 × 60) using strategies based on place value and properties of operations.

3.NF.1 Understand a fraction 1/b as the quantity formed by 1 part when a whole is partitioned into b equal parts; understand a fraction a/b as the quantity formed by a parts of size 1/b.

3.NF.2 Understand a fraction as a number on the number line; represent fractions on a number line diagram.

    b. Represent a fraction a/b on a number line diagram by marking off a lengths of 1/b from 0. Recognize that the resulting interval has size a/b and that its endpoint locates the number a/b on the number line.

3.NF.3 Explain equivalence of fractions in special cases, and compare fractions by reasoning about their size.

    b. Recognize and generate simple equivalent fractions, e.g., 1/2 = 2/4, 4/6 = 2/3). Explain why the fractions are equivalent, e.g., by using a visual fraction model.

    d. Compare two fractions with the same numerator or the same denominator by reasoning about their size. Recognize that comparisons are valid only when the two fractions refer to the same whole. Record the results of comparisons with the symbols >, =, or <, and justify the conclusions, e.g., by using a visual fraction model.

3.MD.2 Measure and estimate liquid volumes and masses of objects using standard units of grams (g), kilograms (kg), and liters (l). (Excludes compound units such as cm^3 and finding the geometric volume of a container.) Add, subtract, multiply, or divide to solve one-step word problems involving masses or volumes that are given in the same units, e.g., by using drawings (such as a beaker with a measurement scale) to represent the problem. (Excludes multiplicative comparison problems [problems involving notions of *times as much*; see Standards Glossary, Table 2]).

FOCUS STANDARDS FOR MATHEMATICAL PRACTICE

MP.2 *Reason abstractly and quantitatively.* Throughout this module, students use area models, tape diagrams, number disks, and number lines to represent decimal quantities. When determining the equivalence of a decimal fraction and a fraction, students consider the units that are involved and attend to the meaning of the quantities of each. Furthermore, students use metric measurement and money amounts to build an understanding of the decomposition of a whole into tenths and hundredths.

MP.4 *Model with mathematics.* Students represent decimals with various models throughout this module, including expanded form. Each of the models helps students to build understanding and analyze the relationship and role of decimals within the number system. Students use a tape diagram to represent tenths and then to decompose one tenth into hundredths. They use number disks and a place value chart to extend their understanding of place value to include decimal fractions. Furthermore, students use a place value chart along with the area model to compare decimals. A number line models decimal numbers to the hundredths.

MP.6 *Attend to precision.* Students attend to precision as they decompose a whole into tenths and tenths into hundredths. They also make statements such as 5 ones and 3 tenths equals 53 tenths. Focusing on the units of decimals, they examine equivalence, recognize that the place value chart is symmetric around 1, and compare decimal numbers. In comparing decimal numbers, students are required to consider the units involved. Students communicate their knowledge of decimals through discussion and then use their knowledge to apply their learning to add decimals, recognizing the need to convert to like units when necessary.

MP.8 *Look for and express regularity in repeated reasoning.* As they progress through this module, students have multiple opportunities to explore the relationships between and among units of ones, tenths, and hundredths. Relationships between adjacent place values, for example, are the same on the right side of the decimal point as they are on the left side, and students investigate this fact working with tenths and hundredths. Further, adding tenths and hundredths requires finding like units just as it does with whole numbers, such as when adding centimeters and meters. Students come to understand equivalence, conversions, comparisons, and addition involving decimal fractions.

MODULE TOPIC SUMMARIES

Topic A: Exploration of Tenths

In Topic A, students use their understanding of fractions to explore tenths. In Lesson 1, students use metric measurement and see tenths in relationship to one whole in the context of 1 kilogram, 1 meter, and 1 centimeter. Using bags of rice, each weighing $\frac{1}{10}$ kilogram, students see that the weight of 10 bags is equal to 1 kilogram. Through further exploration and observation of a digital scale, students learn that $\frac{1}{10}$ kilogram can also be expressed as 0.1 kilogram, that $\frac{2}{10}$ kilogram can be expressed as 0.2 kilogram, and that all expressions of tenths in fraction form (up to one whole) can be expressed in decimal form as well. Students then use their knowledge of pairs to 10 to determine how many more tenths are needed to bring a given number of tenths up to one whole. To bring together this metric measurement experience by way of a more abstract representation, tenths are represented on the number line and with tape diagrams, as pictured below. Students express tenths as decimal fractions, are introduced to decimal notation, and write statements of equivalence in unit, fraction, and decimal forms, for example, 3 tenths = $\frac{3}{10}$ = 0.3 (4.NF.6). Finally, meters and centimeters are decomposed into 10 equal parts in a manner similar to that in which 1 kilogram was decomposed.

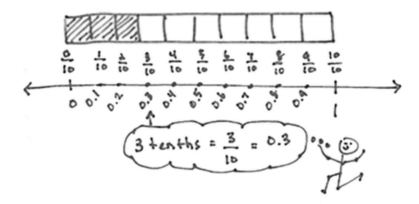

In Lesson 2, students return to the use of metric measurement, this time to investigate decimal fractions greater than 1. They draw lines using a centimeter ruler that measure, for example, $2\frac{4}{10}$ or $6\frac{8}{10}$ centimeters, and recognize that those numbers can also be expressed in unit form as 24 tenths centimeters or 68 tenths centimeters. Students represent decimal numbers using the area model and see that numbers containing ones and fractions (i.e., mixed numbers) can also be expressed using decimal notation, for example, 2.4 or 6.8, and write more sophisticated statements of equivalence, for example, $2\frac{4}{10} = 2 + \frac{4}{10}$ and 2.4 = 2 + 0.4 (4.NF.6).

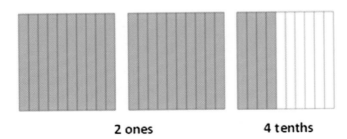

2 ones   4 tenths

In Lesson 3, students work with place value disks and the number line to represent and identify decimal numbers with tenths as a unit. To explore the place value of each unit in a decimal number with tenths, students use number disks to rename groups of 10 tenths as ones. Next, students learn to record the value of each digit of a mixed number in fraction expanded form and then using decimal expanded form, for example, 2 ones 4 tenths = $2\frac{4}{10} = (2 \times 1) + (4 \times \frac{1}{10})$ just as 2.4 = (2 × 1) + (4 × 0.1). Finally, students model the value of decimal fractions within a mixed number by plotting decimal numbers on the number line.

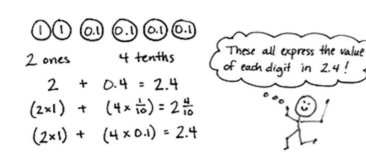

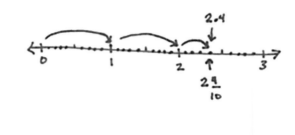

Focus Standard:	4.NF.6	Use decimal notation for fractions with denominators 10 or 100. For example, rewrite 0.62 as 62/100; describe a length as 0.62 meters; locate 0.62 on a number line diagram.
Instructional Days:	3	
Coherence		
Links from:	G3–M2	Place Value and Problem Solving with Units of Measure
	G3–M5	Fractions as Numbers on the Number Line
Links to:	G5–M1	Place Value and Decimal Fractions

Objective 1: Use metric measurement to model the decomposition of one whole into tenths.
(Lesson 1)

Objective 2: Use metric measurement and area models to represent tenths as fractions greater than 1 and decimal numbers.
(Lesson 2)

Objective 3: Represent mixed numbers with units of tens, ones, and tenths with number disks, on the number line, and in expanded form.
(Lesson 3)

Topic B: Tenths and Hundredths

In Topic B, students decompose tenths into 10 equal parts to create hundredths.

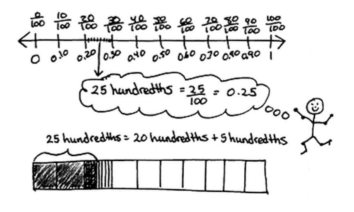

In Lesson 4, they once again use metric measurement as a basis for exploration. Using a meter stick, they locate 1 tenth meter and then locate 1 hundredth meter. They identify 1 centimeter as $\frac{1}{100}$ meter and count $\frac{1}{100}, \frac{2}{100}, \frac{3}{100}$, up to $\frac{10}{100}$, and at the concrete level, they realize the equivalence of $\frac{10}{100}$ meter and $\frac{1}{10}$ meter. They represent $\frac{1}{100}$ meter as 0.01 meter, counting up to $\frac{25}{100}$ or 0.25, in both fraction and decimal form. They then model the meter with a tape diagram and partition it into tenths, as they did in Lesson 1. They locate 25 centimeters and see that it is equal to 25 hundredths by counting up: $\frac{10}{100}, \frac{20}{100}, \frac{21}{100}, \frac{22}{100}, \frac{23}{100}, \frac{24}{100}, \frac{25}{100}$. They represent this as $\frac{20}{100} + \frac{5}{100} = \frac{25}{100}$ and, using decimal notation, write 0.25. A number bond shows the decomposition of 0.25 into the fractional parts of $\frac{2}{10}$ and $\frac{5}{100}$.

In Lesson 5, students relate hundredths to the area model (pictured below), a tape diagram, and number disks. They see and represent the equivalence of tenths and hundredths pictorially and numerically.

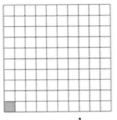 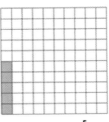 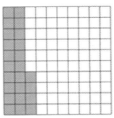

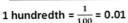

1 hundredth = $\frac{1}{100}$ = 0.01   5 hundredths = $\frac{5}{100}$ = 0.05   25 hundredths = $\frac{25}{100}$ = 0.25

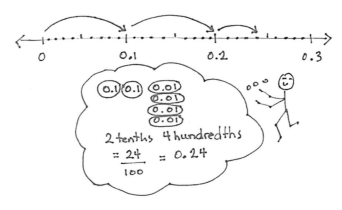

Students count up from $\frac{1}{100}$ with number disks just as they did with centimeters in Lesson 4. This time, the 10 hundredths are traded for 1 tenth and the equivalence is expressed as $\frac{1}{10} = \frac{10}{100} = 0.1 = 0.10$ (4.NF.5, 4.NF.6). The equivalence of tenths and hundredths is also realized through multiplication and division—for example, $\frac{1}{10} = \frac{1 \times 10}{10 \times 10} = \frac{10}{100}$ and $\frac{10}{100} = \frac{10 \div 10}{100 \div 10} = \frac{1}{10}$, establishing 1 tenth is 10 times as much as 1 hundredth. They see too that 16 hundredths is 1 tenth and 6 hundredths and that 25 hundredths is 2 tenths and 5 hundredths.

In Lesson 6, students draw representations of three-digit decimal numbers (with ones, tenths, and hundredths) with the area model.

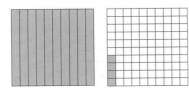

1 one 4 hundredths = $1\frac{4}{100}$ = 1.04   3 ones 24 hundredths = $3\frac{24}{100}$ = 3.24

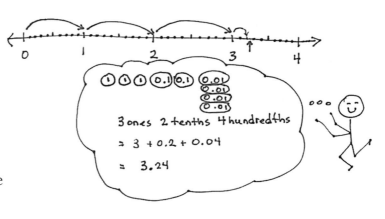

Students also further extend their use of the number line to show the ones, tenths, and hundredths as lengths. Lesson 6 concludes with students coming to understand that tenths and hundredths each hold a special place within a decimal number, establishing that 3.80 and 3.08 are different and distinguishable values.

In Lesson 7, decimal numbers to hundredths are modeled with disks and written on the place value chart where each digit's value is analyzed. The value of the total number is represented in both fraction and decimal expanded form as pictured below.

Hundreds	Tens	Ones	•	Tenths	Hundredths
3	7	8		7	3

3 hundreds   7 tens   8 ones   7 tenths . 3 hundredths

$$\left(3 \times 100\right) + \left(7 \times 10\right) + \left(8 \times 1\right) + \left(7 \times \frac{1}{10}\right) + \left(3 \times \frac{1}{100}\right) = 378.73$$

$$\left(3 \times 100\right) + \left(7 \times 10\right) + \left(8 \times 1\right) + \left(7 \times 0.1\right) + \left(3 \times 0.01\right) = 378.73$$

In the debriefing, students discuss the symmetry of the place value chart around 1, seeing the ones place as the "mirror" for tens and tenths and hundreds and hundredths, thereby avoiding the misconception of the "oneths" place or the decimal point itself as the point of symmetry. This understanding helps students recognize that even as we move to the decimal side of the place value chart, a column continues to represent a unit 10 times as large as that of the column to its right.

In Lesson 8, students use what they know about fractions to represent decimal numbers in terms of different units. For example, 3.2 might be modeled as 3 ones 2 tenths, 32 tenths, or 320 hundredths. Students show these renamings in unit form, fraction form, and decimal form.

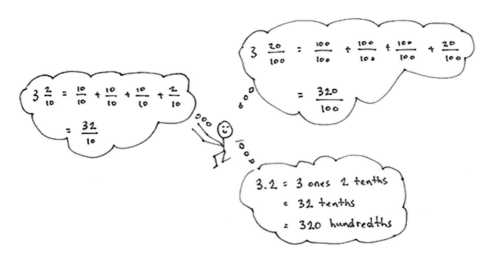

Focus Standard:	4.NF.5	Express a fraction with denominator 10 as an equivalent fraction with denominator 100, and use this technique to add two fractions with respective denominators 10 and 100. *For example, express 3/10 as 30/100, and add 3/10 + 4/100 = 34/100.* (Students who can generate equivalent fractions can develop strategies for adding fractions with unlike denominators in general. But addition and subtraction with unlike denominators in general is not a requirement at this grade.)
	4.NF.6	Use decimal notation for fractions with denominators 10 or 100. *For example, rewrite 0.62 as 62/100; describe a length as 0.62 meters; locate 0.62 on a number line diagram.*
Instructional Days:	5	
Coherence		
Links from:	G3–M2	Place Value and Problem Solving with Units of Measure
	G3–M5	Fractions as Numbers on the Number Line
Links to:	G5–M1	Place Value and Decimal Fractions

Objective 1: Use meters to model the decomposition of one whole into hundredths. Represent and count hundredths.
(Lesson 4)

Objective 2: Model the equivalence of tenths and hundredths using the area model and number disks.
(Lesson 5)

Objective 3: Use the area model and number line to represent mixed numbers with units of ones, tenths, and hundredths in fraction and decimal forms.
(Lesson 6)

Objective 4: Model mixed numbers with units of hundreds, tens, ones, tenths, and hundredths in expanded form and on the place value chart.
(Lesson 7)

Objective 5: Use understanding of fraction equivalence to investigate decimal numbers on the place value chart expressed in different units.
(Lesson 8)

Topic C: Decimal Comparison

The focus of Topic C is comparison of decimal numbers.

In Lesson 9, students compare pairs of decimal numbers representing lengths, masses, or volumes by recording them on the place value chart and reasoning about which measurement is longer than (shorter than, heavier than, lighter than, more than, or less than) the other. Comparing decimals in the context of measurement supports their justifications of their conclusions and begins their work with comparison at a more concrete level.

Students move on to more abstract representations in Lesson 10, using area models and the number line to justify their comparison of decimal numbers (4.NF.7). They record their observations with the <, >, and = symbols. In both Lessons 9 and 10, the intensive work at the concrete and pictorial levels eradicates the common misconception that occurs, for example, in the comparison of 7 tenths and 27 hundredths, where students believe that 0.7 is less than 0.27 simply because it resembles the comparison of 7 ones and 27 ones. This reinforces the idea that in any comparison, one must consider the *size of the units.*

Finally, in Lesson 11, students use their understanding of different ways of expressing equivalent values in order to arrange a set of decimal fractions in unit, fraction, and decimal form from greatest to least or least to greatest.

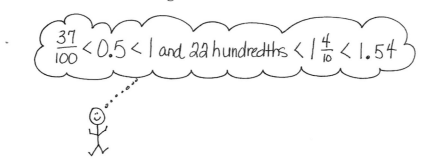

Focus Standard:	4.NF.7	Compare two decimals to hundredths by reasoning about their size. Recognize that comparisons are valid only when the two decimals refer to the same whole. Record the results of comparisons with the symbols >, =, or <, and justify the conclusions, e.g., by using a visual model.
Instructional Days:	3	
Coherence		
Links from:	G3–M5	Fractions as Numbers on the Number Line
Links to:	G5–M1	Place Value and Decimal Fractions

Objective 1: Use the place value chart and metric measurement to compare decimals and answer comparison questions.
(Lesson 9)

Objective 2: Use area models and the number line to compare decimal numbers, and record comparisons using <, >, and =.
(Lesson 10)

Objective 3: Compare and order mixed numbers in various forms.
(Lesson 11)

Topic D: Addition with Tenths and Hundredths

Topic D brings together students' work with addition of fractions and their work with decimals.

In Lesson 12, students begin at the pictorial level, decomposing tenths using the area model and place value chart in order to add tenths and hundredths. They progress to using multiplication to generate equivalent fractions and express the sum in fraction form as a decimal, as pictured below.

$$\frac{3}{10} = \frac{3 \times 10}{10 \times 10} = \frac{30}{100}$$

$$\frac{3}{10} + \frac{4}{100} = \frac{30}{100} + \frac{4}{100} = \frac{34}{100} = 0.34$$

$$\frac{34}{100} = 34 \text{ hundredths} = 0.34$$

They next apply what they know about fraction addition to use multiple strategies to solve sums of tenths and hundredths with totals greater than 1 (see the two examples pictured below), again expressing the solution in decimal form.

$$\frac{9}{10} + \frac{64}{100} = \frac{90}{100} + \frac{64}{100} = 1\frac{54}{100} = 1.54 \qquad \frac{9}{10} + \frac{64}{100} = \frac{90}{100} + \frac{64}{100} = \frac{154}{100} = 1\frac{54}{100} = 1.54$$

In Lesson 13, students add ones, tenths, and hundredths in decimal form by converting the addends to mixed numbers in fraction form, creating like denominators, and applying their understanding of the addition of mixed numbers. Once the decimal fractions are added (4.NF.5), the number sentence is written in decimal notation (4.NF.6).

$$5.6 + 4.53 = 5\frac{6}{10} + 4\frac{53}{100}$$
$$= 5\frac{60}{100} + 4\frac{53}{100}$$
$$= 9\frac{60}{100} + \frac{53}{100}$$
$$= 9\frac{113}{100}$$
$$= 10\frac{13}{100}$$
$$5.6 + 4.53 = 10.13$$

$$5.6 + 4.53 = 5\frac{6}{10} + 4\frac{53}{100}$$
$$= 9 + 1 + \frac{13}{100}$$
$$= 10\frac{13}{100}$$
$$5.6 + 4.53 = 10.13$$

$$5.6 + 4.53 = 5\frac{60}{100} + 4\frac{53}{100}$$
$$= 10\frac{13}{100}$$
$$5.6 + 4.53 = 10.13$$

The addition of decimals is a Grade 5 standard. By converting addends in decimal form to fraction form, Grade 4 students strengthen their understanding of both fraction and decimal equivalence and fraction addition.

In Lesson 14, students apply this work to solve measurement word problems involving addition. They convert decimals to fraction form, solve the problem, and write their statement using the decimal form of the solution, as pictured below:

An apple orchard sold 140.5 kilograms of apples in the morning. The orchard sold 15.85 kilograms more apples in the afternoon than in the morning. How many total kilograms of apples were sold that day?

M [140.5 kg]
A [140.5 kg | 15.85kg] } ?

Solution A
$$140\frac{5}{10} + 15\frac{85}{100} = 155\frac{50}{100} + \frac{85}{100}$$
$$= 155\frac{135}{100}$$
$$= 156\frac{35}{100}$$
$$140\frac{5}{10} + 156\frac{35}{100} = 296\frac{50}{100} + \frac{35}{100}$$
$$= 296\frac{85}{100}$$

The apple orchard sold 296.85 kilograms of apples.

Solution B
$$\left(2 \times 140\frac{5}{10}\right) + 15.85 = 280\frac{10}{10} + 15\frac{85}{100}$$
$$= 296\frac{85}{100}$$

The apple orchard sold 296.85 kilograms that day.

Focus Standard:	4.NF.5	Express a fraction with denominator 10 as an equivalent fraction with denominator 100, and use this technique to add two fractions with respective denominators 10 and 100. *For example, express 3/10 as 30/100, and add 3/10 + 4/100 = 34/100.* (Students who can generate equivalent fractions can develop strategies for adding fractions with unlike denominators in general. But addition and subtraction with unlike denominators in general is not a requirement at this grade.)
	4.NF.6	Use decimal notation for fractions with denominators 10 or 100. *For example, rewrite 0.62 as 62/100; describe a length as 0.62 meters; locate 0.62 on a number line diagram.*
Instructional Days:	3	
Coherence		
Links from:	G3–M5	Fractions as Numbers on the Number Line
Links to:	G5–M2	Multi-Digit Whole-Number and Decimal Fraction Operations

Objective 1: Apply understanding of fraction equivalence to add tenths and hundredths. (Lesson 12)

Objective 2: Add decimal numbers by converting to fraction form. (Lesson 13)

Objective 3: Solve word problems involving the addition of measurements in decimal form. (Lesson 14)

Topic E: Money Amounts as Decimal Numbers

In Topic E, students work with money amounts as decimal numbers, applying what they have come to understand about decimals.

Students recognize 1 penny as $\frac{1}{100}$ dollar, 1 dime as $\frac{1}{10}$ dollar, and 1 quarter as $\frac{25}{100}$ dollar in Lesson 15. They apply their understanding of tenths and hundredths to express money amounts in both fraction and decimal forms. Students use this understanding to decompose varying configurations and forms of dollars, quarters, dimes, and pennies, and express each as a decimal fraction and decimal number. They then expand this skill to include money amounts greater than a dollar in decimal form.

In Lesson 16, students continue their work with money and apply their understanding that only like units can be added. They solve word problems involving money using all four operations (4.MD.2). Addition and subtraction word problems are computed using dollars and cents in unit form. Multiplication and division word problems are computed using cents in unit form. All answers are converted from unit form into decimal form, using the dollar symbol as the unit.

Jack has 2 quarters and 7 dimes. Jim has 1 dollar, 3 quarters, and 6 pennies. How much money do they have together? Write your answer as a decimal.

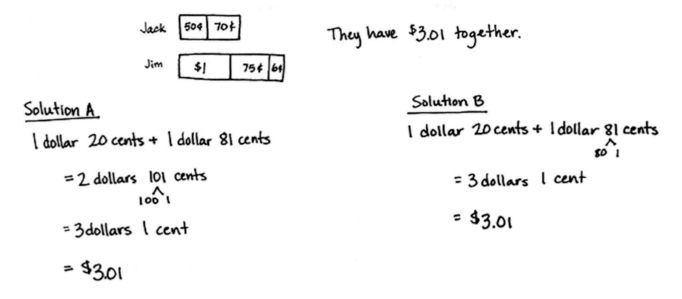

Solution A

1 dollar 20 cents + 1 dollar 81 cents

= 2 dollars 101 cents

= 3 dollars 1 cent

= $3.01

Solution B

1 dollar 20 cents + 1 dollar 81 cents

= 3 dollars 1 cent

= $3.01

Focus Standard:	4.MD.2	Use the four operations to solve word problems involving distances, intervals of time, liquid volumes, masses of objects, and money, including problems involving simple fractions or decimals, and problems that require expressing measurements given in a larger unit in terms of a smaller unit. Represent measurement quantities using diagrams such as number line diagrams that feature a measurement scale.
Instructional Days:	2	
Coherence		
Links from:	G2–M7	Problem Solving with Length, Money, and Data
	G3–M5	Fractions as Numbers on the Number Line
Links to:	G5–M2	Multi-Digit Whole-Number and Decimal Fraction Operations

Objective 1: Express money amounts given in various forms as decimal numbers.
(Lesson 15)

Objective 2: Solve word problems involving money.
(Lesson 16)

MODULE 7: EXPLORING MEASUREMENT WITH MULTIPLICATION

OVERVIEW

In this 20-day module, students build their competencies in measurement as they relate multiplication to the conversion of measurement units. Throughout the module, students explore multiple strategies for solving measurement problems involving unit conversion.

In Topic A, students build on the work they did in Module 2 with measurement conversions. Working heavily in customary units, students use two-column conversion tables (4.MD.1) to practice conversion rates. For example, following a discovery activity where students learn that 16 ounces make 1 pound, students generate a two-column conversion table listing the number of ounces in 1 to 10 pounds. Tables for other measurement units are then generated in a similar fashion. Students then reason about why they do not need to complete the tables beyond 10 of the larger units. They use their multiplication skills from Module 3 to complete the tables and are able to see and explain connections such as $(13 \times 16) = (10 \times 16) + (3 \times 16)$. One student could reason, for example, "Since the table shows that there are 160 ounces in 10 pounds and 48 ounces in 3 pounds, I can add them together to tell that there are 208 ounces in 13 pounds." Another student might reason, "Since there are 16 ounces in each pound, I can use the rule of the table and multiply 13 pounds by 16 to find that there are 208 ounces in 13 pounds."

As the topic progresses, students solve multiplicative comparison word problems. They are then challenged to create and solve their own word problems and critique the reasoning of their peers (4.OA.1, 4.OA.2). They share their solution strategies and original problems within small groups, as well as share and critique the problem-solving strategies that their peers use. Through the use of guided questions, students discuss not only how the problems were solved but also the advantages and disadvantages of using each strategy. They further discuss what makes one strategy more efficient than another. By the end of Topic A, students have started to internalize the conversion rates through fluency exercises and continued practice.

Topic B builds on the conversion work from Topic A to add and subtract mixed units of capacity, length, weight, and time. Working with metric and customary units, students add like units, making comparisons to adding like fractional units, further establishing the importance of deeply understanding the unit. Just as 2 fourths + 3 fourths = 5 fourths, so does 2 quarts + 3 quarts = 5 quarts. Five fourths can be decomposed into 1 one 1 fourth, and therefore 5 quarts can be decomposed into 1 gallon 1 quart. Students realize the same situation occurs in subtraction. Just as $1 - \frac{3}{4}$ must be renamed to $\frac{4}{4} - \frac{1}{4}$ so that the units are alike, students must also rename units of measurements to make like units (1 quart − 3 cups = 4 cups − 3 cups). Students go on to add and subtract mixed units of measurements, finding multiple solution strategies, similar to the mixed-number work in fractions. With focus on measurement units of capacity, length, weight, and time, students apply this work to solve multistep word problems.

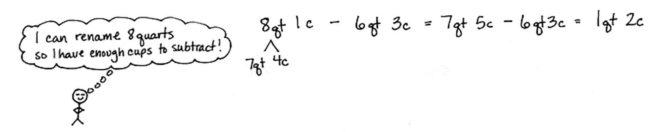

In Topic C, students reason how to convert larger units of measurements with fractional parts into smaller units by using hands-on measurements. For example, students convert $3\frac{1}{4}$ feet to inches by first finding the number of inches in $\frac{1}{4}$ foot. They partition a length of 1 foot into 4 equal parts and find $\frac{1}{4}$ foot equals 3 inches. They then convert 3 feet to 36 inches and add 3 inches to find that $3\frac{1}{4}$ feet = 39 inches. This work is directly analogous to earlier work with fraction equivalence using the tape diagram, area model, and number line in Topics A, B, and D of Module 5. Students partitioned a whole into 4 equal parts, decomposed 1 part into 3 smaller units, and found 1 fourth to be equal to 3 twelfths. The foot ruler is partitioned with precisely the same reasoning. Students close the topic by using measurements to solve multistep word problems that require converting larger units into smaller units.

The End-of-Module Assessment follows Topic C.

Students review their year in Topic D through the practice of skills they have learned throughout the modules and through the creation of a take-home summer folder. The cover of the folder is transformed into the student's own miniature personal whiteboard, and a collection of activities from the lessons within this topic is placed inside the folder for practice over the summer. Students practice the major skills and concepts they learned throughout the year in these final four lessons, including measuring angles and drawing lines, multiplication and division, and addition and subtraction through guided group work, fluency activities, and vocabulary games.

FOCUS GRADE-LEVEL STANDARDS

Use the four operations with whole numbers to solve problems.

4.OA.1 Interpret a multiplication equation as a comparison, e.g., interpret $35 = 5 \times 7$ as a statement that 35 is 5 times as many as 7 and 7 times as many as 5. Represent verbal statements of multiplicative comparisons as multiplication equations.

4.OA.2 Multiply or divide to solve word problems involving multiplicative comparison, e.g., by using drawings and equations with a symbol for the unknown number to represent the problem, distinguishing multiplicative comparison from additive comparison. (See Standards Glossary, Table 2.)

4.OA.3 Solve multistep word problems posed with whole numbers and having whole-number answers using the four operations, including problems in which remainders must be interpreted. Represent these problems using equations with a letter standing for the unknown quantity. Assess the reasonableness of answers using mental computation and estimation strategies including rounding.

Solve problems involving measurement and conversion of measurements from a larger unit to a smaller unit.[22]

4.MD.1 Know relative sizes of measurement units within one system of units including km, m, cm; kg, g; lb, oz.; l, ml; hr, min, sec. Within a single system of measurement, express measurements in a larger unit in terms of a smaller unit. Record measurement equivalents in a two-column table. *For example, know that 1 ft is 12 times as long as 1 in. Express length of a 4 ft snake as 48 in. Generate a conversion table for feet and inches listing the number pairs (1, 12), (2, 24), (3, 36), ...*

4.MD.2 Use the four operations to solve word problems involving distances, intervals of time, liquid volumes, masses of objects, and money, including problems involving simple fractions or decimals, and problems that require expressing measurements given in a larger unit in terms of a smaller unit. Represent measurement quantities using diagrams such as number line diagrams that feature a measurement scale.

FOUNDATIONAL STANDARDS

3.OA.1 Interpret products of whole numbers, e.g., interpret 5 × 7 as the total number of objects in 5 groups of 7 objects each. *For example, describe a context in which a total number of objects can be expressed as 5 × 7.*

3.OA.3 Use multiplication and division within 100 to solve word problems in situations involving equal groups, arrays, and measurement quantities, e.g., by using drawings and equations with a symbol for the unknown number to represent the problem.

3.OA.5 Apply properties of operations as strategies to multiply and divide. Examples: If 6 × 4 = 24 is known, then 4 × 6 = 24 is also known. (Commutative property of multiplication.) 3 × 5 × 2 can be found by 3 × 5 = 15, then 15 × 2 = 30, or by 5 × 2 = 10, then 3 × 10 = 30. (Associative property of multiplication.) Knowing that 8 × 5 = 40 and 8 × 2 = 16, one can find 8 × 7 as 8 × (5 + 2) = (8 × 5) + (8 × 2) = 40 + 16 = 56. (Distributive property.)

3.OA.7 Fluently multiply and divide within 100, using strategies such as the relationship between multiplication and division (e.g., knowing that 8 × 5 = 40, one knows 40 ÷ 5 = 8) or properties of operations. By the end of Grade 3, know from memory all products of two one-digit numbers.

3.NBT.3 Multiply one-digit whole numbers by multiples of 10 in the range 10–90 (e.g., 9 × 80, 5 × 60) using strategies based on place value and properties of operations.

3.NF.3 Explain equivalence of fractions in special cases, and compare fractions by reasoning about their size.

   a. Understand two fractions as equivalent (equal) if they are the same size, or the same point on a number line.

   b. Recognize and generate simple equivalent fractions, (e.g., 1/2 = 2/4, 4/6 = 2/3). Explain why the fractions are equivalent, e.g., by using a visual fraction model.

   c. Express whole numbers as fractions, and recognize fractions that are equivalent to whole numbers. *Examples: Express 3 in the form 3 = 3/1; recognize that 6/1 = 6; locate 4/4 and at the same point of a number line diagram.*

3.MD.2 Measure and estimate liquid volumes and masses of objects using standard units of grams (g), kilograms (kg), and liters (l). Add, subtract, multiply, or divide to solve one-step word problems involving masses or volumes that are given in the same units, e.g., by using drawings (such as a beaker with a measurement scale) to represent the problem.

FOCUS STANDARDS FOR MATHEMATICAL PRACTICE

MP.2 *Reason abstractly and quantitatively.* Students create conversion charts for related measurement units and use the information in the charts to solve complex real-world measurement problems. They also draw number lines and tape diagrams to represent word problems.

MP.3 *Construct viable arguments and critique the reasoning of others.* Students work in groups to select appropriate strategies to solve problems. They present these strategies to the class and discuss the advantages and disadvantages of each strategy in different situations before deciding which ones are most efficient. Students also solve problems that their classmates create and explain to the problem's creator how they solved it to see if it is the method the student had in mind when writing the problem.

MP.7 *Look for and make use of structure.* Students look for and make use of connections between measurement units and word problems to help them understand and solve related word problems. They choose the appropriate unit of measure when given the choice and see that the structure of the situations in the word problems dictates which units to measure with.

MP.8 *Look for an express regularity in repeated reasoning.* The creation and use of the measurement conversion tables is a focal point of this module. Students identify and use the patterns found in each table they create. Using the tables to solve various word problems gives students ample opportunities to apply the same strategy to different situations.

MODULE TOPIC SUMMARIES

Topic A: *Measurement Conversion Tables*

In Topic A, students build on the work they did in Module 2 with measurement conversions. In this module, however, they have the opportunity to work more extensively with tools while creating two-column tables that are then used to solve a variety of measurement problems.

In Lesson 1, students use two-column conversion tables (4.MD.1) to practice conversion rates. They convert from pounds to ounces, yards to feet, and feet to inches. Students begin Lesson 1 by using a balance scale, a 1-pound weight, and individual 1-ounce weights (like fishing sinkers). With the 1-pound weight on one side of the balance, they add 1 ounce at a time to the other side until it balances and students discover that there are 16 ounces in 1 pound. Students then generate a two-column conversion table listing the number of ounces in 2, 3, and up to 10 pounds. They use their multiplication skills from Module 3 to complete the table and reason about why they do not need to complete the table beyond 10 pounds.

Students use various strategies to determine how many smaller units would make up a larger unit not listed in the table. A student could reason, for example, that since the table shows that there are 160 ounces in 10 pounds and 48 ounces in 3 pounds, he can add them together to see that there are 208 ounces in 13 pounds. Another student might reason that since there are 16 ounces in each pound, she can use the rule of the table and multiply 13 pounds by 16 to find that there are 208 ounces in 13 pounds.

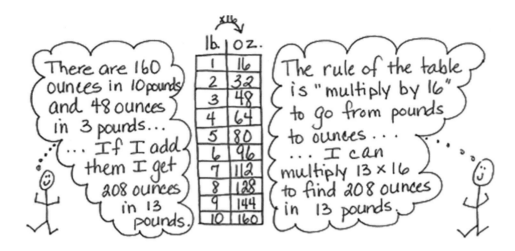

Similar to Lesson 1, in Lesson 2 students complete conversion tables, this time focusing on capacity and converting gallons to quarts, quarts to pints, and pints to cups. Adding to the complexity of the conversions, students explore two-step conversions, solving, for example, to find how many cups are equal to 1 gallon.

In Lesson 3, students investigate the relationships between units of time. They discover a similarity in converting from hours to minutes and minutes to seconds. Students are able to reason that for both sets of conversion, the values in the two tables will be the same because there are 60 seconds in a minute and 60 minutes in an hour. Students also convert from days to hours. The clock and the number line are used as tools to develop the conversion tables.

In Lesson 4, students use the conversions that they discovered in Lessons 1 to 3 in order to solve multiplicative comparison word problems. Working in small groups, they have the opportunity to share and discuss their solution strategies (4.OA.1, 4.OA.2).

Students are given tape diagrams and then challenged to create word problems to match the information displayed within the tape diagrams in Lesson 5. The given information requires students to use the customary or metric units practiced during this topic. After first solving the problems that they create, students share and critique the problem-solving strategies their peers used. In the debriefing, through the use of guided questions, students discuss not only how the problems were solved but also the advantages and disadvantages of using each strategy. They further discuss what makes one strategy more efficient than another.

Focus Standard:	4.OA.1	Interpret a multiplication equation as a comparison, e.g., interpret 35 = 5 × 7 as a statement that 35 is 5 times as many as 7 and 7 times as many as 5. Represent verbal statements of multiplicative comparisons as multiplication equations.
	4.OA.2	Multiply or divide to solve word problems involving multiplicative comparison, e.g., by using drawings and equations with a symbol for the unknown number to represent the problem, distinguishing multiplicative comparison from additive comparison. (See Standards Glossary, Table 2.)
	4.MD.1	Know relative sizes of measurement units within one system of units including km, m, cm; kg, g; lb, oz.; l, ml; hr, min, sec. Within a single system of measurement, express measurements in a larger unit in terms of a smaller unit. Record measurement equivalents in a two-column table. *For example, know that 1 ft is 12 times as long as 1 in. Express length of a 4 ft snake as 48 in. Generate a conversion table for feet and inches listing the number pairs (1, 12), (2, 24), (3, 36), ...*

Instructional Days: 5
Coherence
   Links from: G3–M1   Properties of Multiplication and Division and Solving Problems with Units of 2–5 and 10
                     G3–M2   Place Value and Problem Solving with Units of Measure
   Links to: G5–M1   Place Value and Decimal Fractions
                     G5–M2   Multi-Digit Whole-Number and Decimal Fraction Operations

Objective 1: Create conversion tables for length, weight, and capacity units using measurement tools, and use the tables to solve problems.
(Lessons 1 and 2)

Objective 2: Create conversion tables for units of time, and use the tables to solve problems.
(Lesson 3)

Objective 3: Solve multiplicative comparison word problems using measurement conversion tables.
(Lesson 4)

Objective 4: Share and critique peer strategies.
(Lesson 5)

Topic B: Problem Solving with Measurement

Each lesson in Topic B builds on the conversion work from Topic A to add and subtract mixed units of capacity, length, weight, and time. Unlike the mixed unit work in Module 2, now students work with the two systems of measurement, customary and metric, as well as being posed with fractional amounts of measurement, for example, $2\frac{3}{4}$ feet or $4\frac{3}{8}$ pounds. As students add like units, they make comparisons to adding like fractional units, further establishing the importance of deeply understanding the unit. Just as 2 fourths + 3 fourths = 5 fourths, so does 2 quarts + 3 quarts = 5 quarts. Five fourths can be decomposed into 1 one 1 fourth, and therefore 5 quarts can be decomposed into 1 gallon 1 quart. Students realize the same in subtraction: just as $1 - \frac{3}{4}$ must be renamed to $\frac{4}{4} - \frac{1}{4}$ so that the units are alike, students must also rename units of measurements to make like units (1 quart – 3 cups = 4 cups – 1 cup). Students go on to add and subtract mixed units of measurements, finding multiple solution strategies, similar to the mixed-number work in fractions.

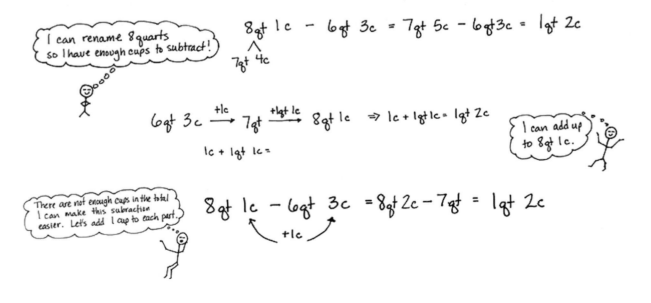

In Lessons 6 through 9, each lesson focuses on a specific type of measurement: capacity, length, weight, or time. Students go on to practice addition and subtraction of mixed units of measurements to solve multistep word problems in Lessons 10 and 11—for example:

Judy spent 1 hour and 15 minutes less than Sandy exercising last week. Sandy spent 50 minutes less than Mary who spent 3 hours at the gym. How long did Judy spend exercising?

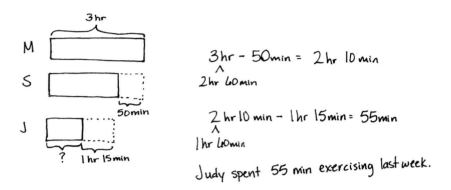

Focus Standard:	4.OA.2	Multiply or divide to solve word problems involving multiplicative comparison, e.g., by using drawings and equations with a symbol for the unknown number to represent the problem, distinguishing multiplicative comparison from additive comparison. (See Standards Glossary, Table 2.)
	4.OA.3	Solve multistep word problems posed with whole numbers and having whole-number answers using the four operations, including problems in which remainders must be interpreted. Represent these problems using equations with a letter standing for the unknown quantity. Assess the reasonableness of answers using mental computation and estimation strategies including rounding.
	4.MD.1	Know relative sizes of measurement units within one system of units including km, m, cm; kg, g; lb, oz.; l, ml; hr, min, sec. Within a single system of measurement, express measurements in a larger unit in terms of a smaller unit. Record measurement equivalents in a two-column table. *For example, know that 1 ft is 12 times as long as 1 in. Express length of a 4 ft snake as 48 in. Generate a conversion table for feet and inches listing the number pairs (1, 12), (2, 24), (3, 36), ...*
	4.MD.2	Use the four operations to solve word problems involving distances, intervals of time, liquid volumes, masses of objects, and money, including problems involving simple fractions or decimals, and problems that require expressing measurements given in a larger unit in terms of a smaller unit. Represent measurement quantities using diagrams such as number line diagrams that feature a measurement scale.
Instructional Days:	6	
Coherence		
Links from:	G3–M1	Properties of Multiplication and Division and Solving Problems with Units of 2–5 and 10
	G3–M2	Place Value and Problem Solving with Units of Measure
Links to:	G5–M1	Place Value and Decimal Fractions
	G5–M2	Multi-Digit Whole-Number and Decimal Fraction Operations

Objective 1: Solve problems involving mixed units of capacity.
(Lesson 6)

Objective 2: Solve problems involving mixed units of length.
(Lesson 7)

Objective 3: Solve problems involving mixed units of weight.
(Lesson 8)

Objective 4: Solve problems involving mixed units of time.
(Lesson 9)

Objective 5: Solve multistep measurement word problems.
(Lessons 10 and 11)

Topic C: Investigation of Measurements Expressed as Mixed Numbers

In Topic C, students convert larger mixed-measurement units to smaller units. Students partition a measurement scale in Lesson 11 to help them convert larger units of measurements with fractional parts into smaller units. For example, students will use a ruler to draw a number line 1 foot in length. Then students will partition the number line into 12 equal parts. Combining fractions and conversions, students will see that 1 twelfth foot is the same as 1 inch. Repeating the same activity, but making different partitions, students will find how many inches are in $\frac{1}{2}$ foot, $\frac{1}{3}$ foot, and $\frac{1}{4}$ foot.

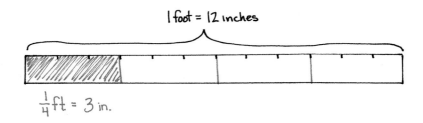

The same hands-on activity can be repeated for the capacity of part of a gallon represented as quarts. That hands-on experience leads students to make abstract connections in Lesson 12 for weight, identifying that $\frac{1}{16}$ pound is equal to 1 ounce, and with respect to time, finding that $\frac{1}{60}$ hour is equal to 1 minute, through the modeling of tape diagrams and number lines. Moving forward, students use their knowledge of conversion tables with this new understanding to convert mixed-number units into smaller units, such as $3\frac{1}{4}$ foot equals 39 inches, by applying mixed-number units to solve multistep problems in Lesson 13.

Erin has $1\frac{3}{4}$ pounds of apples. A recipe for apple tarts requires 4 ounces of apples. How many apple tarts can Erin make?

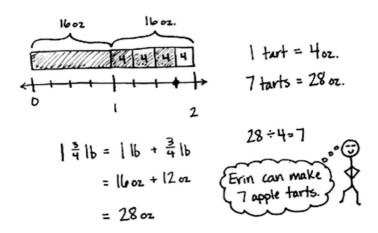

Focus Standard:	4.OA.3	Solve multistep word problems posed with whole numbers and having whole-number answers using the four operations, including problems in which remainders must be interpreted. Represent these problems using equations with a letter standing for the unknown quantity. Assess the reasonableness of answers using mental computation and estimation strategies including rounding.
	4.MD.1	Know relative sizes of measurement units within one system of units including km, m, cm; kg, g; lb, oz.; l, ml; hr, min, sec. Within a single system of measurement, express measurements in a larger unit in terms of a smaller unit. Record measurement equivalents in a two-column table. *For example, know that 1 ft is 12 times as long as 1 in. Express length of a 4 ft snake as 48 in. Generate a conversion table for feet and inches listing the number pairs (1, 12), (2, 24), (3, 36), …*
	4.MD.2	Use the four operations to solve word problems involving distances, intervals of time, liquid volumes, masses of objects, and money, including problems involving simple fractions or decimals, and problems that require expressing measurements given in a larger unit in terms of a smaller unit. Represent measurement quantities using diagrams such as number line diagrams that feature a measurement scale.
Instructional Days:	3	
Coherence		
Links from:	G3–M1	Properties of Multiplication and Division and Solving Problems with Units of 2–5 and 10
	G3–M2	Place Value and Problem Solving with Units of Measure
Links to:	G5–M1	Place Value and Decimal Fractions
	G5–M2	Multi-Digit Whole-Number and Decimal Fraction Operations

Objective 1: Use measurement tools to convert mixed-number measurements to smaller units.
(Lessons 12 and 13)

Objective 2: Solve multistep word problems involving converting mixed-number measurements to a single unit.
(Lesson 14)

Topic D: Year in Review

In Topic D, students review math concepts they learned throughout the year and create a folder with math activities for the summer.

In Lesson 15, students review their work with the area formula as well as their multiplication skills by solving for the area of composite figures. Initially introduced in Grade 3, these problems now require a deeper understanding of measurement and the area formula. Lesson 16, a continuation of Lesson 15, asks students to draw composite figures and solve for a determined area. To review the major fluency work completed in Grade 4, students work in small groups in Lesson 17, taking turns being the teacher and delivering fluency drills to their peers. Finally, Lesson 18 reviews major vocabulary terms taught throughout Grade 4 as students play various games to further internalize these terms.

In Lesson 15, students create a take-home version of a personal whiteboard that they can use during the lessons and at home during the summer. Each page of the homework of these lessons includes a top half and a bottom half that have identical problems. The top half is completed for homework, ultimately becoming an answer key for the bottom half. The bottom half is placed into the student mini-whiteboards for them to complete over the summer. Having already completed the top half, students can check their work by referring back to the top half answer key. Other games, templates, and activities used in the final lessons are also added to the folder so that on the final day of school, students go home with a folder full of activities to practice over the summer in order to keep their Grade 4 math skills sharp.

Objective 1: Create and determine the area of composite figures.
(Lessons 15 and 16)

Objective 2: Practice and solidify Grade 4 fluency.
(Lesson 17)

Objective 3: Practice and solidify Grade 4 vocabulary.
(Lesson 18)

CHAPTER 7

Mathematical Models

A *Story of Units* is a curriculum written by teachers for teachers to help every student build mastery of the new college- and career-ready standards. The theme of the story—creating, manipulating, and relating units—glues seemingly separate ideas into a coherent whole throughout each grade and over the years.

As noted in chapter 2, coherence is supported in A *Story of Units* through the use concrete and pictorial models. Students build increasing dexterity with these models through persistent use within and across levels of curriculum. The repeated appearance of familiar models helps to build vertical links between the topics of one grade level and the next. In addition, the depth of awareness that students have with the models not only ensures that they naturally become a part of the students' schema but also facilitates a more rapid and multifaceted understanding of new concepts as they are introduced.

This information is designed to support teachers as they engage students in meaningful mathematical learning experiences aligned to the standards. This support is provided through the following information:

- The grade levels for which the model is most appropriate
- A description and example of the model
- A collection of instructional strategies for using the model presented in order of the natural progression of the concepts

The following categories indicate the primary application area for each model. Of course, models appear repeatedly across grades and topics. Therefore, instructional strategies include examples spanning several levels of the curriculum.

Numbers through 10	Place Value and Standard Algorithms	Fractions
• Number Towers	• Bundles	• Number Line
• Number Path	• Place Value Chart	• Area Models
• Number Bond	• Base-Ten Blocks	
	• Money	
	• Number Disks (with Place Value Chart)	
Addition and Subtraction	**Multiplication**	**Word Problems**
• Ten-Frame	• Array and Area Models	• Tape Diagram
	• Rekenrek	

ARRAY AND AREA MODELS

GRADE LEVEL 1–5

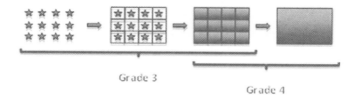

Grade 3

Grade 4

An array is an arrangement of a set of objects organized into equal groups in rows and columns. Arrays help make counting easy. Counting by equal groups is more efficient than counting objects one-by-one. The ten-frame is an array used in Kindergarten (see also the "Ten-Frame" section in this chapter). Students count objects in arrays in Kindergarten and PreKindergarten (PK.CC.4). The rectangular array is used to teach multiplication and leads to understanding area (3.OA.3).

Arrays reinforce the meaning of multiplication as repeated addition (e.g., $3 \times 4 = 4 + 4 + 4$) and the two meanings of division—that $12 \div 3$ can indicate how many will be in each group if I make 3 equal groups and that it can also indicate how many groups I can make if I put 3 in each group. Using arrays also reinforces the relationship between multiplication and division.

Instructional Strategies

- Use number towers to depict multiplication problems in the shape of an array (see also the "Number Towers" section in this chapter).

4 8 12 16

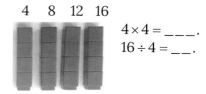

$4 \times 4 = \underline{\ \ \ }.$
$16 \div 4 = \underline{\ \ }.$

5 fours + 1 four = 6 fours
$20 + 4 = 24$
6×4 is 4 more than 5×4.

4 8 12 16 20 24

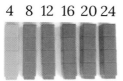

- Use the rectangular grid to model multiplication and division.

$4 \times 6 =$ ____.
$6 \times 4 =$ ____.

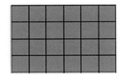

$4 \times$ ____ $= 24.$
____ $\times 6 = 24.$

$24 \div 4 =$ __.
$24 \div 6 =$ __.

- Multiply units with arrays.

  Multiplying hundreds:

4 hundreds $\times 3 = 12$ hundreds.
$400 \times 3 = 1,200.$

$400 \times 3 =$

BASE-TEN BLOCKS

GRADE LEVEL K–2

Base-ten blocks (also referred to as *Dienes blocks*) include thousands "cubes," hundreds "flats," tens "rods," and ones "cubes." Base-ten blocks are a proportional representation of units of ones, tens, hundreds, and thousands and are useful for developing place value understanding. This is a "pregrouped" model for base-ten that allows efficient modeling of larger quantities through the thousands. However, because this place value model requires students to more abstractly consider the 10-to-1 relationship of the various blocks, care must be taken to ensure that they attend to the "ten-ness" of the pieces that are now traded rather than bundled or unbundled.

Base-ten blocks are introduced after students have learned the value of hundreds, tens, and ones and have had repeated experiences with composing and decomposing groups of 10 ones or groups of 10 tens with bundles.

INSTRUCTIONAL STRATEGIES

Instructional strategies for base-ten blocks are similar to those of bundles and place value disks. (See the "Bundles," "Money," and "Number Disks" sections for other teaching ideas.)

- Represent quantities on the mat, and write in standard, expanded, and word form.

- Play "more" and "less" games. Begin with an amount on a mat. At a predetermined signal (e.g., teacher claps or rings a bell), students add (or subtract) a quantity (2, 5, 10, or other) to (or from) the blocks on the mat.

- Give students equivalent representation riddles to be solved with base-ten pieces—for example, "I have 29 ones and 2 hundreds. What number am I?"

- Model addition, subtraction, multiplication, and division.

- Use blocks and mats as a support for teaching students to record the standard algorithms for all four operations.

BUNDLES

GRADE LEVEL K–2

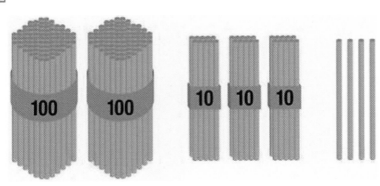

Bundles are discrete groupings of place value units (tens, hundreds, thousands), usually made by placing a rubber band or chenille stem around straws, popsicle sticks, or coffee stirrers. Linking cubes may also be used in this fashion. Ten straws (or cubes) are bundled (or linked) into 1 unit of ten, 10 tens are bundled into 1 unit of one hundred, and so on. These student-made groupings provide the necessary conceptual foundation for children to be successful with pregrouped, proportional, and nonproportional base-ten materials. (See also the "Base-Ten Blocks" and "Number Disks" sections in this chapter.)

Understanding tens and ones is supported in Kindergarten as students learn to compose and decompose tens and ones by bundling and unbundling the materials. Numbers 11 to 19 are soon seen as 1 ten (a bundled set of 10 ones) and some extra ones.

By Grade 2, students expand their skill with and understanding of units by bundling units of ones, tens, and hundreds up to one thousand with sticks. These larger units are discrete and can be counted: "1 hundred, 2 hundred, 3 hundred . . ." Bundles also help students extend their understanding of place value to 1,000 (2.NBT.1). Repeated bundling experiences help students to internalize the pattern that 10 of one unit make 1 of the next larger unit. Expanded form, increased understanding of skip counting (2.NBT.2), and fluency in counting larger numbers are all supported by the use of this model.

Bundles are also useful in developing conceptual understanding of renaming in addition and subtraction. The mat pictured here shows 2 tens and 3 ones. To solve 23 – 9, one bundle of ten is "unbundled" to get 1 ten and 13 ones in order to take away 9 ones.

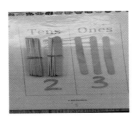

INSTRUCTIONAL STRATEGIES

- Represent various quantities with bundles and "singles."
- Count school days. Each day, a single straw or stick is added to the ones pocket and counted. Sticks are bundled when 10 days have passed and moved to the tens pocket. Have a "100th Day" celebration.
- Bundles may also be used to count down to a significant event (e.g., the last day of school), unbundling as necessary.
- Play Race to Zero with a partner. Students start with a quantity between 30 and 40 in bundles. Roll two dice to determine what can be taken away from the starting quantity (unbundling as necessary). The first partner to reach zero is the winner. This game may also be played as an addition game.
- Count in unit form (e.g., 2 tens, 8 ones; 2 tens, 9 ones; 3 tens).
- Represent quantities on place value mats to be added or subtracted.

MONEY

GRADE LEVEL 2

Dollar bills (1s, 10s, and 100s) are nonproportional units used to develop place value understanding. That is, bills are an abstract representation of place value because their value is not proportionate to their size. Ten bills can have a value of $10 or $1,000 but appear identical aside from their printed labels. Bills can be "traded" (e.g., 10 ten-dollar bills for 1 hundred-dollar bill) to help students learn the equivalence of the two amounts.

As with other place value models, students can use bills to model numbers up to three digits, read numbers formed with the bills, and increase fluency in skip-counting by tens and hundreds.

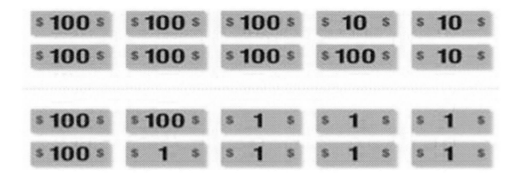

The picture shows that the arrangement of the $100s, $10s, and $1s can be counted in this manner:

For the first frame, the student might say, "100, 200, 300, 400, 500, 600, 700, 710, 720, 730."

For the second frame, the student might say, "100, 200, 300, 301, 302, 303, 304, 305, 306, 307."

The transition from a discrete unit of a bundle to proportional materials, such as base-ten blocks to a nonproportional unit of a bill, is a significant leap in a student's place value learning trajectory.

INSTRUCTIONAL STRATEGIES

- Skip-count up and down by $10 between 45 and 125: "45, 55, 65, 75, 85, 95, 105, 115, 125."
- Practice "making change" by counting on from a starting amount up to a specified total.
- "More" and "Less" games may also be played with money. (See also the "Base-Ten Blocks" section in this chapter.)
- Play equivalency games. "How many $5 bills in a $10 bill? A $20 bill? A $100 bill?"

NUMBER BOND

GRADE LEVEL K–5

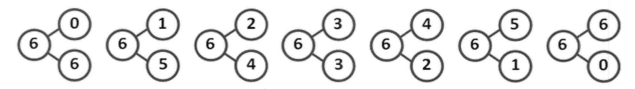

The number bond is a pictorial representation of part-part-whole relationships and shows that, within a part-whole relationship, smaller numbers (the parts) make up larger numbers (the whole). The number bond may be presented as shown in the picture, using smaller circles (or squares) for the parts to distinguish the part from the whole. Number bonds may be presented using the same size shape for parts and whole as students become more comfortable using them.

Number bonds of 10 have the greatest priority because students will use them for adding and subtracting across 10. Students move toward fluency in Grade 1 with numbers to 10 building on the foundation laid in Kindergarten. They learn to decompose numbers to 10 with increasing fluency (1.OA.6). Students learn the meaning of addition as "putting together" to find the whole or total and subtraction as "taking away" to find a part.

Notice in the diagram that the orientation of the number bond does not change its meaning and function ($6+2=8$, $2+6=8$, $8-6=2$, $8-2=6$).

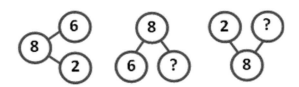

INSTRUCTIONAL STRATEGIES

- Make bonds with a specified whole using concrete objects. Students place all the objects into the "parts" circles of the bond using various combinations. The students can record them pictorially (drawing objects in the bonds), abstractly (writing numerals in the bonds), or using a combination of these representations as appropriate.

- Generate number stories for each number from 5 to 10 from pictures and situations.

- Develop fluency: Show all the possible ways to make ____, for all the numbers from 1 to 10.

- Present bonds in which the whole and one part are visible (using concrete, pictorial, and eventually abstract representations). Students solve for the other part by bonding, counting on, or subtracting.

- Transition students from number bonds to tape diagrams by drawing both representations for number stories.

- Use number bonds as a support for mental math techniques such as "make 10" (grade-specific examples follow).

- Use number bonds to see part-whole fraction and decimal relationships.

Grade 1 Example

Decompose 13 into 10 and 3.

Subtract 9 from the 10.

$$10-9=1$$

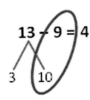

Then, add $1+3$.

$$1+3=4, \text{ so } 13-9=4.$$

Grade 2 Example

Solve 24+33 mentally.
Use bonds to show your thinking.

$$24 + 33$$

20 4   30 3

$$(20 + 30) + (4 + 3) = 57$$

Grade 4 Example 1

Decompose $\frac{4}{7}$ into $\frac{2}{7}$ and $\frac{2}{7}$.

Add $\frac{2}{7}$ to $\frac{5}{7}$ to make 1 whole.

$$\frac{2}{7} + \frac{5}{7} = \frac{7}{7}$$

Then, add $\frac{7}{7}$ to $\frac{2}{7}$.

$$\frac{7}{7} + \frac{2}{7} = \frac{9}{7} \text{ or } 1\frac{2}{7}$$

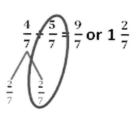

$$\frac{4}{7} + \frac{5}{7} = \frac{9}{7} \text{ or } 1\frac{2}{7}$$

Grade 4 Example 2

T: 98+5=100+____?
S: 98+2+3=100+3.
T: 98+5 is ____?
S: 103.

98 + 5 = 103

② ③

T: 198+54=200+____?
S: 198+54=200+52.
T: 198+54 is ____?
S: 252.

198 + 54 = 152

② ㊼

T: 398+526=400+____?
S: 398+2+524=400+524.
T: 398+526 is ____?
S: 924.

398 + 526 = 924

② ㊾

NUMBER DISKS

GRADE LEVEL 2–5

Number disks are nonproportional units used to further develop place value understanding. Like money, the value of the disk is determined by the value printed on it, not by its size. Students through Grade 5 use number disks when modeling algorithms and as a support for mental math with very large whole numbers. Whole number place value relationships modeled with the disks are easily generalized to decimal numbers and operations with decimals.

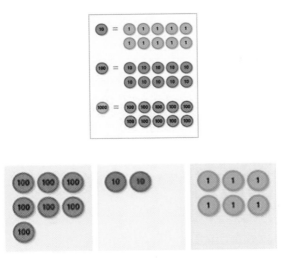

Place Value Chart with Number Disks

INSTRUCTIONAL STRATEGIES

- Play pattern games—for example: "What is 100 less than 253?" Students simply remove a 100 disk and state or record their new number.

- Play partner games. Partner A hides the disks from partner B within a file folder. Partner A says, "I am looking at the number 241. I will make 10 less [physically removing a 10 disk]. What is 10 less than 241?" Partner B writes the answer on his or her personal board or notebook and then states a full response: "Ten less than 241 is 231." Partner A removes the folder, and the partners compare the written response with the disks.

- Perform all four operations with both whole numbers and decimals on mats.

- Use materials to bridge to recording the standard algorithms for all four operations with both whole numbers and decimals.

NUMBER LINE

GRADE LEVEL K–5

The number line is used to develop a deeper understanding of whole number units, fraction units, measurement units, decimals, and negative numbers. Throughout Grades K–5, the number line models measuring units.

INSTRUCTIONAL STRATEGIES

- Measure lengths in meters and centimeters.

- Counting on: Have students place their finger on the location for the first addend, and count from there to add the second addend.

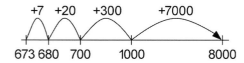

- Have students use a "clock" made from a 24-inch ribbon marked off at every 2 inches to skip-count by fives.

- Compute differences by counting up:

$$8,000 - 673 = 7,327$$

- Multiplying by 10: students visualize how much 5 tens is, and relate it to the number line.

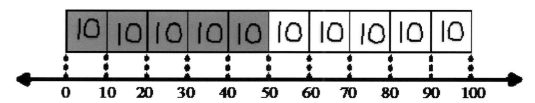

- Rounding to the nearest ten or hundred: students identify which hundreds come before 820: "820 is between 800 and 900."

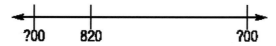

- Model tenths in unit, expanded, fraction, and decimal form.

$$3 \text{ tenths} = 3 \times \frac{1}{10} = \frac{3}{10} = 0.3$$

- Create and analyze line plots.

NUMBER PATH

GRADE LEVEL PREK–1

The number path can be thought of as a visual (pictorial) representation of the number tower (see the "Number Towers" section in this chapter) and is foundational to understanding and using the number line. It also serves as a visual representation of 1:1 correspondence and the concept of whole numbers (one number, one space, and each being equal in size). The color change at 5 helps to reinforce the 5 and 10 benchmarks. The number path also serves as an early precursor to measurement concepts and a support for cardinal counting. (If a student places 7 objects in each of the 7 spaces on the path, he or she must realize that there are 7 objects, not 10. Simply because the path goes up to 10 does not mean there are 10 objects.)

INSTRUCTIONAL STRATEGIES

- Sort, classify, and count up to 5 with meaning, and then work on extending "how many" questions up to 10.

- Match amounts to numerals.

- Write numerals 1 to 5.

- Extend the meaning of 6, 7, and 8 with numerals (6 is 5 and 1; 7 is 5 and 2; 8 is 5 and 3).

- Become fluent with numbers to 10 and practice "before" and "after," as well as relationships of "1 more/less" and "2 more/less"

- Order numbers from 1 to 10.

- Play number order games—for example, partner A closes eyes while partner B covers a number in a number line with a penny; then partner A opens eyes and says the hidden number.

- Fold the number path so that only small sections are visible. Students show 4, 5, 6, 7; the teacher says, "4, 5, hmm, 7. What number is missing?"

- Play I Wish I Had games—for example, "I wish I had 7, but I have only 5." The student answers by placing a finger on 5 and then counting on to say "2"—the amount needed to make the target number.

- Match ordered sets with numerals on the number path.

NUMBER TOWERS

GRADE LEVEL PREK–3

Number towers, also known as number stairs, are representations of quantity constructed by joining together interlocking cubes. At the beginning of *A Story of Units*, these cubes are used to help younger children quite literally build their knowledge of cardinality by erecting towers of various numbers. Number towers are then used to teach concepts of more/less globally and the patterns of 1 more/less and 2 more/less specifically. This model leads to an understanding of comparison and the word *than*, not only in the context of "more than" and "less than," but also in the context of "taller than," "shorter than," "heavier than," "longer than," and so on.

Children are encouraged to build towers for quantities 1 through 5 in one color. For quantities beyond 5, they add on in a second color. This color change provides support for several important developmental milestones. First, it facilitates children's understanding of 5 as a benchmark, which provides an important beginning to their ability to subitize ("instantly see how many"). Second, it allows students to see relationships such as "5 needs 2 more to be 7," "5 is 1 less than 6," and "5 and 4 is 9, which is 1 less than 10." Finally, it encourages students to count on from 5 rather than starting at 1 to count quantities of 6, 7, 8, 9, and 10.

Such comparisons lead to looking at the parts that make up a number ("3 is less than 7; 3 and 4 make 7"). These concepts are foundational to students' understanding of part/whole models (see also the "Number Bond" section in this chapter). This understanding leads naturally to discussions of addition and subtraction, fact fluencies (+1, +2, +3, -1, -2, -3), and even the commutative property ("Flip the tower; 3+4 or 4+3. Does the whole change?"), which are explored in Kindergarten and Grade 1.

In Grades 2 and 3, as students prepare for and study multiplication and division, each unit in the number stair can be ascribed a value other than 1—for example, "Each of our cubes is equal to 3. What is the value of the stair with 5 cubes?"

$$3 \quad 3 \quad 3 \quad 3 \quad 3$$

The use of number stairs can be extended to help children understand more complex properties like the distributive property: "Each of our cubes is equal to three. Make a stair with 5 cubes. Now, add 2 more cubes. The stair with 7 cubes is 2 more threes. So, 5 threes is 15, 2 threes is 6, and together 7 threes is 15 + 6 or 21."

$$5 \text{ threes} + 2 \text{ threes} = (5 + 2) \text{ threes}$$

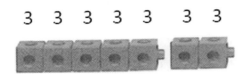

INSTRUCTIONAL STRATEGIES

- Sort, classify, and count up to 5 with meaning, and then begin extending "how many" questions up to 10.
- Build a series of towers from 1 to 10, and then use the towers to relate quantities—for example, "5 is before 6," "6 is after 5," "5 + 1 more is 6," "6 is more than 5," "6 is 1 more than 5," "5 is 1 less than 6," "5 and 2 make 7," and "5 + 2 = 7."
- Build a tower that shows 6.
- Build a specific tower and count the cubes (cardinality).
- Partners roll dice. Then, each partner builds a different tower and states which has more (less).
- Build a tower while stating the "1 more" relationship (e.g., "4; 1 more is 5").
- Deconstruct the tower while stating the "1 less" relationship (e.g., "7, 1 less is 6").
- Count on from 5 (e.g., to count 7, students use the color change to say "5, 6, 7" instead of starting from 1). The color change at 5 may be presented to students as a shortcut by having students slide their finger over a group of 5 as they count (subitizing).
- Count up from numbers other than 0 and 1.
- Count down from numbers other than 10 to numbers other than 0 and 1.
- Compare numbers within 1 and 10.

PLACE VALUE CHART

GRADE LEVEL 2–5

The place value chart is a graphic organizer that students can use (beginning in Grade 1 with tens and ones through Grade 5 with decimals) to see the coherence of place value and operations between different units.

The place value chart without headings is used with labeled materials such as disks:

Place Value Chart without Headings

The place value chart with headings is used with unlabeled materials such as base-ten blocks or bundles:

Place Value Chart with Headings

Hundreds	Tens	Ones

INSTRUCTIONAL STRATEGIES

- Have students build numbers on mats. Place value cards (aka hide zero cards) may be used to show the expanded form of a number that is represented on the place value chart.

- Count the total value of ones, tens, and hundreds with any discrete proportional or nonproportional material such as bundles, base-ten blocks, or number disks.

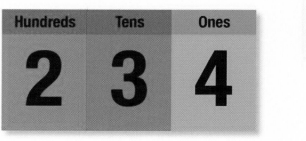 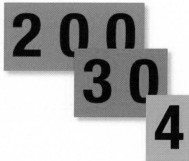

- Model and use language to tell about 1 more/less, 10 more/less on the place value chart with disks when there is change in the hundreds unit.

- Complete a pattern counting up and down.

- Model addition and subtraction using base-ten blocks or number disks.

- Use the mat and place value materials as a support for learning to record the standard algorithms for addition, subtraction, multiplication, and division.

REKENREK

GRADE LEVEL PREK–5

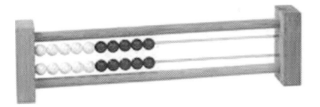

20-Bead Rekenrek

100-Bead Rekenrek

The Rekenrek has a 5 and 10 structure, with a color change at 5 (eliciting the visual effect of grouping 5 and grouping 10). The 20-bead Rekenrek consists of 2 rows of 10 beads, allowing students to see numbers to 10 as a number line on one row or a ten-frame (5 beads on two rows). A 100-bead Rekenrek has 10 rows of 10 beads. Other names for the Rekenrek are *calculating frame, Slavonic abacus, arithmetic rack,* and *math rack.*

INSTRUCTIONAL STRATEGIES

Grades PreK–1

- Count up and down in short sequences (1, 2, 3, 2, 3, 4, 3, 2, . . ., simulating the motion of a roller-coaster).

- Think of 7 as "2 more than 5."

- See "inside" numbers.

- Count in unit form (1 ten 1, 1 ten 2, 1 ten 3, . . . , 2 tens 1, 2 tens 2, and so on).

- Skip-count with complexity, such as counting by 10s on the 1s (3, 23, 33, 43, . . .).

- Group numbers in 5s and 10s. Compare the Rekenrek to the ten-frame.

- Build fluency with doubles.

- Make 10.

- Add across 10; subtract from 10.

- Build numbers 11 to 20.

- Show different strategies for adding $7+8$ ($5+5+2+3$, $7+7+1$, $10+5$, $8+8-1$).
- Compose and decompose numbers.
- Solve addition and subtraction story problems (e.g., putting together, taking away, part-part-whole and comparison).

Grades 2–5

- Show fluency with addition and subtraction facts.
- Find complements of numbers up to 10, 20, 30, . . . , 100.
- Skip count by 2, 3, 4, 5, 6, 7, 8, and 9 within 100.
- Identify doubles plus one and doubles minus one.
- Model rectangular arrays to build conceptual understanding of multiplication.
- Demonstrate the distributive property. Think of 3×12 as 3×10 plus 3×2.

TAPE DIAGRAM

GRADE LEVEL 1–5

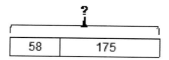

Rachel collected 58 seashells. Sam gave her 175 more. How many seashells did she have then?

Tape diagrams, also called *bar models*, are pictorial representations of relationships between quantities used to solve word problems. Students begin using tape diagrams in Grade 1, modeling simple word problems involving addition and subtraction. It is common for students in Grade 3 to say that they no longer need the tape diagram to solve the problem. However, in Grades 4 and 5, students begin to appreciate the tape diagram because it enables them to solve increasingly more complex problems.

At the heart of a tape diagram is the idea of *forming units*. In fact, forming units to solve word problems is one of the most powerful examples of the unit theme and is particularly helpful for understanding fraction arithmetic.

The tape diagram provides an essential bridge to algebra and is often called *pictorial algebra*.

Like any other tool, it is best introduced with simple examples and in small, managable steps so that students have time to reflect on the relationships they are drawing. For most students, structure is important. RDW, or Read, Draw, Write, is a simple process used for problem solving and is applicable to all grades:

1. Read.
2. Draw and label.

3.   Write a number sentence.

4.   Write a word sentence (statement). The more students participate in reasoning through problems with a systematic approach, the more they internalize those behaviors and thought processes. What can I see? Can I draw something? What conclusions can I make from my drawing?

There are two basic forms of the tape diagram model. The first form, sometimes called the *part-whole model*, uses bar segments placed end-to-end (the Grade 3 example that follows depicts this model). The second form, sometimes called the comparison model, uses two or more bars stacked in rows that are typically left justified (the Grade 5 example that follows depicts this model).

Rather than talk to students about the two forms, simply model the more suitable form for a given problem and allow flexibility in the students' modeling. Over time, students will develop their own intuition for which model will work better for a given problem. It is helpful to ask students as a class, "Did anyone do it differently?" so they can see more than one way to model the problem. Then, perhaps ask, "Which way makes it easier for you to visualize this problem?"

Grade 3 Example

Priya baked 256 cookies. She sold some of them. 187 were left. How many did she sell?

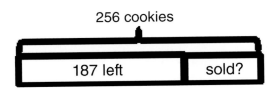

256 – 187 = ___

Priya sold <u>69</u> cookies.

Grade 5 Example

Sam has 1,025 animal stickers. He has 3 times as many plant stickers as animal stickers. How many plant stickers does Sam have? How many stickers does Sam have altogether?

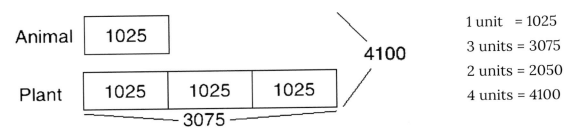

1.   He has <u>3,075</u> plant stickers.

2.   He has <u>4,100</u> stickers altogether.

INSTRUCTIONAL STRATEGIES

- Modeling two discrete quantities with small individual bars where each individual bar represents one unit. (This serves as an initial transition from the Unifix cube model to a pictorial version.)

  Bobby's candy bars:

  Molly's candy bars:

- Modeling two discrete quantities with incremented bars where each increment represents 1 unit:

  Bobby's candy bars

  Molly's candy bars

- Modeling two quantities (discrete or continuous) with nonincremented bars:

  Bobby's candy bars

  Molly's candy bars

- Modeling a part-part-whole relationship where the bars represent known quantities, the total is unknown.

- Modeling a part-part-whole relationship with one part unknown.

- Modeling addition and subtraction comparisons.

- Modeling with equal parts in multiplication and division problems.

- Modeling with equal parts in fraction problems.

TEN-FRAME

GRADE LEVEL PREK–3

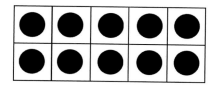

A ten-frame is a 2-by 5-grid (array) used to develop an understanding of concepts such as 5-patterns, combinations to 10, and adding and subtracting within 20. The frame is filled beginning on the top row, left to right, then proceeding to the bottom row, building left to right. This pattern of filling supports subitizing by building on the 5 benchmark, as well as providing a pattern for placing disks on place value mats in later grades. Concrete counters, as well as pictorial dots, may be used to represent quantities on the frame.

In Kindergarten and early in Grade 1, a double ten-frame can be used to establish early foundations of place value (e.g., 13 is 10 and 3 or 1 ten and 3 ones). It can also be used on place value mats to support learning to add double-digit numbers with regrouping. The "completion of a unit" on the ten-frame in early grades empowers students in later grades to understand a "make 100 (or 1,000)" strategy, to add 298 and 37 (i.e., 298+2+35), and to more fully understand addition and subtraction of measurements (e.g., 4 ft 8 in+5 in).

INSTRUCTIONAL STRATEGIES

- Flash a ten-frame for 3 to 5 seconds, and then ask students to recreate what was filled/not filled on their own personal ten-frame. (Students may also tell how many they saw or match the flash with a numeral card.)

- Use the flash technique, but ask students to tell 1 more or less than the number flashed.

- Roll dice and build the number on the ten-frame.

- Partner games: Partner A rolls a die and builds the number on the frame. Partner B rolls and adds that number to the frame (encouraging "10" and "leftovers" or using two ten-frames to represent the sum).

- Play Crazy Mixed-Up Numbers. Have children represent a number on the ten-frame. Then, give various directions for changing the frame (e.g., start with 4: "2 more," "1 less," "1 fewer," "double it," "take away 3"). This activity has the added benefit of providing the teacher with the opportunity to observe how students count—who clears the mat and starts over each time and who is counting on and/or subtracting.

- Write number stories about the filled and "unfilled" parts of the ten-frame.

- Counting in unit form:

Regular	Unit Form
Eleven	1 ten one
Twelve	1 ten two
Thirteen	1 ten three
Twenty	2 tens
Twenty-six	2 tens six

- Represent a number between 5 and 10 on the frame with one color counter. Have students add a quantity between 6 and 9, represented by a second color, to it (e.g., 7+6). Encourage students to "fill the frame" and restate the problem as 10+3.

CHAPTER 8

Terminology

The terms listed in this chapter were compiled from the New or Recently Introduced Terms portion of the Terminology section of the Module Overviews in A *Story of Units*. All grade levels are represented, from Prekindergarten to Grade 5. This list serves as a reference for teachers to quickly determine at which point in the curriculum terms are introduced. We provide descriptions, examples, and illustrations. It should be noted that, especially during the early years of learning, students are often spared exposure to formal definitions of terms due to their complexity.

GRADE PREK

Module 1

- 1 less (e.g., 1 less than 4 is 3)
- 1 more (e.g., 1 more than 4 is 5)
- After (position word)
- Count (with reference to use of number core)
- Counting the Math Way (count fingers from left pinky to right pinky)
- Different (way to analyze objects to match or sort)
- Exactly the same (way to analyze objects to match or sort)
- Group (objects sharing one or more attributes)
- How many (with reference to counting quantities or sets)
- Line (with reference to counting configuration)
- Mark (with reference to starting point for count)
- Match (group items that are the same or have the same given attribute)

- Number (numeral)
- Partners (embedded numbers)
- The same, but . . . (way to analyze objects to match or sort)
- Size (generalized measurement term)
- Sort (group objects according to a particular attribute)

Module 2

- Above, behind, below, between, down, in, in front of, next to, off, on, under, up (position words)
- Circle (two-dimensional shape whose boundary consists of points equidistant from the center)
- Corner (where two sides meet)
- Face (flat side of a solid)
- Flat (as opposed to round)
- Model (a representation of something)
- Pointy (having a sharp point)
- Rectangle (two-dimensional shape enclosed by four straight sides)
- Roll (attribute of a shape)
- Round (circular; shaped like a circle, sphere, cylinder)
- Shape (external boundary of an object)
- Side (position or with reference to a shape)
- Slide (attribute of a shape)
- Square (two-dimensional shape enclosed by four straight, equal sides)
- Stack (attribute of a shape)
- Straight (without a curve or bend)
- Triangle (two-dimensional shape enclosed by three straight sides)

Module 3

- 0, 6, 7, 8, 9, 10 (numerals)
- Shapes (rectangle, triangle, square, circle)
- Sides
- Tally marks
- Zero

Module 4

- About the same length/height/weight as (way to compare measurable attributes)
- Are there enough . . . ? (comparative question)

- Balance scale (tool for weight and measurement)
- Bigger than (volume or size comparison)
- Compare (specifically using direct comparison)
- Empty (volume comparison)
- Equal to (e.g., 5 is *equal to* 5.)
- Exactly enough/not enough (comparative term)
- Extra (leftovers)
- Fewer/fewer than (way to compare number of objects, e.g., "There are fewer apples than oranges.")
- First (comparing numbers related to order or position)
- Full (volume comparison)
- Greater/greater than (number comparison)
- Heavy/heavier/heavier than (weight comparison)
- Height (measurable attribute of objects, described as tall or short)
- Last (comparing numbers related to order or position)
- Length (measurable attribute of objects, described as long or short)
- Less than (with reference to volume, numbers of objects, or numbers, e.g., 3 is *less than* 4.)
- Light/lighter/lighter than (weight comparison)
- Long/longer/longer than (length comparison)
- More than (with reference to volume and numbers of objects)
- Same (with reference to volume, holding the same amount)
- Set (group of objects)
- Short/shorter/shorter than (length comparison)
- Smaller than (volume or size comparison)
- Tall/taller than (height comparison)
- Weigh/weight (measurable attribute of objects, described as heavy or light)

Module 5
- Add/addition
- Addition story
- All together
- Are left
- Equals
- In all
- Math drawing
- Number sentence

- Pattern
- Plus
- Put together
- Repeating part
- Sixteen, seventeen, eighteen, nineteen, twenty (number words)
- Subtract/subtraction
- Subtraction story
- Take away
- Total

GRADE K

Module 1

- 1 less (e.g., 4: 1 less is 3)
- 1 more (e.g., 4: 1 more is 5)
- 5-group (pictured)
- Counting path (with reference to order of count)
- Exactly the same/not exactly the same/the same, but . . . (ways to analyze objects to match or sort)
- Hidden partners (embedded numbers)
- How many (with reference to counting quantities or sets)
- Match (group items that are the same or have the same given attribute)
- Number path (pictured)
- Number sentence (e.g., 3 = 2 + 1)
- Number story (stories with *add to* or *take from* situations)
- Rows/columns (often used in reference to horizontal/vertical groups in a rectangular array)
- Sort (group objects according to a particular attribute)
- Zero

Module 2

- Above, below, beside, in front of, next to, behind (position words)
- Circle
- Cone (three-dimensional shape)
- Cube (three-dimensional shape)
- Cylinder (three-dimensional shape)
- Face (flat side of a solid)

- Flat (two-dimensional shape)
- Hexagon (flat illustration enclosed by six straight sides)
- Rectangle (flat illustration enclosed by four straight sides)
- Solid (three-dimensional shape)
- Sphere (three-dimensional shape)
- Square (flat illustration enclosed by four straight, equal sides)
- Triangle (flat illustration enclosed by three straight sides)

Module 3

- Balance scale (tool for weight measurement)
- Capacity (with reference to volume)
- Compare (specifically using direct comparison)
- Endpoint (with reference to alignment for direct comparison)
- Enough/not enough (comparative term)
- Heavier than/lighter than (weight comparison)
- Height (vertical distance measurement from bottom to top)
- Length (distance measurement from end to end; in a rectangular shape, length can be used to describe any of the four sides)
- Longer than/shorter than (length comparison)
- More than/fewer than (discrete quantity comparison)
- More than/less than (volume, area, and number comparisons)
- Taller than/shorter than (height comparison)
- The same as (comparative term)
- Weight

Module 4

- Addition (specifically using *add to with result unknown, put together with total unknown, put together with both addends unknown*)
- Addition and subtraction sentences (equations)
- Make 10 (combine two numbers from 1 to 9 that add up to 10)
- Minus (−)
- Number bond (mathematical model; pictured)
- Number pairs or partners (embedded numbers)
- Part (when used in the context of number—an addend or embedded number)
- Put together (add)
- Subtraction (specifically using *take from with result unknown*)

- Take apart (decompose)
- Take away (subtract)
- Whole (total)

Module 5

- 10 and ____
- 10 ones and some ones
- 10 plus
- Hide zero cards (in later grades, called place value cards; pictured)
- Regular counting by ones from 11 to 20 (e.g., 11, 12, 13, . . .)
- Regular counting by tens to 100 (e.g., 10, 20, 30, 40, 50, 60, 70, 80, 90, 100)
- Say ten counting by tens to 100 (e.g., 1 ten, 2 tens, 3 tens, 4 tens, 5 tens, 6 tens, 7 tens, 8 tens, 9 tens, 10 tens)
- Teen numbers

Module 6

- First, second, third, fourth, fifth, sixth, seventh, eighth, ninth, tenth (ordinal numbers)

GRADE 1

Module 1

- Addend (one of the numbers being added)
- Count on (students count up from one addend to the total)
- Doubles (e.g., 3 + 3 or 4 + 4)
- Doubles plus 1 (e.g., 3 + 4 or 4 + 5)
- Expression (e.g., 3 + 2, 7 − 1 as opposed to a number sentence, e.g., 3 + 2 = 5, 6 = 7 − 1)
- Track (students use different objects to track the count on from one addend to the total)

Module 2

- A ten (pictured)
- Ones (basic units of the place value system, 10 ones = 1 ten)

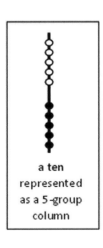

a ten represented as a 5-group column

Module 3

- Centimeter (standard length unit within the metric system)
- Centimeter cube (pictured)
- Length unit (e.g., centimeters, inches)

Module 4

- \> (greater than)
- \< (less than)
- Place value (the unit associated with a particular digit due to its position within a number; also used in reference to the place value system)

Module 5

- Attributes (characteristics of an object, such as color or number of sides)
- Fourth of (shapes), fourths (1 out of 4 equal parts)
- Half of, halves (shapes)
- Half past (expression for 30 minutes past a given hour)
- Half-hour (interval of time lasting 30 minutes)
- Hour (unit for measuring time, equivalent to 60 minutes or 1/24 of a day)
- Minute (unit for measuring time, equivalent to 60 seconds, 1/60 of an hour)
- O'clock (used to indicate time to a precise hour, with no additional minutes)
- Quarter of (shapes) (1 out of 4 equal parts)
- Three-dimensional shapes:
  - Cone (pictured)
  - Cube (pictured)
  - Cylinder (pictured)
  - Rectangular prism (pictured)
  - Sphere
- Two-dimensional shapes:
  - Circle (pictured)
  - Half-circle (pictured)
  - Hexagon (flat shape enclosed by six straight sides)
  - Parallelogram (a flat, four-sided shape in which both pairs of opposite sides are parallel)
  - Quarter-circle (pictured)
  - Rectangle (flat shape enclosed by four straight sides and four right angles)
  - Rhombus (flat shape enclosed by four straight sides of the same length)

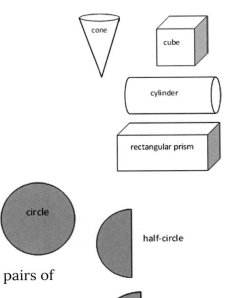

○ Square (a rectangle with all sides of equal length—viewed as a "special rectangle")

○ Trapezoid (pictured)

○ Triangle (flat illustration enclosed by three straight sides)

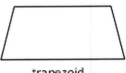

trapezoid

Module 6

- Comparison problem type
- Dime
- Nickel
- Penny
- Quarter

GRADE 2

Module 1

No new or recently introduced terms

Module 2

- Benchmark (e.g., "round" numbers like multiples of 10)
- Endpoint (e.g., the point where something begins or ends)
- Estimate (an approximation of a quantity or number)
- Hash mark (the marks on a ruler or other measurement tool)
- Meter (m, a standard unit of length in the metric system)
- Meter stick
- Meter strip (pictured)
- Number line (pictured)
- Overlap (extend over, or cover partly)
- Ruler (tool used to measure length)

Module 3

- Base-ten numerals (e.g., a thousand is 10 hundreds, a hundred is 10 tens; starting in Grade 3, a one is 10 tenths, and so on)
- Expanded form (e.g., 500 + 70 + 6)
- Hundreds place (e.g., the 5 in 576 is in the hundreds place)

- One thousand (1,000)
- Place value or number disk (pictured)
- Place value chart (pictured)
- Standard form (e.g., 576)
- Word form (e.g., five hundred seventy-six)

Say Ten form modeled with number disks: 7 hundreds 2 tens 6 ones = 72 tens 6 ones

Module 4

- Equation (a statement that two expressions are equal, e.g., $3 \times \underline{\quad} = 12$, $7 = 21 \div b$, $5 \times 4 = 20$. Note that, while an equation may or may not contain an unknown number, once the unknowns are filled in, one is left with a number sentence.)
- Minuend (e.g., the 9 in $9 - 6 = 3$)
- New groups below (pictured)
- Number sentence (an equation or inequality for which both expressions are numerical (can be evaluated to a single number)—for example, $4 \times 3 = 6 \times 2$, $21 > 7 \times 2$, $5 \div 5 = 1$. Number sentences are either true or false—for example, $4 \times 4 < 6 \times 2$ and $21 = 7 \times 4$—and contain no unknowns.
- Subtrahend (e.g., the 6 in $9 - 6 = 3$)
- Totals below (pictured)

Place Value Chart with Headings
(use with numbers)

hundreds	tens	ones
7	2	6

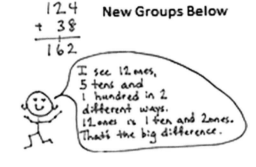

New Groups Below

I see 12 ones, 5 tens and 1 hundred in 2 different ways. 12 ones is 1 ten and 2 ones. That's the big difference.

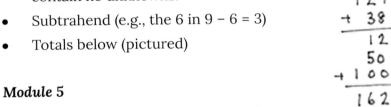

Totals Below

Module 5

- Algorithm (a step-by-step procedure to solve a particular type of problem)
- Compensation (simplifying strategy where students add or subtract the same amount to or from both numbers to create an equivalent but easier problem)
- Compose (e.g., to make 1 larger unit from 10 smaller units)
- Decompose (e.g., to break 1 larger unit into 10 smaller units)
- Simplifying strategy (e.g., to solve $299 + 6$, think $299 + 1 + 5 = 300 + 5 = 305$)

Module 6

- Array (e.g., an arrangement of objects in rows and columns)
- Columns (the vertical groups in a rectangular array)
- Even number (e.g., a whole number whose last digit is 0, 2, 4, 6, or 8)
- Odd number (any number that is not even)

- Repeated addition (e.g., 2 + 2 + 2)
- Rows (the horizontal groups in a rectangular array)
- Tessellation (tiling of a plane using one or more geometric shapes with no overlaps and no gaps)
- Whole number (e.g., 0, 1, 2, 3 . . .)

Module 7

- Bar graph (pictured)
- Category (group of people or things sharing a common characteristic, e.g., bananas are in the fruit category)
- Data (a set of facts or pieces of information)
- Degree (used to measure temperature, e.g., degrees Fahrenheit)
- Foot (ft, unit of length equal to 12 inches)
- Inch (in, unit of length)
- Legend (notation on a graph explaining what symbols represent)
- Line plot (graphical representation of data; pictured)
- Picture graph (representation of data like a bar graph, using pictures instead of bars; pictured)
- Scale (a number line used to indicate the various quantities represented in a bar graph; pictured)
- Survey (collecting data by asking a question and recording responses)
- Symbol (picture that represents something else)
- Table (representation of data using rows and columns)
- Thermometer (temperature measuring tool)
- Yard (yd, unit of length equal to 36 inches or 3 feet)

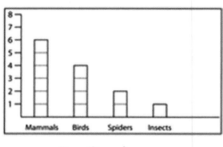

Bar Graph

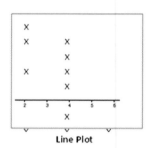

Line Plot

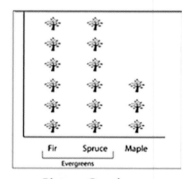

Picture Graph

Scale

Module 8

- a.m./p.m.
- Analog clock (pictured)
- Angle (e.g., illustration formed by the corner of a polygon)
- Digital clock
- Parallel (used to describe opposite sides of a parallelogram, e.g., "These sides are parallel, because if they kept on going, they'd never intersect!")
- Parallelogram (quadrilateral with both pairs of opposite sides parallel)

- Polygon (closed illustration with three or more straight sides, e.g., triangle, quadrilateral, pentagon, hexagon)
- Quadrilateral (four-sided polygon, e.g., square, rhombus, rectangle, parallelogram, trapezoid)
- Quarter past, quarter to
- Right angle (e.g., a square corner)
- Second (unit for measuring time, 60 seconds is equivalent to 1 minute and 1/60 of a minute)
- Third of (shapes), thirds (1 out of 3 equal parts)
- Trapezoid (a quadrilateral in which at least one pair of opposite sides is parallel)
- Whole (used in reference to fractions, e.g., 2 halves make 1 whole, 3 thirds make 1 whole)

GRADE 3

Module 1

- Commutative property/commutative (e.g., $3 \times 5 = 5 \times 3$)
- Distribute (with reference to the Distributive Property, e.g., in $12 \times 3 = (10 + 2) \times 3 = (10 \times 3) + (2 \times 3)$)
- Divide/division (e.g., $15 \div 5 = 3$, which is interpreted as either 15 divided into groups of 5 equals 3 or 15 divided into 5 groups equals 3)
- Equal groups
- Expression (a number, or any combination of sums, differences, products, or divisions of numbers that evaluates to a number, e.g., $3 + 4$, 8×3, $4 + b$, $3 \times 4 + 5 \times 4$ as distinct from an equation or number sentence; see Grade 2 Module 4)
- Fact (used to refer to multiplication facts, e.g., 3×2)
- Factors (numbers that are multiplied to obtain a product)
- Multiply/multiplication (e.g., $5 \times 3 = 15$, which is interpreted as 5 groups of 3 equals 15)
- Number of groups (factor in a multiplication problem that refers to the total number of equal groups)
- Parentheses ( ) (the symbols used around a fact or numbers within an equation)
- Quotient (the answer when one number is divided by another)
- Rotate (turn; used with reference to turning arrays 90 degrees)
- Row/column (in reference to rectangular arrays)
- Size of groups (factor in a multiplication problem that refers to how many in a group)
- Unit (used to refer to one part of a tape diagram partitioned into equal parts)
- Unknown (used to refer to the missing number in a number sentence)

Module 2

- About (with reference to rounding and estimation; used to indicate an answer that is not precise)
- Addend (e.g., in 4 + 5, the numbers 4 and 5 are the addends)
- Capacity (the amount of liquid that a particular container can hold)
- Continuous (with reference to time as a continuous measurement)
- Endpoint (used with rounding on the number line; the numbers that mark the beginning and end of a given interval)
- Gram (g, a unit of measurement for weight in the metric system)
- Halfway (with reference to a number line, the midpoint between two numbers, e.g., 5 is halfway between 0 and 10)
- Interval (e.g., an amount of time passed or a segment on the number line)
- Kilogram (kg, a measurement unit for mass—not distinguished from weight at this stage)
- Liquid volume (the space a liquid takes up)
- Liter (L, a unit of measurement for liquid volume)
- Milliliter (mL, unit of measurement for liquid volume)
- Plot (locate and label a point on a number line)
- Point (used to refer to a specific location on the number line)
- Reasonable (with reference to how plausible an answer is, e.g., "Is your answer reasonable?")
- Rename (regroup units, e.g., when solving with the standard algorithm)
- Round (estimate a number to the nearest 10 or 100 using place value)
- Standard algorithm (for addition and subtraction)
- ≈ (symbol used to show than an answer is approximate)

Module 3

- Multiple (specifically with reference to naming multiples of 9 and 10, e.g., 20, 30, 40)
- Multiplier (the factor representing the number of units)
- Product (the quantity resulting from multiplying two or more numbers together)

Module 4

- Area (the amount of two-dimensional space in a bounded region)
- Area model (a model for multiplication based on area; pictured)

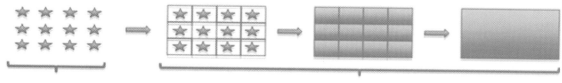

Module 1 and Module 3   Module 4

- Square unit (a unit of area—specifically square centimeters, inches, feet, and meters)
- Tile (to cover a region without gaps or overlaps)
- Unit square (e.g., given a length unit, it is a 1 unit by 1 unit square)
- Whole number (the numbers: 0, 1, 2, 3, . . .)

Module 5

- Copies (refers to the number of unit fractions in 1 whole)
- Equal parts (parts with equal measurements)
- Equivalent fractions (fractions that name the same size or the same point on the number line)
- Fractional unit (half, third, fourth, and so on)
- Nonunit fraction (fractions with numerators other than 1)
- Unit fraction (fractions with numerator 1)
- Unit interval (the interval from 0 to 1)

Module 6

- Measurement data (e.g., length measurements of a collection of pencils)
- Most frequent (most common measurement on a line plot)
- Scaled graphs (bar or picture graph in which the scale uses units with a value greater than 1)
- Survey (collecting data by asking a question and recording responses)

Module 7

- Attribute (any characteristic of a shape, including properties and other defining characteristics, e.g., straight sides, and nondefining characteristics, e.g., blue)
- Diagonal (e.g., the line drawn between opposite corners of a quadrilateral)
- Perimeter (boundary or length of the boundary of a two-dimensional shape)
- Property (e.g., squares have the property that all sides are equal in length)
- Regular polygon (polygon whose side lengths and interior angles are all equal)
- Tessellate (to tile a plane without gaps or overlaps)
- Tetrominoes (four identical squares arranged to form a shape so that every square shares at least one side with another square)

GRADE 4

Module 1

- Algorithm
- One million, ten millions, hundred millions (as places on the place value chart)
- Ten thousands, hundred thousands (as places on the place value chart)

Module 2

- Kilometer (km, a unit of length measurement)
- Mass (a measurement of the amount of matter in an object—not distinguished from weight at this stage)
- Milliliter (mL, a unit of measurement for liquid volume)
- Mixed units (e.g., 3 m 43 cm)

Module 3

- Associative Property (e.g., 96 = 3 × (4 × 8) = (3 × 4) × 8)
- Composite number (positive integer having three or more whole number factors)
- Distributive Property (e.g., 64 × 27 = (60 × 20) + (60 × 7) + (4 × 20) + (4 × 7))
- Divisor (e.g., the 3 in 37÷3)
- Partial product (e.g., in the calculation 24 × 6 = (20 × 6) + (4 × 6) = 120 + 24, 120 and 24 are partial products)
- Prime number (positive integer greater than 1 having whole number factors of only 1 and itself)
- Remainder (the number left over when one integer is divided by another)

Module 4

- Acute angle (angle that measures less than 90 degrees)
- Acute triangle (triangle with all interior angles measuring less than 90 degrees)
- Adjacent angle (e.g., ∠ADC and ∠CDB are called adjacent angles; pictured)

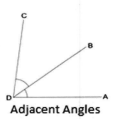
Adjacent Angles

- Angle (union of two noncollinear rays sharing a common vertex)
- Arc (connected portion of a circle; pictured)

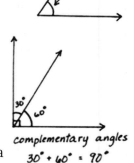

- Collinear (three or more points are *collinear* if there is a line containing all of the points; otherwise, the points are *noncollinear*)
- Complementary angles (two angles with a sum of 90 degrees; pictured)
- Degree measure of an angle. (Subdivide the length around a circle into 360 arcs of equal length. A central angle for any of these arcs is called a *one-degree angle* and is said to have angle measure 1 degree.)

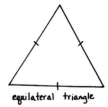
complementary angles
30° + 60° = 90°

- Diagonal (straight lines joining two opposite corners of a straight-sided shape)
- Equilateral triangle (triangle with three equal sides; pictured)
- Illustration (set of points in the plane)

equilateral triangle

- Interior of an angle (pictured)
- Intersecting lines (lines that contain at least one point in common)
- Isosceles triangle (triangle with at least two equal sides; pictured)
- Length of an arc (circular distance around the arc)
- Line (straight path with no thickness that extends in both directions without end)
- Line of symmetry (line through an illustration such that when the illustration is folded along the line, two halves are created that match up exactly; pictured)
- Line segment (two points, A, B, together with the set of points on the line $\overleftrightarrow{AB}$ between A and B)
- Obtuse angle (angle with a measure greater than 90 degrees but less than 180 degrees)
- Obtuse triangle (triangle with an interior obtuse angle)
- Parallel (two lines that lie in the same plane and do not intersect)
- Perpendicular (two lines that intersect and any of the angles formed between the lines is a 90 degree angle.)
- Point (precise location in the plane)
- Protractor (instrument used in measuring or sketching angles)
- Ray. (The *ray* $\overrightarrow{OA}$ is the point O and the set of all points on the line $\overleftrightarrow{OA}$ that are on the same side of O as the point A)
- Right angle (an angle that measures 90 degrees, introduced earlier as "a square corner")
- Right triangle (triangle that contains one 90 degree angle)
- Scalene triangle (triangle with no equal sides)
- Straight angle (an "angle" that measures 180 degrees, i.e., a line)
- Supplementary angles (two angles whose measurements add up to 180 degrees; pictured)
- Triangle (consists of three noncollinear points and the three line segments between them; the three segments are the *sides* of the triangle, and the three points are the *vertices*)
- Vertex (a point, often used to refer to the point where two lines meet, such as in an angle or the corner of a triangle)
- Vertical angles (when two lines intersect, any two nonadjacent angles formed by those lines; also called *vertically opposite angles*)

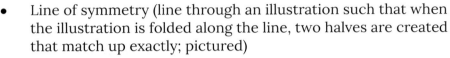

isosceles triangle
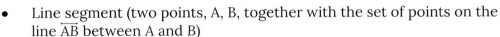
Line of Symmetry
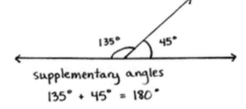
supplementary angles
135° + 45° = 180°

Module 5

- Benchmark fraction (e.g., $\frac{1}{2}$ is a benchmark fraction when comparing $\frac{1}{3}$ and $\frac{3}{5}$)
- Common denominator (when two or more fractions have the same denominator)

- Denominator (bottom number in a fraction)
- Like denominators (e.g., $\frac{1}{8}$ and $\frac{5}{8}$)
- Mixed number (e.g., $3\frac{1}{4}$, which is an abbreviated form for $3 \times \frac{1}{4}$)
- Numerator (top number in a fraction)
- Unlike denominators (e.g., $\frac{1}{8}$ and $\frac{1}{7}$)

Module 6

- Decimal expanded form (e.g., $(2 \times 10) + (4 \times 1) + (5 \times 0.1) + (9 \times 0.01) = 24.59$)
- Decimal fraction (fraction with a denominator of 10, 100, 1,000, and so on)
- Decimal number (number written using place value units of ones, tens, hundreds, and so on, as well as decimal fraction units, e.g., tenths, hundredths)
- Decimal point (period used to separate the whole number part from the fractional part of a decimal number)
- Fraction expanded form (e.g., $(2 \times 10) + (4 \times 1) + \left(5 \times \frac{1}{10}\right) + \left(9 \times \frac{1}{100}\right) = 24\frac{59}{100}$)
- Hundredth (place value unit such that 100 hundredths equals 1 one)
- Tenth (place value unit such that 10 tenths equals 1 one)

GRADE 5

Module 1

- Equation (two expressions with an equal sign between them, i.e., a statement that two expressions are equal, though without a guarantee that the statement is true)
- Exponents (e.g., $10^3 = 10 \times 10 \times 10$)
- Millimeter (mm, a metric unit of length equal to 1 thousandth of a meter)
- Thousandths (related to place value)

Module 2

- Multiplier (a quantity by which a given number is to be multiplied)
- Parentheses (the symbols used to indicate the order in which operations should be carried out)

Module 3

No new or recently introduced terms

Module 4

- Decimal divisor (the number that divides the whole and has units of tenths, hundredths, thousandths, and so on)
- Simplify (using the largest fractional unit possible to express an equivalent fraction)

Module 5

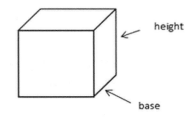

- Base (e.g., in a right rectangular prism, a choice of one face–often thought of as the face on which the prism rests; pictured)

- Bisect (divide into two equal parts)

- Cubic units (cubes of the same size used for measuring volume)

- Height (in a right rectangular prism, the length of an edge perpendicular to the chosen base; pictured)

- Hierarchy (pictured)

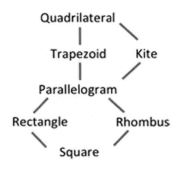

- Unit cube (cube whose sides all measure 1 unit; cubes of the same size used for measuring volume)

- Volume of a solid (measurement of space or capacity)

- Rectangle (a parallelogram having four right angles)

- Rhombus (a parallelogram in which all sides are of equal length)

- Kite (quadrilateral in which two adjacent sides have equal lengths and the remaining two sides also have equal but possibly different lengths)

Module 6

- Axis (fixed reference line used in the context of the coordinate plane)

- Coordinate (a number used to identify a location)

- Coordinate pair/ordered pair (two numbers that are used to identify a point on a plane; written (x, y) where x represents a distance from 0 on the x-axis and y represents a distance from 0 on the y-axis)

- Coordinate plane (a plane equipped with a coordinate system, and in which any point may be located by a coordinate pair)

- Origin (the point at which the x-axis and y-axis intersect, labeled $(0, 0)$ on the coordinate plane)

- Quadrant (any of the four regions created by the intersection of the x-axis and y-axis)

Notes

CHAPTER 3

1. When a cluster is referred to in this chart without a footnote, the cluster is addressed in its entirety.
2. The balance of this cluster is addressed in Modules 3 and 7.
3. From this point forward, fluency practice is part of the students' ongoing experience. The balance of this cluster is addressed in Module 3.
4. The focus of this module is on the metric system to reinforce place value, mixed units, and word problems with unit conversions. Decimal and fraction word problems wait until Modules 6 and 7. Standard 4.MD.3 is addressed in Module 3.
5. Standard 4.NBT.4 is addressed in Module 1 and then reinforced throughout the year.
6. Multiplying two two-digit numbers is addressed in Module 7.
7. Standard 4.MD.1 is addressed in Modules 2 and 7. Standard 4.MD.2 is addressed in Modules 2, 6, and 7.
8. Tenths and hundredths are important fractions in this module, represented in decimal form in Module 6.
9. In this module, we continue to work with fractions, now including decimal form.
10. Standard 4.MD.1 is addressed in Modules 2 and 7. Standard 4.MD.3 is addressed in Module 3.
11. The focus now is on customary units in word problems for application of fraction concepts. Standard 4.MD.3 is addressed in Module 3.

CHAPTER 6

1. Grade 4 expectations in the NBT standards domain, however, are limited to whole numbers less than or equal to 1,000,000.
2. Only addition and subtraction multistep word problems are addressed in this module. The balance of this cluster is addressed in Modules 3 and 7.
3. The balance of this cluster is addressed in Modules 3 and 7.
4. This standard is limited to problems posed with whole numbers and having whole number answers. Students should know how to perform operations in the conventional order when there are no parentheses to specify a particular order (i.e., the Order of Operations).

5. Pounds, ounces, time, and money are covered in Module 7.

6. Standard 4.MD.3 is addressed in Module 3.

7. Pounds, ounces, and time are addressed in Module 7. This is a nontested standard, but expressing metric measurements of length, mass, and capacity from larger to smaller units strengthens the upcoming modules.

8. Time and money are addressed in Module 7. This is a nontested standard, but the context of operating on distance, volume, and mass strengthens the upcoming modules.

9. Pounds, ounces, time, and money are covered in Module 7.

10. Pounds, ounces, and time are addressed in Module 7. This is a nontested standard, but expressing metric measurements of length, mass, and capacity from larger to smaller units strengthens the upcoming modules.

11. Time and money are addressed in Module 7. This is a nontested standard, but the context of operating on distance, volume, and mass strengthens the upcoming modules. This module focuses on only addition and subtraction. Multiplication and division are addressed in future modules.

12. Pounds, ounces, and time are addressed in Module 7. This is a nontested standard, but expressing metric measurements of length, mass, and capacity from larger to smaller units strengthens the upcoming modules.

13. Time and money are addressed in Module 7. This is a nontested standard, but the context of operating on distance, volume, and mass strengthens the upcoming modules.

14. Students become fluent with the standard algorithm for multiplication in Grade 5 (5.NBT.5). Grade 4 students are introduced to the standard algorithm in preparation for fluency and as a general method for solving multiplication problems based on place value strategies, alongside number disks, partial products, and the area model. Students are not assessed on the standard algorithm in Grade 4.

15. Note that care must be taken in the interpretation of remainders. Consider the fact that $7 \div 3$ is not equal to $5 \div 2$ because the remainder of 1 is in reference to a different whole amount ($2\frac{1}{3}$ is not equal to $2\frac{1}{2}$).

16. Students become fluent with the standard division algorithm in Grade 6 (Standard 6.NS.2). For adequate practice in reaching fluency, students are introduced to, but not assessed on, the division algorithm in Grade 4 as a general method for solving division problems.

17. Standard 4.NBT.4 is addressed in Module 1 and then reinforced throughout the year.

18. Standard 4.MD.1 is taught in Modules 2 and 7. Standard 4.MD.2 is taught in Modules 2, 6, and 7.

19. Note that care must be taken in the interpretation of remainders. Consider the fact that $7 \div 3$ is not equal to $5 \div 2$ because the remainder of 1 is in reference to a different whole amount (2⅓ is not equal to 2½).

20. Students become fluent with the standard division algorithm in Grade 6 (Standard 6.NS.2). For adequate practice in reaching fluency, students are introduced to, but not assessed on, the division algorithm in Grade 4 as a general method for solving division problems.

21. Standard 4.MD.1 is addressed in Modules 2 and 7. Standard 4.MD.3 is addressed in Module 3.

22. The focus now is on customary units in word problems for application of fraction concepts. Standard 4.MD.3 is addressed in Module 3.

Board of Trustees

Eureka Math Study Guide: A Story of Units Contributors

Katrina Abdussalaam, Curriculum Writer

Tiah Alphonso, Program Manager–Curriculum Production

Kelly Alsup, Lead Writer / Editor, Grade 4

Catriona Anderson, Program Manager–Implementation Support

Debbie Andorka-Aceves, Curriculum Writer

Eric Angel, Curriculum Writer

Leslie Arceneaux, Lead Writer / Editor, Grade 5

Kate McGill Austin, Lead Writer / Editor, Grades PreK-K

Adam Baker, Lead Writer / Editor, Grade 5

Scott Baldridge, Lead Mathematician and Lead Curriculum Writer

Beth Barnes, Curriculum Writer

Bonnie Bergstresser, Math Auditor

Bill Davidson, Fluency Specialist

Jill Diniz, Program Director

Nancy Diorio, Curriculum Writer

Nancy Doorey, Assessment Advisor

Lacy Endo-Peery, Lead Writer / Editor, Grades PreK-K

Ana Estela, Curriculum Writer

Lessa Faltermann, Math Auditor

Janice Fan, Curriculum Writer

Ellen Fort, Math Auditor

Peggy Golden, Curriculum Writer

Maria Gomes, PreKindergarten Practitioner

Pam Goodner, Curriculum Writer

Greg Gorman, Curriculum Writer

Melanie Gutierrez, Curriculum Writer

Kelley Isinger, Curriculum Writer

Nuhad Jamal, Curriculum Writer

Mary Jones, Lead Writer / Editor, Grade 4

Halle Kananak, Curriculum Writer

Tam Le, Document Production Manager

Susan Lee, Lead Writer / Editor, Grade 3

Jennifer Loftin, Program Manager—Professional Development

Soo Jin Lu, Curriculum Writer

Nell McAnelly, Project Director

Ben McCarty, Lead Mathematician / Editor, PreK–5

Cristina Metcalf, Lead Writer / Editor, Grade 3

Susan Midlarsky, Curriculum Writer

Pat Mohr, Curriculum Writer

Victoria Peacock, Curriculum Writer

Jenny Petrosino, Curriculum Writer

Terrie Poehl, Math Auditor

Robin Ramos, Lead Curriculum Writer / Editor, PreK–5

Cecilia Rudzitis, Curriculum Writer

Tricia Salerno, Curriculum Writer

Chris Sarlo, Curriculum Writer

Ann Rose Sentoro, Curriculum Writer

Colleen Sheeron, Lead Writer / Editor, Grade 2

Gail Smith, Curriculum Writer

Shelley Snow, Curriculum Writer

Kelly Spinks, Curriculum Writer

Marianne Strayton, Lead Writer / Editor, Grade 1

Theresa Streeter, Math Auditor

Lily Talcott, Curriculum Writer

Kevin Tougher, Curriculum Writer

Saffron VanGalder, Lead Writer / Editor, Grade 3

Lisa Watts-Lawton, Lead Writer / Editor, Grade 2

Erin Wheeler, Curriculum Writer

MaryJo Wieland, Curriculum Writer

Jessa Woods, Curriculum Writer

Hae Jung Yang, Lead Writer / Editor, Grade 1

Index

Page references followed by *fig* indicate an illustrated figure.